STONE JOURNALS

Journeys to the mysterious standing stones of Europe

Patrick Ford

Stone Journals
Copyright ©2018 Patrick Ford

ISBN 978-1506-912-28-8 PRINT

LCCN 2018954956

April 2019

Published and Distributed by
First Edition Design Publishing, Inc.
P.O. Box 20217, Sarasota, FL 34276-3217
www.firsteditiondesignpublishing.com

ALL RIGHTS RESERVED. No part of this book publication may be reproduced, stored in a retrieval system, or transmitted in any form or by any means — electronic, mechanical, photo-copy, recording, or any other — except brief quotation in reviews, without the prior permission of the author or publisher.

Cover design by Joseph Dionne
Front cover photo - Stonehenge
Back cover photo - Callanish Stone Circle
Title page photo - Swinside Stone Circle

The author can be contacted at:
pkford@pacific.net or
PO Box 383, Redwood Valley, Ca 95470

All quotes from Julian Cope:
Reprinted by permission of Harper Collins Publishers Ltd
C Julian Cope 1998 (Modern Antiquarian) & 2004 (Megalithic European)

Acknowledgements

Thank you Sharon for your support with this endeavor and for coming along on many of the journeys. This book could never have happened without you.

Much thanks to John at Appleseed Consulting for making sense of my Pages chaos. You are a hero.

I can never repay the kindness shown me by Joe Dionne. We met by chance on my first Stone Journey back in 1999. He was on his way back from Boscawen-Un Stone Circle as I was hiking towards it. Though our paths have not crossed again since that day, he has remained a dear friend. We are "brothers of the stones." As I began putting this book together he gave me advice. Then, wanting to see my book become a reality he offered, at no charge, to design the cover for me. I will always be in his debt.

I am also indebted to Paula Ridley for reading my first rough draft and pointing out its many flaws. I tried to do better.

Special thanks to Julian Cope whose *The Modern Antiquarian* inspired me more than anyone or anything else.

Last, and most importantly, I thank the stones. I have found such joy in their company.

"Stonehenge pleases like a magical spell."
William Stukeley

Table of Contents

PREFACE 2
INTRODUCTION 5

Stone Journey 1 SOUTHERN ENGLAND 13
Stone Journey 2 SCOTLAND, STONEHENGE 51
Stone Journey 3 SCOTLAND 79
Stone Journey 4 SOUTHERN ENGLAND, SCOTLAND, NORTHERN ENGLAND 91
Stone Journey 5 SWEDEN 119
Stone Journey 6 SCOTLAND, NORTHERN ENGLAND 127
Stone Journey 7 ENGLAND, SCOTLAND 165
Stone Journey 8 IRELAND, NORTHERN IRELAND 181
Stone Journey 9 IRELAND, ENGLAND, SCOTLAND 231

AFTERTHOUGHTS 287
GLOSSARY 290

Stone Journey 1
Southern England

Avebury
Boscawen-Un Stone Circle
Brisworthy Stone Circle
Carn Euny
Duloe Stone Circle
King Stone
Men An Tol
Merrivale Stones
Old Sarrum
Rollright Stone Circle
Silbury Hill
Soussans Common Stone Circle
Stanton Drew Stone Circles
Stonehenge
The Blind Fiddler
The Bowl Rock
The Hurlers Stone Circles
The Merry Maidens Stone Circle
The Pipers
Trencrom Hill
West Kennet Long Barrow
Whispering Knights

Stone Journey 2
Scotland, Stonehenge

Cairnholy 1
Callanish Stone Circle
Little Meg Stone Circle
Long Meg & Her Daughters Stone Circle
Maeshowe
Ring of Brodgar
Scara Brae
Stonehenge
Stones of Stenness
The Twelve Apostles Stone Circle
The Watchstone
Tomb of The Eagles
Torhouse Stone Circle (Torhouskie)

Stone Journey 3
Scotland

Cairnholy 1 and 2
Glenquicken Stone Circle
Loupin Stanes Stone Circle
The Twelve Apostles Stone Circle

Stone Journey 4
Southern England, Scotland, Northern England

Avebury
Beltane
Cherhill White Horse
Girdle Stanes Stone Circle
Glastonbury
Kirkmadrine Stones
Loupin Stanes Stone Circle Machrie Moor
Mayburgh
Silbury
Stoney Littleton Long Barrow
The Longstones (Adam and Eve)
West Kennet Long Barrow

Stone Journey 5
Sweden

Ales Stenar
Disa's Ting
Havangsdosen
Kivik Kungagraven

Stone Journey 6
Scotland, Northern England

Ballymeanoch Stones
Balnuaran of Clava
Borve Alignment
Corrimony Cairn
Cullerlie Stone Circle
Druids Circle
Dunadd Fort
Dunchraigaig Cairn
Eire Pair
Fairy Glen
Janus Stones

Kenmare Stone Circle
Knockdrum Stone Fort
Knocknakilla Stone Circle Complex
Knocknarea
Knockraheen Stone Circle Complex
Knowth
Listoghil
Loanhead Of Daviot Stone Circle
Loughcrew Cairns
Maiden Stone
Midmar Kirk Stone Circle
Nether Largie Cairns
Punchestown Longstone
Racecourse Longstone
Seven Sisters Stone Circle
Shronebirrane Stone Circle
St Brigids Well
Sunhoney Stone Circle
Swinside Stone Circle (Sunkenkirk)
Temple Wood Stone Circle
Templebryan Stone Circle
The Fingers Stone Row (Gurranes)
The Great X (Nether Largie Stones)
The Twelve Apostles Stone Circle
Uragh Stone Circle

Stone Journey 7
England, Scotland

Avebury
Belas Knap Long Barrow
Brimham Rocks
Devil's Arrows
Glenquicken Stone Circle
Minchinhampton Stone
Rollright Stones
Stanton Drew Stone Circles & Cove
Stonehenge
Wayland's Smithy Long Barrow

Stone Journey 8
Ireland, Northern Ireland

Ardgroom Stone Circle
Beaghmore Stone Circles
Blarney Castle
Block & Bluid
Bohonagh Stone Circle
Broadleas Stone Circle

Brown's Hill Dolmen
Burgatia Stone
Carrowmore Megalithic Cemetery
Castleruddery Stone Circle
Church of St. Barrahane
Cong Stone Circles (Glebe)
Creevykeel Court Tomb
Dowth
Drombeg Stone Circle
Giants Grave
Glantane Stone Circle (Glanthane)
Grange Stone Circles
Hill Of Tara

Stone Journey 9
Ireland, England, Scotland

An Diseart
Ardgroom Stone Circle
Ardmore Stone Row
Athgreany Stone Circle (Piper Stones)
Ballycommane Stones
Ballymeanoch Stones
Balnachraig Stone
Bonane Heritage Park & Stone Circle
Boscawen-Un Stone Circle
Callanish I
Callanish II
Callanish III
Callanish IV
Clach Stein Stones
Colaiste Ide Ogham Stones
Creagantairbh Standing Stone
Croft Moraig Stone Circles
Danes Stone
Derreen Gardens
Derreenataggart Stone Circle
Drift Standing Stones
Dun Carloway Fort
Dunadd Hill Fort
Dunchraigaig Cairn
Feaghna Bullaun Stone
Fortingall Stone Circles
Fortingall Yew
Gallarus Oratory
Glebe Cairn
Graigue Stone
Hurlers Stone Circles
Kealkill Stone Circles and Stones

Kenmare Stone Circle
Kilmakader Church grounds
Kintraw Stone and Cairn
Lanyon Quoit
Lugnagappul Ogham Stones
Lundin Farm Stone Circle
Men An Tol
Merrivale Stone Complex
Ru Cruin Cairn
Soussans Common Stone Circle
South Zeal Stone
St. Michael's Mount
St. Nectan's Glen
Stanton Drew Stone Circles & Cove
Steinacleit Cairn and Circle
Temple Wood Stone Circles
The Blind Fiddler
The Great X (Netherlargie Stones)
The Piper Stones
The Truiseil Stone
Tobar Eoin (St. John's Well)
Uragh Stone Circle

"Laugh not so lightly O King, for in these stones is a mystery and healing virtue."
Merlin
The History of Britain

Preface

By way of introduction, let me start by saying that in the beginning I was just a traveler with an interest in the "big standing rocks" of Europe. I had no real expectations and certainly no hopes that I might have any kind of life changing experiences. I just had a strong desire to go and see for myself the amazing large stone monuments I had first seen in pictures when I was a young boy. However, after several trips to the UK, and one to Brittany, that changed. I changed. There came a point in time when I was going more as a seeker, looking for real experiences with the stones and in search of any knowledge I might gain about them, or from them.

Most of the text of this book is taken directly from, or based upon, the journals I kept during what I came to call my "Stone Journeys." The photographs are ones I took myself, with a few exceptions when my wife Sharon took the shot.

May of 2009 was the first of these "Journeys." Though I had been to the UK many times before this trip, and had, in fact, visited many stone sites, the stones had been an interest, not a passion. This journey was quite different. In planning for the trip there were three books I had obtained that were to be of great value to me. The first I had acquired was *Mysterious Britain* by Janet and Colin Bord. On my first trip to England, I had picked it up off a "used" rack in a book store. Though it covers a variety of subjects from stone circles, to sacred wells, to ley lines, and so on, it was the information on standing stones and stone circles that really excited me. Each page was like fuel for the fire that I found smoldering deep inside. Following the purchase of this book, over the next few years I often found myself pulling it off a bookshelf in my library, gazing at the old black and white photographs, and reading and rereading the descriptions of the different stone sites. Each time I did this the fire inside burned a little hotter until one day I knew that it was time to make another trip to Europe. Time to visit the stones.

Also of great assistance as I began making plans were *A Guide To The Stone Circles Of Britain, Ireland, and Brittany* by Aubrey Burl and *Circles Of Stone* by Max Milligan, text by Burl, both having been purchased off the internet.

In Burl's *Guide* you have a straight forward and informative guide with descriptions, minimal directions, and maps for more than 400 stone sites. There are also some mediocre photos.

While Maxwell's book also contains some good information, the real prize here is his photographs. The book describes 70 stone circles from around the UK and Ireland with stunning black and white photographs of each.

All three books include Ordinance Survey map coordinates which can be very helpful when trying to find some locations. But you have to get the right maps and understand how to use them. I set out on my first Journey with just the large edition AA Britain Road Atlas.

I also gained some information from the web site www.stonepages.com. This is a limited site put together and maintained by an enthusiastic couple from Italy who have actually been to the stone sites featured.

By the time I made my second "Journey," I had found many other publications (most notably *The Modern Antiquarian* by Julian Cope) and web sites, (I especially appreciate the efforts of Andy at the Megalithic Portal web site) which provided valuable information, including maps and directions to the sites. That information along with Road Atlases by Collins, AA, and Phillip's, as well as information obtained from locals, provided enough to find most of the locations I went in search of.

On my last two "Journeys" I did purchase Ordinance Survey maps for parts of Cornwall and southwest Ireland that were quite helpful. They really do give you much more detailed information about roads and terrain, as well as often showing the circles, standing stones, etc. on the maps.

Another valuable tool would be a handheld GPS but I have yet to purchase one.

When writing about my journeys I stayed away from the many myths and legends and most of the historical, astronomical, and geological information as it is all explored and explained rather thoroughly in other publications and on many web sites. In these pages I have stayed with the information recorded in my journals as much as possible. I talk about the sites I visited, the experiences I had, and what I learned.

I apologize for writing this in a jumble of first and second person, as well as, past and present tenses. Sometimes one just felt better than the other, but also, moving to the second person seemed, at times, to include the reader more in the experience.

Lastly I hope this book strikes a comfortable chord with anyone who has felt a desire to listen to, and to follow, the call of an inner more personal voice, and to open themselves to possibilities that the "practical" mind would either ignore or run away from. To such a person I would suggest that there is much to be learned in the company of stones.

Introduction

Though I did not take my first "Journey to the Stones" until I was almost 60 years old, I realize now that I began preparing for that moment when I was about 10, as by that time I was already quite fascinated with rocks. I loved to climb on the big ones and to collect the smaller ones. There was, and still is, something very special about climbing to the top of a large rock formation and gazing out over the surrounding terrain. Or just sitting quietly on top of a big boulder, mind open to possibilities. Or holding a large crystal in your hand and staring into its depths.

As a youth I would sometimes spend part of my summers with my grandparents and they would take me on trips to Sequoia National Park. It was not just the magnificent redwoods that were a wonder, there was also the awesome presence of Morrow Rock. It is a massive granite formation that has a hiking trail winding up its side to the top. Once you get there, the views are unbelievable. I loved that rock. Though we would take the long walk together, when we would get to the top my grandparents would find a place in the shade to sit and rest. I would then find someplace out of their sight where I could leave the trail and proceed to run full out across the uneven surface, jumping from rock to boulder, filled with excitement, joy, and a dose of fear. The fall, should one occur, was forever. Then, when I would find the right place, I would sit with my back to the rock and just feel happy.

That feeling is as real for me today as it was when I was that young boy. To just stand or sit on some large rock and feel the rock's strength, a sense of permanence, and to know all is well with the world.

When I was in the fifth grade, I took some of my hard earned paper route money and purchased a copy of the *Golden Nature Guide - Rocks and Minerals*. After reading it from cover to cover, I took it with me to the local sports and hobby store in Ukiah and showed the owner a picture of the rock hammer I wanted. I was told they would have to order it for me and every other day for the next couple of weeks I would stop by the store only to have my hopes dashed yet again. When it finally arrived, I held it like it was some precious, holy relic, and I was anxious to set off into the hills in search of the gems and minerals I knew were just waiting for me to find them.

Leaving the hobby store, I went straight to the Army Surplus store. After sifting through a variety of packs and bags used to carry everything from ammo to medical supplies, I found just what I was looking for. It was a canvass bag that had been used to carry ammunition. It had a long strap which hung comfortably across my shoulder, a flap which snapped to keep the contents of the bag from falling out, and inside, two compartments. In one I would place my rock specimens and in the other I would carry my little book of knowledge. At last I was ready to begin my search.

Now I really had no idea what I was doing, but book in bag and hammer in hand I took off into the hills to the west of the Ukiah Valley. It did not take long before I began to feel disappointed. It seemed that everything I picked up was just an old rock no different than any other and I was not finding anything that looked like the wonders I had seen in my book. Still, over the coming weeks and months I continued to bring home bag after bag of rocks and in fact, began to find some that I thought must surely be special. I would clean them up and place the "good" ones in shallow boxes lined with cotton. Then searching through pictures in my book I would try to name each specimen, making paper labels for those I felt sure of. Among the rocks in my boxes I had some nice pieces of milky quartz, a couple of quartz crystals, obsidian, serpentine, jade, and even some nice small crystals I didn't know the name of that I found at the back of an abandoned mine shaft. Though there was nothing there of value to anyone else, I loved my little rock collection.

When a rock and mineral show was held at the fairgrounds, I purchased a ticket and while my friends were all out playing baseball or shooting marbles I was walking in awe from booth to booth, down aisle after aisle, dazed by the beauty and the variety of the specimens on display. I did not have a lot of money, but I was able to purchase a nice chunk of pyrite and a good sized terminated quartz crystal. Returning home I placed each lovingly in their own cotton lined box. To me it was like having a large gold nugget and a giant diamond in my collection. I could not have been happier!

Over the next couple of years I continued to add to my collection. Sadly it was all lost in a move my family made when I was 13. Though it was years before I began to collect in earnest again, I was always picking up rocks and bringing them home to place around the house or in the garden.

It was not until I was about 35 that I made my first trip to England. My wife, Sharon, and I had decided to take a summer vacation there, and as we began making our plans, there was for me no doubt that our first stop after arriving would be Stonehenge. I had first seen pictures of these wondrous stones in a slide presentation when I was in the fourth grade and in the following years I kept my eyes open for any information I might find on this remarkable stone monument. It was one of those places I dreamed of someday visiting. So, when the opportunity came, I was determined to make that dream a reality. We flew into London and after giving ourselves a few days to settle in, we rented a car and headed out. I can still visualize with clarity my first sighting of those incredible stones. Traveling down A303 we came over a rise and standing there quite alone on a wide open grassy field was Stonehenge, a sight like no other, and it shook me.

Upon parking and paying for admittance we took the walk through the tunnel under the road and to the circle. Approaching the stones I was excited but also slightly apprehensive. It was like going to meet a relative for the first time and hoping to find them warm and welcoming.

Stonehenge was fenced off by a rope placed quite a ways out from the stones and running a couple of feet off the ground, but even the disappointment of not being able to walk among the stones (and the never ending mass of tourists) did not diminish the obvious "presence" of this place. I was in complete awe of those stones and it just felt right to be there. Over the years, with each return visit, I have experienced the same wonderful feeling of belonging, and the same strong desire for everyone else to just go away and leave me alone with the stones.

The next stop on this trip was to Avebury, and what a truly incredible place it is. Avebury is the largest stone circle/henge in the UK. A henge is a circular earthen inclosure consisting of an outer bank and in most cases an inner ditch, with one or more entrances. In the case of Avebury it also has an inner circle of giant standing stones. Even with all the destruction that has happened there in the past (the majority of the stones have been destroyed, buried, or broken up to be used in building homes or fences) it is still a very, very special place. Its megaliths are some of the most massive in all of the UK and the earth ring and ditch that surround the complex are impressive to say the least. Though this site is protected, you can walk freely among the stones and even go up to them and give them a hug if you like. I did not hug the stones that first time but I did spend enough time moving from stone to stone to realize that there was something going on there that intrigued me. I could not really explain the feeling but it was as if there was something waking inside of me that had been slumbering for many years, but that I was still too groggy to understand.

When we left Avebury I felt a sense of sadness. It was kind of like visits I made to my grandparents as a young man. When it came time to go I would feel sad that I could not stay longer. With them there was a wisdom, an understanding of life, and a joy in living that I could feel nourishing me when just setting in their company, and there was always a sense of loss when leaving them. It was the same feeling when I left Avebury.

Over the next many years I made several return return visits to the UK, either on tour with my band or on vacation with Sharon. On those trips I often made stops at Stonehenge and Avebury, but was always in a hurry. On one trip to Cornwall with Sharon, we did visit many stone sights including Men An Tol (which left me quite puzzled), Lanyon Quoit, and the Nine Maidens Stone Alignment. Though I was not yet "all in" when it came to the stones, I was becoming very intrigued.

At the end of a European tour that my band had just completed Sharon joined me in France. Though our travels would take us all over France it was our visit to Brittany that really changed my world. I would never look at the "stones" the same way again.

It began with a visit to Carnac. I had seen information about this site in a French tourism booklet and had immediately felt the pull of the stones. There were photos of row upon row of standing stones and of individual tall standing megaliths (a megalith is a single standing stone), and I knew we had to check it out. Upon arrival we spent about half a day exploring the stones in the Carnac area. In some locations there are huge tall stones called menhirs standing all alone and quite magnificent. In other places you find rows and rows of stones standing like large dominoes all lined up and waiting for a push. (In fact there are some 3000 of these standing stones around Carnac.) Throughout the area there are also many burial chambers of various sizes and styles of construction. It really is a wonderful place. But as great as it is, I did not get any of the inner tug I had received when at Avebury. I had hoped to have a more personal experience, a connection of some kind to these stones, but it was not the case.

Deciding it was time to move on we drove west. After visiting a couple of interesting sites, including one very impressive passage grave the name of which I sadly cannot remember, we found ourselves nearing a small town called Erdeven. On the right side of the road, we saw another grouping of stones standing in rows. So, parking the car, we got out and began walking among them. The stones were large, rather chunky in appearance, in a variety of sizes and shapes, and some appeared to be as much as 10 feet tall. There was no one else around, the traffic on the road was light, and I was excited to notice a good "feeling" that came from being with these stones.

I saw a small wood arrow pointing towards a hedge lined path that headed off to the north. Painted on the arrow was "les geants." Off we went, excited to see where this path might lead us.

A short walk found us entering a group of more than 20 large megaliths, both standing and fallen, and some were as much as maybe 20 feet in length. Unlike Carnac, this place definitely had something "going on." As we wandered through the stones I began getting a tingling sensation all over. Sharon did not seem to notice anything.

We walked towards a massive fallen stone, at least three feet thick, that lay on the earth like a large altar stone. I began to notice that the closer I got to this "altar stone" the stronger the tingling sensation was. It was kind of like having a light electrical current running throughout my system. Stepping up to the stone, it suddenly felt as if I had a blow torch placed under my feet. The heat was unbelievable as it rushed up my legs and through my body. Sharon, seeing that I was very flushed and breaking out in a sweat asked if I was ok? A good question!

Along with the intense heat, I was also filled with an exhilaration, a feeling of serious power, and looking at Sharon leaning against the stone, a raw lust. Reaching out I pulled Sharon into my arms and she said, "Pat, you're burning up!" Without getting too graphic, suffice it to say that in no time I had placed Sharon on the stone and was in the process of trying to remove her clothing. I had never experienced anything like that before and only three times, in a more subdued manner, since. I was like a body of energy wanting to explode. I must say that Sharon handled the situation remarkably well. She had no idea what was happening, but in a calm and soothing voice I could hear her saying, "Not a good time, Pat."

At about this moment we heard the voices of people approaching. Though I was still in a daze, thanks to Sharon, all appeared quite normal as three people walked into the group of stones and greeted us with, "Bonjour!"

Moving away from the "altar stone," I began getting myself under control. As my temperature and pulse dropped, I walked up to one of the standing stones, placed my hands on it and felt a cool peace roll over me. As the other visitors showed no sign of leaving, and I was still a bit confused, we began walking back to the car. Sharon had a look of concern on her face and asked if I was ok. Though the "rush" was gone, I continued to have a subtle tingling throughout my body for hours after the experience. There was also a sense of loss. Whatever had happened, I was wanting more.

Later that night, lying in a hotel bed I kept thinking about what had happened. At that small, little known site of standing and fallen stones, I had had the most incredible experience of my life. What had caused this? Was it the size of the stones? The location of the stones? The composition of the stones? Was it their placement? Was it any or all of the above? After years of visiting these megalithic sites I must confess, I am still puzzled.

When I had walked among the stones at Carnac earlier in the day, I had felt nothing. No hit of any kind. Then, I did get a good feeling when we first got to the Erdeven stones but that was all. Walking the path to "the giants" there had been only a sense of anticipation. But walking into that gathering of stones was like turning the volume of the stereo all the way up. The intensity of that rush of energy was incredible. Over the years since this experience I have become convinced that certain stones must have been placed in precise locations where they became a conduit for earth energies, a place where those energies can flow freely up and out or down and in. The thing is, of course, that someone a very, very, long time ago figured this out. Pretty impressive.

It was not until I was working on writing this book that I obtained a copy of Aubrey Burl's *Megalithic Brittany*. I had, up until then, never seen any information about this location near Erdeven in any other books. What a joy to find on page 145 the listing "187a, Kerzerho, Erdeven, stone rows." In his description of the stones to the north he described the stone at the end of the row as "the Table of Sacrifice," and there is a photo. He explained that locals say, "that's the place where the blood used to flow." I was blown away. This was my "altar stone," and I had felt the power of this place.

Over the years following that trip to Brittany, I have greatly increased the amount of time I spend studying and working with earth energies, stones, gems, etc. I have become much more attuned to those energies and use them for dowsing, to improve health issues, and to further my own spiritual growth.

A few years ago I even went so far as to build my own stone circle. It is approximately 46 feet across. In the center there is a six and a half foot tall pillar stone some three feet in diameter. Around the outer edge is a circle of smaller stones six inches to a foot tall, set stone against stone. About three feet in from the outer ring is an inner circle of 16 larger stones of various sizes and shapes which are evenly spaced. The four largest stones in this inner circle are about three feet in height and placed at the north, south, east, and west. There are two entrances to the circle, one in the north and the other in the east.

When I decided to build this circle I first walked the land with my dowsing rods looking for the right place. I found a spot where two energy lines crossed each other making an X. One line ran east/west and the other north/south. I knew this was the place for my circle and I placed my center stone where X marked the spot. This circle has become a real place of peace for me and over the last several years the stones and I have developed quite a bond. It is a magical place.

A few words about dowsing. While I do not have the skills of a professional, I can find energy lines and water lines easy enough and have had some success with health issues and life questions. Though I do sometimes use a pendulum, usually I work with one or two L shaped rods. I hold one loosely in each hand, about chest high, with the short part of the L in the hand and the long part facing forward. When I cross an energy line, the rods turn inward to line up with each other and when I pass over the energy line they return to the forward position. Should I choose to follow a line, I use just one rod and follow its lead. I have found that the ability to dowse this way seems to run in about half the people I have tested. You either seem to have it or you don't. Whether it can be learned by practice, I do not know.

The rods can also be used to ask yes or no questions to great effect. I use one rod to do this. In my case, a yes response is the rod moving to the right and a no is the rod moving to the left. More on this later.

Early in 2009 I found the desire to return to those wondrous standing stones of Europe growing too strong to ignore. I began making my plans to return to England. It was time for a "Journey to the Stones."

Stone Journals

This is pretty much everything I need for one of these journeys. Well, almost everything. I do all my planning on the front side and have copious notes on how to find the locations I will be in search of, whether it be a stone circle or a B&B. I also have often booked my rooms in advance so as to make sure I am not wandering around looking for a room in an area that is fully booked because of the local sheep dog trials. Then of course there are the plane tickets, the passport, and the ATM and credit cards. Pack light, be ready for cold and rain, and enjoy!

"There is no use merely touching our heads indifferently against the surface of any stone, feeling around it with our fingertips and expecting all sorts of information to come pouring out in vividly pictorial or other fashion.

What we want we must go in and get ourselves. There is no other real way of obtaining anything worthwhile.

Until we learn how to do this in the spirit of love for the life forces connected with the stones, they will remain uncommunicative or merely misleading."

William Gray
The Rollright Ritual

Stone Journey 1
SOUTHERN ENGLAND

STONE JOURNEY 1 - May 10, 2009

Leaving for England I had my itinerary pretty much laid out and was prepared with site info and locations, road directions and maps, compass, tape measure, and dowsing rods. Flying out of SFO (San Francisco) my spirits and hopes were high. At last I was going back. It was time to get up close and personal with the stones.

Arriving at London Heathrow at 6:50 AM, I was through customs and in my Hertz rental car by 8:00. After a couple of hours driving and several stops for directions, I arrived at my destination in Oxfordshire. The Rollright Stone Circle is located just north of Chipping Norton along the A436.

By the time I finally did arrive at the Rollright Circle, an overall feeling of exhaustion had set in. Though it was still early in the day, I was pretty much reconciled to a short walk through the circle and then off to find a room somewhere to get some much needed sleep. But as I opened the posted gate and walked through, I looked to the right and there through the trees I saw the stones. I almost laughed as I was flooded with a feeling of joy. I was really here, and I was quite excited!

Passing through a short stretch of woods I came out into an open field and turning to the right walked to the edge of the circle. What a circle it is. This is nothing like the Stonehenge or Avebury sites with their massive, shaped and smoothed stones. Standing there staring at my discovery the first words to come to my mind were actually "ancient" and "gnarly". There are 77 stones in this perfect shaped circle and they are all very rough, misshaped, and pockmarked. Cope, in *The Modern Antiquarian,* referred to their appearance as being "leprous." Some even have holes worn all the way through the soft limestone, like worm eaten wood. They are also much smaller than the stones at those better known sites. The tallest stone is about seven feet tall and quite spindly while most are four feet or less. Green grass and weeds had grown up around the base of the stones along with lovely long stemmed yellow wild flowers which stood proudly alongside their stone companions.

I began with a walk around the outside of the circle, getting the feel of the place. It is 104 feet in diameter and has a very seductive charm about it. There is an entrance on the southeast side of the circle and the moment I walked through it and into the circle, I had a sense of being lighter, like I had just released myself of some burden. I began wandering around with no thought, plan, or expectation. I soon found myself talking to one stone or another, and though they did not respond it just sort of felt right. I then became aware of a sensation of energy flowing up from the ground, through my feet, legs, and body. Unlike my experience at Erdeven this was a subtle, soothing energy. It was like my legs were straws, slowly sucking energy out of the earth.

Feeling better by the minute, I spent quite a while just enjoying the company of these wonderful old rocks, wandering from stone to stone. I was next drawn to one particular stone on the east side. Reaching out I touched the stone, and it was like I had just plugged into a battery charger. My feet seemed to be absorbed into the earth and as I stood there, hand on stone, I experienced a free flow of energy from the ground into my body. Where just a short time before I had been exhausted, I was now completely rejuvenated. It was quite amazing.

Sadly, at this moment I noticed that a couple of other people had arrived. Their arrival kind of "messed with my groove" but I was back on track physically and mentally, and spiritually I was on cloud nine. I stayed for a while longer and as I continued to walk from one stone to another I did feel a slight tug from one of the stones on the northeast side. When I got out my dowsing rods and walked the circle, both of the stones I had been drawn to give my rods a strong pull. As this was the first stop of my journey I didn't quite have my act together yet and neglected to check the site for energy lines crossing the circle.

By now even more people had arrived. The circle's location right next to the road is a bit of a drawback as people can easily stop by for a quick photo op. There is also the intermittent traffic noise which can be a little bothersome. So, saying goodbye to these marvelous old stones I exited the circle and went to visit the other two stone sites close by.

On the edge of this same field, about a half mile walk or so from the Rollright Circle there are the remains of a burial chamber called the Whispering Knights and just across the road from Rollright is a tall standing stone called the King Stone. Both sites are impressive but they are also both fenced off with pointed metal fencing and I could get no sense of them. I understand protecting the stones but this just seemed wrong on several levels. The stones felt caged rather than protected. The wind was really picking up, and it was getting quite cold so I decided it was time to go. Being fully charged I was ready for more, and so I headed south towards Avebury.

As I drove south I thought to myself that I was off to a really good start on this "journey to the stones." It had begun with only a few hours' sleep, then three hours getting to the airport and waiting for my flight, and 10 non sleep hours in the air to London. It was about another hour clearing customs and getting my rental car. Then another two hours driving on the wrong side of the road in fast moving morning traffic, while trying to read maps, road signs, and to figure out the roundabouts. That's about 16 exhausting hours to the Rollright Stone Circle on very little sleep, not to mention the jet lag. But then to walk into the circle, to be welcomed by the stones, and to be recharged by the life energies of the earth itself, that was a wonderful thing. I had left Rollright with a smile on my face and a peaceful heart.

I stopped for lunch in Burford at a lovely restaurant called Hufkins. Everything was prepared with locally grown produce and they baked their own breads. I had a sandwich, soup and tea for 10 pounds, and it was delicious.

Arriving in Marlborough, which is near Avebury, I decided to find a room for the night. Right on the main drive through town I found the Ivy House Hotel (now closed) and checked in. It was 60 pounds with breakfast, and the room was quite comfortable. After a short walk around town I decided to drive on to Avebury, just 15 minutes away.

What a joy to return to this wonderful place once again. The first thing you encounter is the earth mound and ditch, or henge that surrounds the site. It is about a quarter of a mile across, and it is the largest such earth ring in the world. The ditch, which is on the inside of the mound, is about 12 feet deep, but was originally closer to 30, and the 15 foot high mound was once 18 feet. Imagine that. It would have been almost 50 feet from the bottom of the ditch to the top of the mound. Very impressive!

Standing there looking at the henge, I thought about how very different this site was from Stonehenge. Stonehenge stands alone and majestic out on flat land, and the awe inspiring stones could have been seen from long distances away, even when its small henge was intact. Here at Avebury however, the earth henge completely hid what was inside. Only by entering within did you experience the mystery of this massive stone complex. This was a very sacred place. Whereas Stonehenge challenged you with its presence, Avebury dared you.

I climbed up on the mound and walking the perimeter you find there are four entrances to the henge through which two roads pass, crossing near the circle center. Just inside the ditch are the remains of the main stone circle and looking down on these massive stones you get just a hint of what once was. Not only is this the largest stone circle in all of Europe but in its full glory there were two more stone circles within it that would have been the fifth and seventh largest. Only a few of the stones of those inner circles remain. Nonetheless, Avebury remains quite impressive.

And the stones! The stones! They are like sculptures done by some modern artist and placed on display. No Rollright rocks here. These massive megaliths are as tall as 19 feet, weigh as much as 60 tons, and are dramatically (an for the most part naturally) shaped. Their gray surfaces are smoothed as if buffed by some modern power tool.

Standing there looking down on the circle stones I remembered that what I was seeing was only a portion of each stone. In fact, about one third of each stone is buried in the ground. So, when I was looking at a stone close to 20 feet tall, it was actually more like 30 feet in length. That makes this all even harder to comprehend. These stones were transported over long distances and then carefully and purposefully positioned, and this without the use of flatbed trucks, backhoes, and cranes. Unreal!

Sadly, the winds which began earlier in the day were becoming a real event. I had trouble standing still to take photos as the winds jerked me back and forth, and it was also getting dark and very cold. Still, I was determined to walk among the stones for as long as I could handle it. Moving in and out of the stones I did have a chuckle when I noticed that the many large black sheep wandering around did not seem bothered at all by the degrading weather conditions. At one point I found myself envying a big ram, who stood there seemingly quite content, covered in his heavy coat of wool. He returned my gaze as if wondering, "What is this guy's problem?"

The chill began getting into my bones, and the long journey was catching up with me. I did stand with a few of the giants long enough to get a comforting tingle but that was it. It was about time to go. The warmth of the bed back in Marlborough beckoned.

I walked back up on the earth ring and stood looking down on the Devil's Chair, a massive circle stone, and on to the other stones running off to the north. As I teetered to and fro in the wind, I felt a sadness. Not for me, but for these last surviving standing stones. All that remains of what was once an enormous complex of giant stone circles and avenues. I was reminded of an occasion when as a boy I had sat listening to a couple of old timers telling stories of when they were young, when they were strong and when life was glorious, and how sad it was that so many of their friends were gone. It was easy for me to imagine these same conversations being shared from stone to stone.

Turning, I looked to the south, where the stones of West Kennet Avenue disappeared over the rise. Sadly, I would not be visiting them this time. I was done, and walked back to my car with mixed emotions.

I had a great night's sleep but was up at 5:30 AM. After a nice breakfast, I headed for the Stanton Drew Circle. My route along the A4 took me right past the West Kennet Long Barrow so I parked alongside the road, walked through the signed gate, and started up the path. It is about a half mile across farm land and up a hill to the barrow. The fields were covered with a radiant yellow flowered plant much like

mustard plants back home. (I later learned that this plant was rape from which comes rapeseed oil.) It really was a beautiful walk and once at the top there was a most spectacular view across the yellow fields to Silbury Hill, the largest man-made earth mound in Europe. At 130 feet tall, it really is majestic and they have no idea why it was built. This walk was worth it just for the view.

West Kennet Long Barrow is also very impressive. The earth mound is more than 100 yards long and in excellent condition. The entrance to the barrow is fronted with huge standing stones, and I was struck by their size, shape, and placement. This was no hap-hazard construction. Nor was the inside, where there were five separate chambers connected by a central passage. It really is quite spacious inside, and I was able to walk throughout this tomb without bending over. The walls and ceiling were created by stacking blocks of

Stone Journals

stone, some pieces being quite large. The stone work was amazing to me. The people who built this obviously did so with concern for both detail and durability and with respect for those who would be buried within. They wanted it right.

I know there are many people who hold this site in the highest reverence, and many have had a variety of experiences there. Though I too walked this site with reverence, I was not blessed with any experiences while there other than the joy of just seeing this marvelous place. It was enough.

I was struck by a realization. This is a massive open rock tomb located in the countryside, at the top of a hill, with no guards or protection, and yet I found no litter or graffiti anywhere. No chance back home. It is really sad that many Americans have so little respect for cultural and natural sites such as this one. This would be a party place back home, and there would be beer cans, broken bottles, cigarette butts, and graffiti everywhere.

As impressed as I was with West Kennet, yesterday's weather was still holding. According to my car's outside temperature gauge, it had been 41 degrees F and the winds were blowing. It was only 8:00 in the morning, and I was already cold all the way through my warm jacket. I had hoped to be in an open and contemplative frame of mind when I arrived at the barrow, and planned to sit inside for a while to see what might come to me. But that was not to be the case. The cold won out, and I walked back down the hill.

Returning to the car, I headed west. The drive took about an hour longer than it should have due to some direction problems, but eventually, just off the B3130, I arrived at the Stanton Drew Stone Circles, named after the little village alongside which they sit. The location is quite beautiful. The terrain consists of green rolling hills and open farm land which is crossed by the River Chew. Near the river, located close together there are three stone circles, two avenues, and a cove. A cove is a group of three stones set up sort of like an arbor with no roof, one on each side with a back.

As with many stone sites in the UK, I found I was also sharing this location with sheep, so I had to pay a bit of attention to where I stepped as sheep have no concerns with where they leave their droppings. That said, the sheep were quite interesting to watch. They like to settle up against the larger rocks, seeming to draw comfort from their presence and of course warmth from the stones. Especially fun to watch are the young ones who love chasing each other around and around the massive rocks.

Sadly, most of the stones in the largest of the Stanton Drew circles (called the Great Circle) have been removed, or fallen, or buried, and of the original 27 to 30 stones, there are only a few still standing. You can just barely find several of the fallen stones as over time they have been almost completely swallowed up by the earth. Still, this circle is very impressive in its size, being 369 feet across, and it is actually only second in size to Avebury.

When I am at stone sites like this one, I can't help but wonder why no one bothers to dig up and then reposition some of these buried stones? With the technologies available today, they can pretty much set them in their proper place and even in the original position. What harm would be done? In fact, I think it would be beneficial to the stones and to those who can appreciate their energies. There is of course just the esthetic value of a seeing a standing stone verses a buried one. Just one man's opinion.

The stones at Stanton Drew are not so large as those at Avebury but they are of serious size with the largest being almost 10 feet in height. For the most part they are block shaped and showing serious signs of weathering, though nothing like the stones I had seen at the Rollright Circle. Many do however have a similar leprous condition, red coloration, and are covered with lichen much like the Rollright stones.

The northeast circle is only 97 feet in diameter but all eight of its stones are still there and half are still standing. As I walked the circle I found myself drawn to one

Stone Journals

stone on the east side that had fallen and was lying at an angle protruding from the ground. I enjoyed the warmth I felt emitting from this stone and climbed up on it to lie for a while. I did not get an energy boost, but on a cold blustery day the warmth was enough. I lay there for about half an hour and during that time, along with the warmth, came some wonderful visualizations of common looking people, from some age long ago, moving along a stone avenue to the east and entering the circle to stand with heads and hands raised. No sound, but wonderful imagery. I got up and seeing the remains of that same avenue off to the east, I walked out to its end, and turning, followed it back into the circle, making the same walk I had seen. As I entered the circle, it just felt right. Was it a real window into the past? I have no idea, but I thanked the circle for the gift.

There was one couple that did pay the site a brief visit while I was there but for the most part it was just me, the stones, the sheep, the wind, and the cold. Though I liked this spot, I headed back to the car and its heater. The weather really was having a negative impact on me.

Driving south towards Cornwall on the A37, I realized that I had forgotten to visit the Stanton Drew "Cove" and I was quite unhappy with myself. But then I had also neglected to visit the third circle. It was obvious I was beginning to get burned out. I had begun this drive by getting lost for close to an hour. Bad start. I was getting tired of driving on the wrong side of narrow little roads with no shoulders, praying that the rapidly approaching trucks would not take me out. I was also feeling guilty about the short stays at the last several stone sites, as I had come a long way to have this experience. But mostly I was just letting the weather get to me. The winds would just not let up. I had heard on the radio that the high winds were being blamed for having blown the roof off a large building on a local college campus. On two occasions the gusts blew my little car right into the next lane and thankfully there was never another car already occupying said space.

Arriving on the southern peninsula of Cornwall my first stop was to be The Bowl Rock which I had found mentioned in *Mysterious Britain* by Janet and Colin Bord. Once again my map proved not to be very accurate. I found myself driving a narrow, wooded lane up what appeared to be the highest hill in the area. Near the top the trees were replaced by brush and boulders. Pulling into a parking area at the end of the lane, I saw a hiking trail leading off up the hill and decided to check it out before resuming my search. This proved a fortunate choice.

The trail led off into the brush which grew thickly up and over, forming a tunnel of green. It was well laid out and was a comfortable hike. Breaking out of the brush field, I saw the summit before me strewn with large boulders and stone outcroppings. At the very top was a magnificent stack of stones done by nature herself, with the cap stone being a huge granite cube. Climbing up on top of this monument was like stepping on to a large altar, with the landscape around me being the temple and the gorgeous blue sky with its billowing white and gray clouds, the dome which covered it all. No European cathedral could be more impressive.

It was at this point I realized that the angry winds had died down and that the sun was breaking through the clouds. Each time the sun's rays would shine down on me, it was like a blessing with a hope for more to come. As I stood there alone on nature's altar, the vista across the Cornish countryside seemed never ending and once again I could feel the energies of the earth begin recharging my inner battery. I thanked the powers that be for bringing me to this wonderful place. I stood still, absorbing the revitalizing energies being offered.

I think I should say that it is my belief that the "life force," called *nwyfre* by the ancient Welsh, exists in everything, and that it flows through everything, though maybe a little slower through a stone. We humans are masters of none. We are just a part of the mix and should respect that life force in all its manifestations.

Later, when the skies began to darken once again, I climbed down off the rocks and began the walk back to the car. I felt so much better and even had a bounce in my step. At one point I began jogging down the path, jumping from boulder to boulder like that young boy on Morrow Rock. I had once again found my center and was ready to continue my journey.

It was not until I had been back in the States awhile, collecting my notes and looking at maps, that I realized that this hill I had climbed was Trencrom Hill, considered one of the most important "spiritual" sites in Cornwall. It is said to once have been the home of giants and spriggans. Though I cannot speak to any of that, I do know that the earth energies there are real and they are powerful.

Back in my car I tried several different roads before I found The Bowl Rock, but when I did it actually took my breath away. The setting was quite special. There it sat, just a little ways off to the side of the road. A huge rounded boulder nestled up against a lovely babbling creek, whose banks were overgrown with a variety of lush green plants. Between the road and the rock was a small grassy meadow interwoven with colorful wild flowers. Growing around the base of the rock were several ferns and there was one small leafed ivy climbing up its surface. The backdrop to this wondrous setting was a deep wood.

The Bowl Rock is about 12 feet across the base and maybe 10 feet tall. It sits there like a slightly deflated stone ball that has settled into the earth. Actually, it sort of reminded me of a large stone brain sitting on the ground.

Walking the site and viewing the rock from various angles, I was filled with joy. I really liked this place. The closer I got to the rock, the more I could "feel" it welcoming me. When I reached out and touched it, the rock felt warm, and this on a cold, overcast day in a shaded wood. The stone on which I lay at Stanton Drew had a warmth to it, but nothing like this, and that stone had been right out in the sun. I had an overwhelming sense of peace flood my body. Like sliding into a warm bath on a cold day, I had a feeling I was sliding into the stone itself, and it was very comforting. I was sensing much more than a rock before me. I sensed a presence and a surety that it had much to offer.

I stood calmly, hand on stone, open to anything that might occur. I had a moment there when I imagined Spock doing a Vulcan mind-meld with the Horta and I had a little chuckle. As I waited, a voice filled my head with the message, "First you must be quiet," and then I felt compassion flowing from the rock. Yes, strange as that might seem, I did say compassion. It was like I was a disciple sitting at the

master's feet, and the master knowing I was not nearly ready. In fact, I have been about 40 years now trying to still my mind and I have yet to have much success. Meditation practices are not easy for me and coupled with the occasional traffic sounds from the road nearby it just wasn't happening. As I began to get frustrated with the sense of missed opportunity, that warm feeling once again flooded me, and I knew it was ok, I had been blessed. Everything was just fine. I need only accept the gift of the stone. I stepped away from the rock with mixed emotions, both sadness and joy. I had experienced something I cannot fully explain and which I know most will see as nonsense or an overactive imagination. But for me, it was an experience I shall always cherish. And this from a rock.

After spending the night at a B&B in Penzance, I took off around 9:00 AM. It was cold, and the mist was heavy enough to require windshield wipers. I must say the mist hanging heavy over the English countryside provided a bit of intrigue. Maybe I've watched too many Sherlock Holmes films with Basil Rathbone, but it did provide a mysterious edge to things.

According to the map, my first stop was not far away. I was in search of a single standing stone called The Blind Fiddler. Driving along the A30 I had gone well past the village of Drift, near which it should have been located, and I began looking for a turn around. I saw a slight turnout, and as I pulled into it I also saw an entry gate in the hedge which ran alongside the road. There was a post there in which was carved Boscawen-Un. I was quite surprised and very happy as this stone circle was on my list of places to find. I parked and began the hike into the mist shrouded countryside.

The narrow path was lined with gorse, heath, and beautiful bluebells, and with every step my anticipation grew. As I walked up over a hill and across open fields there was an occasional break in the mist revealing wonderful views of the rolling farm lands below. It was only then that I realized I was on top of a ridge.

Approaching a large brush field where the plants were some 10 feet high and very dense, I followed the path as it entered into a tunnel cut into, and through, the brush. After just a short distance, the path split left and right and opened up overhead. To the right I saw a wooden gate, beyond which I could see stones standing in the mist. Opening the gate I entered a clearing that was completely surrounded by a high brush barrier and in the center of which sat a most lovely stone circle. The mist was so thick that I was already thoroughly coated with a layer of moisture. It dripped off my nose and ran in rivulets off my rain proof jacket. I must say, it made for a very mysterious and mystical atmosphere, and as I walked into the circle I did so with a Cheshire grin on my face.

The circle is actually an oval some 82 feet by 73 feet. It has 19 standing stones which are three to five feet in height and which are spaced fairly evenly apart, except that is, in the west where there is what appears to be an entry. I also noticed that the stones all seem to have been smoothed flat on the inside of the circle. In the middle, but setting noticeably off center, is a taller stone over seven feet tall which leans at quite a dramatic angle. When I walked the circle with my dowsing rods, it was interesting to find an energy line running through the circle passing right under the (not quite) center stone. One had to wonder what had happened with the builders. It is like they built the circle first and then realized they had not properly placed it so as to have the energy line running through its middle. So, rather than move the whole circle they just placed the center stone on the energy line instead of in the actual center. Whatever the reason, it only added to the intrigue of this location.

I did notice another really cool thing about this circle. One of the stones standing off to the west side was not granite like all the others but was in fact a large block of quartz. Similar in size and shape to the others but definitely quartz. What was that all about? Why just the one?

Wandering the circle, going from stone to stone, I received no special feelings or reactions from this site. But that really was ok because just being there in that place, at that moment, was more than enough. Each stone was wonderful in and of itself, and though they were probably carved by nature, they had the appearance of having been shaped somewhat by human hands. And the setting, a meadow of dark green grass surrounded by a tall hedge of yellow flowered gorse, added to the richness of the place. Though the grass was, for the most part, kept low by people walking the site, it did manage to grow in tall, thick rings, like fur collars, around the base of each stone. Protruding from these collars were lovely blue wildflowers creating a beautiful effect. It was a wonderful circle in a wonderful location, and I had it to myself. Life was good!

My jacket and shoes were water repellant and were doing a great job. My pants, however, were not, and they were getting quite wet. I was once again getting cold down to the bones and decided it was time to leave. Had it been a nice sunny day, I could have stayed for hours. Boscawen-Un was that good.

Returning to my car I headed back in search of The Blind Fiddler. I saw a sign pointing to Carn Euny which I knew to be the site of a prehistoric village and decided to check it out. After driving down a narrow lane, walled in by tall hedges, I came to its end at a farm house. There was a small parking area with a sign reading Carn Euny pointing towards a path. So, I parked and once again walked off into the mist.

It was a short hike to Carn Euny which is the stone remains of what was once a prehistoric village. With the passage of time this ancient village now sits below ground level. Over much of the site you can walk along the surface looking down into what remains of the homes in which the villagers lived and the passages that connected them. However, there is one central, dome shaped room, that stands out from all the rest. It is still completely intact, and is in fact, totally underground and accessed by entering a long tunnel. To get into this room I walked down the 33 foot long stone lined tunnel, which required me to bend over just a little. I came to another side tunnel which went off to the left, so I took this 10 foot long passage and entered the main room which is circular in shape, quite large, open, and comforting. It measured 16 feet in diameter and was eight feet high. The interior is completely constructed of rocks on the walls, and the corbbelled ceiling, and they still fit snuggly together. It was quite dry inside and in my case it was a pleasant break from the wet mist. These types of enclosed spaces are called fogous. They are found in several locations around Cornwall, and it really is not known what their purpose was. It was very impressive to think of folks thousands of years ago having the skills to design and build this place.

Back outside the mist had once again become a light rain, but, undaunted, I took the time to walk the remainder of the site and was glad that I did.

Returning to the car I had an extra pair of Levis which I gladly changed into while the car heater provided a much appreciated warmth to my cold body. I was very pleased with myself for having purchased my lightweight water repellant jacket and water repellant walking boots before leaving for England. Wearing them kept both my top side and my feet quite dry. I know, you are wondering why not rain proof pants as well? As I can come up with no good or logical explanation, I will just move on.

Soon I was once again back in search of the Fiddler, and it was not long before I came to a portion of the A30 alongside which I thought the stone should be located. However, this whole stretch of road was lined on both sides by large "can't see over them and can't see through them" hedges. I parked in a small turnout across the road from a metal gate that was an entry to farm land beyond. Walking over to the gate, I could see sprawling before me acres of some kind of leafy green vegetable crop that had been planted in long meandering earth mound rows. These earth mounds were about 10 inches high and were separated by narrow ditches. The vegetables popping up through the top of the mounds were only three or four inches high and too young for me to identify.

Climbing up on the gate and looking along the hedge to my right, there it was! Tall and majestic, surrounded by rows of green vegetables gathered around it like subjects before their king. I actually cheered. Gazing at the panorama before me, I thought the visual of this tall, dark, lonely stone surrounded by its green minions, was as beautiful as some painting done by an impressionist master. Actually, the more I looked, what came to mind was a Japanese Zen garden with a lone stone surrounded by rows of tilled brown earth rather than raked white sand. The image is still vivid in my mind today.

Though the cold winds continued to blow, the sun had begun to peek through the clouds, and the drizzle had stopped. I was hopeful that as I was now dry all over, I might stay that way for a while. Climbing over the gate I walked down the rows to the lone giant, being very careful to stay in the ditches and not to damage the mounds. Once at the stone I was more than a little impressed. It is a good five feet at the base and stands about 11 feet in height. Though the traffic noise from the A30 just over the hedge was somewhat bothersome, there was something very peaceful and calming about this old boy and his field of new born veggies. As with many such stones, The Blind Fiddler is tall, wide, and thin. It does have a more triangular shape than most, however. Checking my compass I found it was placed in the earth with its broad sides facing due east/west, its narrow sides facing north/south. Then with my dowsing rods in hand, I walked around the stone and found that it had been placed right on an energy line which ran under it in an east/west direction.

I sat down with my back to the Fiddler, partially to get out of the cold wind but mostly to get close to the stone. I was sitting facing to the east, right on the energy line, and I could feel it flowing through the ground below me. I was suddenly aware of others standing by this rock, looking to the east, waiting for the morning sunrise. What was going on? It seemed so real. When I had first looked beyond the gate and seen this stone, I had immediately felt a strong pull as if the Fiddler had something to share with me. Now, sitting there leaning back up against the stone, I was awed by this vision and flooded with a feeling of well-being. Soon a comforting warmth began infusing my whole body and I knew I was not the first.

Though the mist and resulting damp had lifted, the temperature was still quite cold. I, however, was feeling very comfortable with my Fiddler friend. I soon became overwhelmed with a desire to sleep, and it seemed as though the stone was opening up his arms and enfolding me, like I was being absorbed into the rock itself. I felt sooo, verrry, content. Suddenly, shaking myself, I wondered if indeed I had slept. I had this image of the Hobbits, Pippin and Merry, leaning against Old Man Willow, being lulled to sleep, and then the tree opening and trapping them inside. Though I felt no concern or sense of danger here, I turned to look up at the stone, chuckled, and said, "So what are you getting up to Fiddler?"

Standing to leave I noticed about two thirds of the way up the stone a lone snail. It looked so small and insignificant. But it was working its way up this giant like a pilgrim going to the top of the mountain in search of its God. I wanted to stay and see if it made it, but, alas, at the pace it was moving I was going to be there a very long time, and I was ready to go.

I gave the Fiddler a big hug and thanked him for sharing his energies with me. Cold day and all, I was feeling quite good. Carefully walking the rows back to the car, I on several occasions turned to look back at my new friend. I hope that one day I will get back for another visit and another restorative rest.

Since the weather was a little better I decided to go back to Boscawen-Un. As I was walking down the path, I came upon a fellow who was taking pictures. I knew right away he was a kindred spirit, and as I approached him he smiled and took my photo. His name was Joseph, and he was from Michigan. He explained he had been visiting stone sites in the UK since the 90's and was in fact just returning from having visited Boscawen-Un. I liked him right away and we stood there in the cold for quite a while getting acquainted. As he left we parted company as friends who walked a similar path, and I knew those paths would cross again.

Arriving at the circle I found a man there with his two dogs. He was quite a nice fellow and his dogs, which were kind of like a smaller greyhound, were having a grand time chasing each other around and around the circle at amazing speeds. While watching them I had many a laugh and enjoyed a pleasant conversation with the fellow. He told me he lived nearby and before he left he gave me directions to The Merry Maidens Stone Circle that was to be found not far from Boscawen-Un. It would be my next stop.

Once again I had this wonderful ring of stones to myself, and the weather was much improved from just a few hours before. I checked compass points, did a little more dowsing, and just sat calmly on a stone here and there, in no hurry and happy not to be. When in the company of stones I have come to realize one must have patience. If you are in a hurry, you may miss what the stones have to offer. Once again I think of those dear hobbits Pippin and Merry and their frustration with the Ents who took days just greeting each other. So it is with stones. Unless you come across a stone that is erupting energy like the "altar stone" I experienced near Carnac, you need to be patient and approach each stone with no expectations. After an hour or so, I walked the path back to my car, thankful to have been blessed with the opportunity to meet this wonderful ring of rocks.

In route to the Merry Maidens, I stopped to check out the remains of the Tregiffion Chambered Tomb. Its location right alongside (and under) the B3315 sort of kills the charm factor a bit but it was worth the stop.

The Merry Maidens Stone Circle sits up on a rise in a large grassy field and can easily be seen from the B3315. It really is an intriguing view, those impressive standing stones with nothing but the sky for a backdrop. Upon closer inspection it is a near perfect circle, 78 feet in diameter. Rarely do circles get this accurate. There are 19 stones about four feet tall and for the most part of a similar rectangular shape. Like at Boscawen-un, and maybe even more so here,

the inner face of each of the stones has been worked to be very smooth. However, here at the Maidens they also made a point of flattening the tops of most of the stones. They are placed 12 feet apart except in the east where there is a gap of about 20 feet. An entrance maybe?

Though it is quite simple in its design, this circle seems to have been very carefully thought out by its builders with serious attention given to a clean, orderly, minimalism. If I had anything negative to say about this circle it would be that maybe it was a bit too proper. No edge.

Walking the stones, I dowsed a strong east/west energy line running through the circle. Going from stone to stone I noticed on

Stone Journals

closer inspection that though the stones were mostly of a similar rectangular shape, each was an individual with its own peculiarities, and, in fact, one stone was actually quite different in shape. It was shaped like the hour glass figure of a woman, hips to neck. Was there a reason for this? I imagine so, but who knows what?

There was also an outlier stone to the south of the circle that piqued my interest and I spent a little time with it. In the end, while I enjoyed my time at the Merry Maidens I received no special feelings or experiences. Still I left these stones happy to have been in their company.

Deciding to call it a day, I went to Penzance in search of a room with a phone so I could call home. This turned out to be a much more difficult task then I had presumed. The places I checked only had phones in the lobbies. After trying eight different B&Bs/hotels, I was finally directed to the Mount Haven which was built up on the hillside above Marazion, only a few miles away. It was a little pricy but they had one room available and it had a phone, so I grabbed it. While filling out the booking form, I heard a lady's voice call, "Hello Patrick!" Looking up I was surprised to see a woman with a big smile and a head of bright orange hair. When I asked, "Do we know each other?" she responded, "You're a blues musician, and I was just looking at a photo of you." She then went on to explain that her name was Orange (of course), she was an owner of the hotel, and she had just been talking with Joseph whom I had met earlier in the day at Boscawen-Un. Joseph was staying at the Mount Haven as well, and he had been sharing with her his story about meeting me on the path to the circle and had shown her the photo he had taken of me. What were the odds?

Orange then showed me to my room which had a wonderful view overlooking Saint Michael's Mount and the southern Cornwall Coast. Sharon and I had visited this marvelous place many years ago and looking down on the island fortress brought back some fond memories. Knowing of my interest in the stones, Orange also presented me with a copy of *Spirits Of The Stones* by Alan Richardson to browse, thinking it might help me along my journey. Sure enough, after tea and scones, I sat in my room for hours reading this lovely book, and what an inspiring read it was. I shall always be in debt to Orange. When I got home from this trip, I ordered a copy for myself.

That evening I met up with Joseph, and we spent hours over dinner getting to know each other better, sharing many personal stories. We were linked by the stones, and I shall always be grateful.

The next morning as I was preparing to check out, Orange told me I might want to take the path down to the beach as it was only a ten minute walk. She said I could find chunks of quartz there that had been smoothed by the action of the ocean waves rolling in and out on the beach, and she referred to them as quartz lingams. Evidently a large vein of quartz runs out to sea at that location. As I have several shiva lingams (from western India) at home, I was intrigued. It was raining again so I borrowed an umbrella, took the walk, wandered along the beach, and found four wonderful rounded quartz stones sized between an egg and a papaya. Happy with my finds I went back to Mount Haven, checked out, and set out to renew my stone journey. The egg sized stone I have since polished up, and it sits on the table next to my bed. The largest can be found resting upon one of the stones in my stone circle, moved according to my whim.

I must say that if an individual is going to be in that part of the world, they could not find a more wonderful place to stay then Mount Haven. It may be pricey if your budget is limited but Orange and staff will make your stay memorable.

The first stop of the day was to be at one of the most unique stone sites in the UK. I had visited this location many years ago when Sharon and I were traveling Cornwall, and I could not wait to see it again. Located on the Penwith Peninsula, Men An Tol seems to me to be what remains of a small stone circle. What makes it so unique is the three stones that are still above ground and upright. Standing alongside each other, they form the numerals 101. Though you can still find several of the circle's other stones partially protruding from the ground, these three stand fully exposed about three and a half feet in height. The thing is, the center stone of the three is remarkably round with a hole in its middle large enough for a small adult to crawl through. It looks like a large stone doughnut or inner tube. On each side of this big O, several feet away, sits a narrow, straight standing stone. It really does look like 101 and as I have spent most of my life living within a few miles of US 101 (the main highway along the West coast), it seemed quite comforting to me and only right that I should be there.

I had no trouble finding the place to park my car as I kind of remembered it from our previous visit and there is a small sign posted. The walk to the stones is along a rough dirt road lined on both sides with those wonderful English stone walls. I am always impressed by the craftsmanship involved in making them. The height, width, and placement of the stones. Really great!

It is less than a mile to the site itself, set off to the right of the road a ways. Because the stones are short in stature, they are easy to miss if you are not looking. Sitting out in this desolate landscape, they do look kind of lonely and insignificant, especially if

the gorse is grown up tall. It was quite cold and windy, and I did not spend a lot of time at Men An Tol. I wandered around trying to locate other stones of the circle, and while dowsing the site, I found an east/west line running right through what would have been the center. I had no special experiences at this site, but it is a really unique place, and I enjoyed my visit.

Back in my car I spent quite a lot of time driving around trying to find a couple of different circles. I was unsuccessful in my search and decided that, as the rain had increased, I would take a break. I found a great little mineral shop/museum in Pendeen (The Pendeen Mining Museum) and thoroughly enjoyed looking at their wonderful collection. I also must say I enjoyed being out of the rain. I did purchase a piece of stilbite/chabasite, a nice fan of black kyanite, and a sample of a local rock the name of which I have forgotten.

Having warmed up and dried out as well, I decided to have a go at finding two standing stones located between Penzance and Lands End called The Pipers. Not only did I find them with no problem, I felt quite silly as they were located just off the B3315, across the road and down about 100 yards from the Merry Maidens Circle that I visited the day before. Oh well.........

The Pipers stones (see page 36) actually stand a little ways apart from each other in separate fields. The one closest to the Maidens is over 13 feet tall, standing very erect, and in fact, has a strong phallic appearance. This stone has a very serious energy flowing from it, but the pouring rain (and I do mean pouring) left me with little desire to explore it any further. I apologized to the stone for being such a wimp and moved on to the other Piper which is 15 feet tall and said to be the tallest in Cornwall. It protrudes from the earth at quite an angle as if a giant standing in the distance had thrown it there like a javelin. As with The Blind Fiddler, I found that both of these megaliths had flat east/west facing surfaces and both had east/west energy lines running directly under them. This must have been intentional.

    As I was really cold and really wet, it was back to Marazion for tea and scones. After a walk through the village, I saw the tide was out and decided to take a stroll across the walkway to Saint Michael's Mount. As at Mont St. Michel on the north coast of France (and before they built a permanent road), when the tide is out you can walk all the way across to the island using the causeway. However, when the tide is in, you must take a boat. Though it was too late to get inside the keep, it was none the less a beautiful walk and brought back fun memories of Sharon and I taking the tour of this magical place. It is a must see if one is in the area.

    I spent the night at the Glenleigh Hotel. It was simple but very nice, reasonably priced, and provided a pleasant breakfast. I rose early and was soon ready to continue my journey.

    There is something very special about walking among stones shrouded in mist, but day after day of this cold, wet, and windy thing was keeping me from spending much time at the sites. When I got up this morning it was with high hopes of seeing some sunshine, but in fact, it was the worst day yet. I did, nonetheless, resume my search and eventually found myself in the village of Duloe, on the B3254, parked across the street from a sign on which was posted "stone circle." It pointed down a gravel road.

    Leaving the warmth of the car, with umbrella open and facing into the unrelenting wind, I set out. The road was lined on both sides by tall trees whose branches had grown across and intertwined with each other, forming a large dark green tunnel. It was just a short walk and at the end was a wooden gate beyond which was a lush

Stone Journals

grassy pasture. Looking out across this field of green, I was struck by what I saw awaiting me. Standing on the far side of the pasture was the Duloe Stone Circle and even on this miserable rainy day, it was magnificent.

There are seven standing stones and one that is lying on the ground. The largest of the stones stands eight and a half feet tall and along with his friends (this stone definitely has a strong masculine energy), they form a small but significant circle about 38 feet across. In fact this is the smallest stone circle in Cornwall. The stones vary in size, are rough and naturally shaped, and though not nearly as large as the megaliths of some other circles, several of these stones do have some good size to them. To just glance at them you might not notice, but if you look closer you find that all eight stones are really very unique and I sensed that each had its own story to tell. But, how long would it take to get it?

That said, what really makes the stones of this circle stand out is their color. I had been seeing dull grays and rusty reds everywhere but here that changed, and with dramatic effect. These wondrous stones are in fact large hunks of quartz. I had seen the one small but impressive quartz stone at Boscawen-Un, but here was a complete circle of a subdued but glorious white.

At one point the wind was gusting so strong that the rain was being blown sideways and pelting my face so hard that it hurt. I huddled up against the large stone which sits to the east, and thanked him for giving me cover. I sensed the stone smiling, and I felt warmth radiating from this massive rock. On this cold rainy day, I was thankful and I said so.

When the gusts would die down for a moment or two, I

would walk the circle trying to get acquainted with these intriguing white stones and when possible attempting to dowse. I had the feeling that the stones were getting quite a chuckle watching my attempts to dowse while the winds twisted the rods in my hands every which way. When the gusts would get too strong, I would run back behind "big fella," as I named him, and wait for them to subside.

I think at this point I should clarify that, yes, I know that rocks do not have eyes to watch with or mouths to speak or laugh with. Let's call it awareness, and there is no doubt in my mind that the "spirit" of the stone can be very aware and can in fact communicate on some levels. You have to be open, and even then there is no assurance, but what joy when the connection is made.

While dowsing, in between gusts, I did find a strong energy line running right through the center of the circle in a north/south direction. This consistent pattern of finding stone circles or single stones with energy lines running through or under them is obviously not chance. These placements had a purpose.

In the end the weather won out, and I was forced to leave long before I would have liked. This is another location where on a nice sunny day I would have spent hours. Before leaving the Duloe Circle, I thanked the spirits of the circle and gave "big fella" a hug. As I left, I thought once again that I could hear a subtle laughter coming from the stones as they watched me forcing my way into the wind and rain in an attempt to return to my car.

Almost a year later I obtained a copy of Cope's *The Modern Antiquarian* and in his description of his visit to Duloe, he finishes with, "Now I must leave, as I can hardly breathe in this wind and my hands are like icicles." There you have it.

From Duloe I was headed for a village called Minions to find The Hurlers Stone Circles. In route I stopped to check out King Doniert's Stone which was located right alongside the B3254, a narrow country road. There are actually two granite Christian cross bases sitting there which have carvings on them. One is believed to have been built by the order of Doniert, the King of Cornwall. It is said Doniert "ordered this cross for the good of his soul." Ah, the good old days, when you could buy your way into heaven.

On to the Hurlers Stone Circles. This is a site where three good sized stone circles sit alongside each other in pretty much a north/south alignment. Located on the bleak Bodmin Moor, with dark skies overhead and explosive gusty winds hurling rain in my face, it really was a desolate place and one where I knew I would not last long.

In the short walk from the parking lot to the first circle, not much more than a quarter mile, my pants were already soaked through. Hurrying through the circles I did take enough time to appreciate the unique shapes of these granite stones. Though smaller in stature, most three to five feet in height and the tallest just under six feet, they are some of the most interestingly shaped stones I have encountered. These rocks definitely seemed to me to have been worked by human hands. But alas, with the wind literally howling, I turned and ran back to the car, not caring as I splashed through one puddle after another. I was done for the day, and I rushed toward the simple pleasure of the car heater.

Once again I give really high marks to my Keen hiking boots which appeared soaked on the outside but on the inside kept my socks and feet completely dry.

Arriving in Tavistock I got a room at the Westward B&B and quickly changed into dry clothes. Then it was off for a wonderful cream tea and a little shopping. In a crystal/New Age shop I found and purchased a silver ring with a nice Moldevite setting, as well as several other fun gifts. It was a nice break just wandering in and out of shops and staying dry.

That evening I sat in my room thinking about my experiences up to that point in my journey. It dawned on me that at many of the sites I had visited, I had encountered other people. In most cases it might have only been one or two but at Avebury there had been quite a lot. Even in miserable weather there are those souls who feel a strong enough "calling" to dare the elements and visit one of these stone sites. I think it is just something you either feel or you don't. For example, while looking for the Rollright Circle I asked directions from a "local" who had no idea where it was. And yet while I was at that circle I met a couple from Canada who were there specifically to see those very stones.

I also found myself wondering why my experiences here in the south of England had been so different from the one I had in Brittany. Though I really only had that one heavy experience in France, it was so very intense and even sexual in its manifestation. In England I have had many more experiences, and even a few where I felt that strong Male energy, but for the most part they have been much more "controlled," much more of an inner, spiritual experience than an outward release of energy. But then, when I think about these two different peoples, what comes to mind when I think of the French is "Amour!" and when I think of the British my first thought is "proper." Maybe the stones are like the people. Maybe they are conduits of the energies of the earth on which they cohabit and as the energies of these places are different so too would be the people. Just thinking.

When I awoke on the morning of the 16th, I looked out the window to see the wind howling through the trees, and sheets of rain blowing in every direction. I thought to myself, "Well, Patrick old chap, here we go again!"

After a nice breakfast and visit with other guests, I ran to the car (it was pouring) and started off in search of a place called Sheepstor and its stone circle. Though it looked quite close on the map, it was almost an hour before I was parked at what I presumed was my starting point.

Compass in hand and following the directions I found in Burls' *A Guide to Stone Circles of Britain, Ireland, and Brittany,* I began the trek up the tor. Thankfully the rain had become a sprinkle, but the winds continued with ferocious gusts which made it difficult to walk at times and on occasion would blow me sideways. It was also very cold. After about 45 minutes of being battered about by the winds, I gave up and made to return to the car. This was not quite as simple a task as I had thought. Nothing was looking familiar and I admit I was getting a bit nervous when I finally saw my car parked under the trees.

Driving back down the narrow road I entered a heavily wooded area where I came across a small parking lot. I parked and got out my maps to try to figure out what I had done wrong. Looking around me I was struck by the beauty of this woody, mossy, lush green place, and as I was still a little wound up, I got out of the car and took a short walk. I soon came across a group of Dartmoor horses. These are wild horses that have been wandering around the moor for over a thousand years. They are a bit short and stocky but have an almost magical look and manner about them. They were in no way afraid of me, and I spent some time just walking among them, enjoying their company. It was great fun and helped me to settle.

Back in the car, looking at the maps, I really could not figure out for sure where I was, so I decided to start back down the road in hopes of finding a point on the map I could work from. Not too far along I came across two old timers out for a walk. Down under the canopy of the thick forest, the winds were no concern, and they were enjoying their stroll. When I asked if they might have any idea where I could find the Sheepstor Stone Circle, they thought they knew of it and gave me what seemed to be clear directions. They then wished me well and continued along. Fifteen minutes later I pulled into a small parking area that matched the description I had been given right down to the stone walls, the gate, and the "Sheepstor Farm" sign posted alongside the road. I had been on the right tor but evidently on the wrong side, or at least so I thought. A tor by the way, is just a cone shaped hill as far as I can figure.

Leaving the warmth and calm of the car, I once again entered the tempest. My spirits were high, and I was optimistic. But after half an hour climbing over rock strewn terrain and being buffeted about by strong winds I could feel the cold setting in along with the pessimism. So I decided to go to the top of the tor where I would have a 360 degree view. Surely then I would find my goal. I climbed the slope fighting a strong head wind all the way. Arriving at the summit, I found a collection of big boulders and right on the very top was a big stone slab looking like a table top without the legs. This was the perfect place from which to spy my circle.

As I lifted my foot to step up onto the slab a gust of wind literally grabbed me and tossed me backwards through the air about eight feet down the tor. It was just lucky for me I landed on soft grass rather than against one of the many boulders strewn across the hillside. The rain began falling again in earnest, and as I pulled myself up off the wet ground I knew I had had enough. Surrendering to the elements I stood, hands in the air, and with as strong of a voice as I could muster I yelled, "You win!" But as I began marching back down the tor, I turned and in a more subdued voice said, "This time."

As an aside, I have since spent a fair amount of time searching out information on this circle, and I am pretty sure I was still not in the right place. I hope to try again another day.

Returning to the car I changed into dry pants and shoes and drove to Buckland Abbey which I had noticed was located nearby. This had been the home of Sir Francis Drake, the great English privateer/explorer from the 16th century whose adventures had thrilled me when I was a young boy, both in book and in movies. He was famous for routing the Spanish fleet but he had also explored the Coast of California not too far south of where I live. There is even a bay near San Francisco where it is believed he landed, called Drakes Bay.

Arriving at Drake's home I found it to be not only a lovely place, but once I was inside, it was dry, warm, and there were no winds. The house had very few furnishings in it but it did have the one item I was most interested in seeing: Drake's Drum.

Drake's Drum is a huge snare drum that he took with him on many of his voyages around the world. As he lay on his death bed in Panama in 1596, he ordered it returned to Buckland Abbey in England where it still is today. He was said to have vowed that if England was ever in danger someone was to beat the drum, and he would return to defend the country. Throughout the years since, people have claimed to have heard the drum beating during times of danger, one such occasion being the outbreak of World War I.

Though the paint is faded, it is still very impressive and being a drummer by profession I really appreciated the overall condition and construction of this drum. Also, its size was impressive, it being rather large. It is quite a drum, and quite a legend.

Once again dry, with spirits restored, I decided to try my luck at finding another stone site. I really did want to touch bases with some stones this day. In the same area as the Abbey, the Brisworthy Stone Circle was said to be located. So, after studying my maps, I was back in the car and on the road again.

After about 30 minutes of driving back and forth I was about to give up when I saw a road I had not yet been down. After a short distance, I saw on the right a small white sign reading Brisworthy which pointed up this narrow, tall hedge lined country lane. I drove up the lane until it ended at a large farm complex. I saw no one to speak to, so I parked the car and once again checked the directions found in Burl's *Guide*, hoping this time to have better luck.

I walked down a dirt road, climbed over a gate, and with an occasional check of my compass headed northeast across the moor. After climbing over a stone wall or two and going only about another half mile, I found, there alone on this very desolate moorland was the most charming ring of small stones. There were 24 rather plain looking standing granite stones, and though small in stature (the largest only three and a half feet tall) they are in no way shy. The ring, too, is small, being only 81 feet in diameter, but this small circle of stones gives off a strong vibe of confidence that is noticeable even from quite a distance away. Although it was not raining, the wind was roaring in my ears, my eyes were watering, my nose running, and it was really cold. Even so, I was excited as I arrived at the circle's edge.

Walking the perimeter of the circle, which was built on a bit of a slope, I gazed out across the wide, open, barren moor on which these stones sat. I wondered, "Why had this particular location been chosen?" I then made a second circuit paying attention to each individual stone. And again I wondered, "Why had each stone been chosen?" While making this lap I had the strongest feeling of being watched. I then walked into the circle and standing in the center I opened myself to whatever I might experience.

With the wind howling around me and the cold fighting to get through my clothing, I stood alone and still, waiting. I did not wait long before I began to "understand" that these stones were in fact very happy to meet me! I was not alone at all. I was in the company of stones. Indeed, I felt as if I was standing among 24 very individual beings but that they were of one mind as to my presence there. I was very welcome. They get very few visitors and were pleased I had made the effort.

I then walked the inside of the circle giving thanks to each of the stones, asking for their blessing, and being rewarded with a subtle warmth coming up through my legs. As it was really cold, this was most sincerely appreciated and as it was beginning to sprinkle I knew I would not last much longer. I felt directed to the largest stone as if it were the spokesperson, or rather the spokestone for the group. Standing there looking at this oddly shaped stone, the message came through very clearly. "Even on this dark and blustery day I could find comfort here in the company of the stones. They were always there. When troubled I need only think of them and my spirits would be lifted and my resolve strengthened." For a period of time I just stood there absorbing the message, energies, and blessings of the circle. I thanked them all and exited the circle calling, "I am really sorry that I've got to go!" I could sense them smiling as I walked away, or actually jogged away, as it was looking like serious rain again.

When I had left Buckland Abbey in search of Brisworthy I was feeling tired and my hips were very soar, the result of a bursitis which flairs up now and again, especially in cold weather. Leaving the Brisworthy Circle, I did so feeling no pain or fatigue and with my batteries once again fully charged.

It has now been many years since I visited that precious circle of stones and I have often thought of it, and them, and know I was in fact "blessed."

Waking the next morning in Tavistock, I was thinking of the stones. They were on my mind constantly it seemed. It was sort of like having the television on in your house while you are doing other things. You are paying it no attention until suddenly you find yourself staring at the TV, pulled into some news story or bit of action. So it was with my mind. I keep being drawn back to the stones.

My first thoughts were of Brisworthy. A grouping of small, rather insignificant looking stones gathered in a circle on a cold, desolate moor. Alone. Just waiting for any soul lucky enough to find their way there.

Then there was The Blind Fiddler, standing tall and proud, surrounded by his veggies. When I think of him, I cannot help but smile.

And then my mind wandered to The Bowl Rock, the sleeping giant. The very heart and soul of Cornwall. I miss him. It is sad that the rock is located so close to the road like that, and even sadder that so very few people stop or care. But then, I imagine that if you were to place an enlightened soul like, say, the Dali Lama, on a rug alongside of US Highway 101, who would notice, and even if they did, how many would stop? You might think my comparison odd, but then again, have you ever met The Bowl Rock?

I had enjoyed my stay in Tavistock but saying my farewells to the nice folks at the Westward B&B I drove off into the rain. I was now looking for Merrivale, a vast site with stone hut ruins, long stone rows, cairns, standing stones, and circles. It was said to be located not too far off the B3357, a main road running east/west through Dartmoor, and the directions I had seemed very simple and straightforward. I should have known better.

I made several passes back and forth along a stretch of road where I thought the site should be located, having no luck at all. The wind and the rain were really getting serious, and I had hoped to explore this site before it got too bad. Pulling into a stone wall enclosed parking area, I saw a couple of fellows putting camping gear into their car. I pulled alongside them and asked if they knew where the Merrivale site was. They pointed across the moor and said it was about a 10 minute walk. They told me that they had been on a camping trip out on the moor, but the previous night it had rained so hard that the water coming off the hillside formed a current which had run right into their tent soaking everything in it, them included. They were giving it up and heading home.

By the time I began my trek the weather had turned really awful. An umbrella was useless in these winds. I pulled my hood tight around my face leaving just my eyes uncovered. Still I had to walk with my head down to keep the wind driven rain out of my eyes. The grass moorland was so soaked it was like walking on waterlogged sponges. Each step forward my boot would sink into the boggy soil and water would gush out. Then the trailing foot would make its effort to pull free and to take the next step. There was nothing fun about this. Dartmoor can be a very oppressive place.

After about 10 minutes I did find myself walking among what appeared to be the remains of old stone huts barely visible in the bog. I soon found my first stone rows. There were actually two stone rows made up of rather small and insignificant looking stones. The rows were only about three and a half feet apart forming a narrow avenue about two hundred yards long. There was also a small cairn in the middle of the avenue. If it had been a nice day I am sure I would have been excited about my find, but on this day, not so much. Looking out in the distance I saw a lone, tall, narrow, standing stone, and I knew from a small Merrivale guide booklet I had picked up in Tavistock that there should be a stone circle located near it. Head down I once again began sloshing along from puddle to puddle.

Arriving at the solitary stone, which was about 10 feet tall, I could see a small circle of stones a short distance away. Standing there getting soaked, I did feel some kind of empathy from this lonely sentinel, a sort of recognition. Still, after only a few minutes I hollered, "Sorry, but I have to keep moving," and I headed towards the circle.

Rising from the grass there are 11 short stones one to one and a half feet tall and together they make up an oval 58 feet by 67 feet. As I stumbled around the outside of the circle, I asked for the stones' blessings and hoped that as with the Rollright and Brisworthy circles, I might even get some comfort. I got nothing, and I was done in.

Returning to the car, I got out of my soaked pants and put on some dry cords. As I sat there with the indispensable heater on high I thought about my Merrivale experience. While I could say I was there, I couldn't say it meant very much. With the exception of a good, but brief, connection I had with the tall standing stone, and I did feel potential there, the remainder of this visit I could chalk up to "Been there, done that!"

Once the chill was gone from my bones, I drove on to Princetown in search of an information center and was surprised to find a very nice one. The staff was quite pleasant and when asked if anyone could recommend a stone circle in the area that would not require a long slog through the wind and rain, they had a good laugh. They then talked it over and came up with Soussans Common, which they said was situated quite close to a road, just out of Postbridge. I remembered it mentioned in Burl's *Guide*, so I thanked them and headed out.

I arrived at the stone circle in short order, and, in fact, it sat nestled up against a forest tract just 50 yards or so off a quiet country road. The forest surrounded it on three sides like a horseshoe, and from its cozy enclosure Soussans Common Stone Circle faced out on the desolation of Dartmoor, seemingly quite content. Looking out from the protection of the car, I could see that the rains had let up and that the trees formed a natural break from the wind. So, out I jumped.

This is a small but complete circle with the remains of a cairn in the center. It is only about 30 feet across, and it is made up of 22 short stones, six inches to maybe two and a half feet tall. They are placed quite close together except for one large gap in the southwest that appears to be an entrance. Most are thin and many look like they were set on their sides. There is also a pink color to many of them that I had not seen before. Really quite lovely. As I walked the ring wittershins (counter clockwise), saying my little blessing, I forgot all about the cold drizzle and was in that moment at peace. The way the forest wrapped around the stones it felt as if it was protecting them and as long as I was within the circle I was safe as well. Walking the circle I felt a strong energy boost and remained quite content as the rain began falling once again. There was a real "presence" here, and I enjoyed its company, appreciated its warmth, and was in no hurry to leave.

Feeling quite good after my visit to Soussons, I went in search of the circle on Scorhill Tor, outside of Chagford. This was to be the last stone circle before returning to London and then home. Finding what I assumed to be the parking area and trailhead, I made one final trek into the elements. While the rain fell at a steady pace, the wind would at times gust so strong as to stop me in my tracks. Peering out from under my hood, I searched in vain for the circle. After maybe 20 minutes my bones ached from the cold and I turned to look back down the tor to get a sense of where I was. This proved to be a big mistake, as a gust of wind shoved me so hard from behind that it was all I could do to keep my feet under my body as I was pushed down the hill. Propelled by the relentless wind I was drawing on hurdling skills that I had not used since I was on the high school track team, and even then I had not been very good. I was leaping over boulders like hurdles and splashing through puddles like running cross country. The thing was, I could not stop. With the rough, rock strewn, soggy ground I knew at any moment I would lose my footing and take a brutal fall, or even worse twist or break an ankle. As I was being hurled down the tor I began yelling, "All right, I give, I'm leaving!"

After what seemed like forever the winds began to let up and I actually slowed to a walk. I could not believe my luck to have survived this experience with no harm done. Even so, my walk soon became as close to a trot as I could manage. I wanted off this mountain! Coming over a small rise I saw the parking area and this time at my own choice, I began running for the protection, and the soon to be warmth, of my little Ford car. My quest for the stones had come to an end.

I guess this was really just about the only way for this stone journey of mine to end. Fighting my way through adverse weather conditions on a barren moor in an unsuccessful search for a stone circle. Scorhill remained for me to find another day. Silly as it sounds, I was beaten up, but I was not beaten. I relish the very thought of returning.

I spent the night in Salisbury at Sarum Heights B&B. It is so named because Old Sarum, a massive Iron Age hill fort, is right across the street. In the morning I began the day by visiting the fort. As it is an earth fort, it was covered with lush green grass mixed with the joyous bright yellow of buttercups. It was built in the form of a giant circle covering around 25 acres.

First you encounter a tall and steep earth mound followed by a very deep ditch. Climbing up out of the ditch there is a large flat area. In the center is another deep ditch encircling a flat topped mound which rises above the surrounding terrain. This was the fort's stronghold. It really was impressive and quite beautiful.

While strolling the grounds and thinking back on my journey, I decided I needed to make one more stop before going on to London. How could I get this close and not stop at Stonehenge?

I did not expect a lot from this visit based on past experiences there. And now after having wandered in and out of all those wonderful circles and having sat with my back to tall standing stones, it would be disappointing to stand outside the fence looking in. And, there would be the inevitable large masses of people. Nonetheless, it is Stonehenge and so off I went.

Even though the crowd situation was just as I expected, there is nothing else like this stone monument to be found on the entire planet. It is really a unique site and more complex than any other. As described by Chippindale in *Stonehenge Complete*, there are actually five major elements to its construction.

Though many stones are now broken or missing, starting from the outside you first encounter a ring of sarsen stones 100 feet in diameter. Each has been shaped, stands about 13 and one half feet above the ground, is seven feet wide and about three and three fourths feet thick. They stand about three and a half feet apart and are topped with snuggly fit lintel stones which originally formed a complete flat surface around the circle top, about two and a half feet thick. This arial walkway would have been really cool to have seen when it was all there. Only a portion remains today.

Just inside this ring is a smaller circle of evenly spaced bluestones, each only about six and a half feet in height, about four feet wide, and two and one half feet thick. Many are, sadly, missing now.

Next you find the five inner sarsen trilithons. A trilithon is two massive stones, these up to 24 feet tall, (and remember another third is underground) standing side by side with a huge cut stone placed on top creating large stone archways. It is amazing that using just antlers and other stones, people long ago shaped and smoothed these trilithons and then put them into place.

The top of each of the uprights had been flattened, leaving a large nipple in their center. Two cups had been carved in the bottom of, and at each end of, the cap stones so that when they were flipped, lifted and placed on top, the nipples would set snuggly into the cups, locking the three stones together. It is a wonder to see, and it is very difficult to comprehend how in the world they did it. These were placed in the center of the circle in a large horseshoe shape about 45 feet across with the open end facing the northeast. What is even more impressive is that after thousands of years three of the five trilithons still stand.

Mimicking the outer circle, just inside the sarsen horseshoe is a bluestone horseshoe of individual stones between six and eight feet in height.

The last element is what is called the Altar Stone, a 16 foot long individual stone which lies broken in two near the closed end of the horseshoe. It may have stood there as an upright originally.

All in all this is, in fact, quite complex even by today's standards, and I have not even included the "Heel", "Slaughter", or "Station" stones, nor the possible astronomical alignments, the Avenue, the Cursus, the barrow burials, and more! It's an amazing place.

I did stop to say hello to the Heel Stone, standing alone out to the East. It is a really cool old stone. It is also the point from behind which the sun announces itself at Summer Solstice.

Slowly walking the perimeter, I was, as always, awed by what had been created there and wished I could transport myself back in time to see this marvel in its full glory.

This was also the first time I paid attention to the fact that there was actually a henge, with an exterior earth mound and ditch. As the mound has been worn down by the elements over time, you do not even notice the henge as you stand, staring in awe at the stones themselves. Returning to the car, I was glad I had stopped.

This stone journey was over and it was time to go home. This had been an experience I shall never forget and one which had altered me forever. I had met the stones and been blessed by them. I would miss them.

These are just a few more photos from this, my first, "Journey to the Stones."

Merry Maidens Stone Circle

Avebury Stone Circle

West Kennet Long Barrow / Silbury Hill

The Hurlers Stone Circles

Stonehenge Stone Circle

Stanton Drew NE Stone Circle

"Perhaps the energies *behind the* stones *can* enable something *within ourselves that is very* odd, *old, bright and pure,* to enter *the* avenues *of our consciousness.*"
Alan Richardson
The Inner Guide to the Megaliths

Stone Journey 2

SCOTLAND, STONEHENGE

STONE JOURNEY 2 - June 26, 2010

It had been a little over a year since my solo journey to the stones of southern England.

Sharon had just recently retired from her career as an educator and our 40th anniversary was coming up. So, we decided to celebrate with a trip to Europe, spending the first couple of weeks in the UK. As we made our plans, Sharon really wanted to go to Scotland to see if she could find out anything about her Scottish heritage. All she really knew was that her great grandfather had moved to the US from the Dumfries area. Not much to go on but it gave us somewhere to start. I thought it was a great idea and asked if she would mind visiting a few stone circles while there. Knowing my interest and having heard my stories, she was intrigued and said it sounded fun. I was going back to the Stones!

Flying into Edinburgh, we stayed the first two days at the York B&B while we adjusted to the time change. It was pleasant enough, in the city center, and we enjoyed our stay. Edinburgh is a lovely city and always great to visit. Along with enjoying the many wonderful sights the city offers, we also took a bus ride out to Rosslyn Chapel. What a special place it is. DaVinci Code aside, it is really impressive in both construction (the stone work is amazing) and its overall sense of peace. Being there helped to put our hearts and minds in just the right place to begin our journey.

Upon leaving Edinburgh our first stop was Dumfries in the south of Scotland. As this is where Sharon's family on her mom's side, the Kirkpatricks, were said to have come from, it seemed the logical place to start, and there was a really well ordered heritage/ancestry center there where she was able to find help. Lucky for me, just north of the town was the Twelve Apostles Stone Circle and it was to this site that we went first. The circle sits in a field just off the A76 on a minor road and was easily spotted through the fence that enclosed the field. Pulling into a turnout we saw a plaque there acknowledging this to be the Twelve Apostles. And, it was a lovely day!

I was like a little kid as I leaped out of the car, jumped the fence, and set off at a brisk walk to the stones 150 yards away. I looked back to see if Sharon was coming, and with a smile on her face, she said,

"I'll wait here." I could sense the stones urging me on. They actually seemed to be as happy with my presence as I was happy to be there with them, and I was a bit giddy as I approached the first stone. Greeting the stone I placed my hand on it and was amazed at how smooth and silky it felt, almost as if it had been waxed and buffed. I had never felt such a texture on a standing stone before. As I stood there, hand on stone, my feet began to settle into the earth. You would not have physically seen it, but that is just how it felt. I had this same experience on my last journey. It is like I am plugging into the earth, and once again I could feel the energy begin a subtle pulse up through my legs. What joy!

This is the largest circle in Scotland, being about 100 yards across. There are only 11 stones here, five standing and six lying on the ground. Where the twelfth Apostle went I have no idea. Each stone was an individual with different shapes, textures, markings, and sizes, and the largest was about 10 feet long. As I walked from stone to stone I noticed that several had that waxed feeling and it puzzled me. I reasoned maybe it was from the cows (there were quite a few lying at the circle's edge) rubbing against the rocks but then realized that could not explain it as the smoothness also appeared on the top of several rocks and obviously the cows did not get up there. I never did resolve this puzzle.

Another curious thing was the various markings on the stones. Some had long, deep slashes running across them as if they had been attacked by Freddy Kruger. It could be the result of glacier action but in any case it really is a strange effect. Others had cup marks in them. There is a stone lying in the southeast that has a long row of large cup marks on it, but whether they were created my nature or man I could not tell.

I think I should say a word or two about cup markings. At many of the stone sites I have visited, I have come across stones into which cups have been carved. These "cups" are small, spherical bowls, usually two or three inches across. Sometimes there might be only a few cups but in some stones it can be dozens. No one really knows why these cups were carved in the stones though many opinions are out there. While I find them interesting, they don't seem to hold my attention, and I often do not comment about them when I see them.

As for the shapes of the stones, some were rounder, others squarer, and one was cone shaped, but all seemed to be of a natural form rather than having been shaped by the hands of humans.

The cows that had been watching me seemed comfortable with my presence and most had lain down around a couple of the larger stones. One, however, decided to check me out and walked straight towards me, stopping on the opposite side of a huge fallen stone I was inspecting. We just stood there staring at each other across the stone. After several minutes of this, I wished my friend well and moved on to the next stone while she returned to lounge with her friends.

As I walked this marvelous circle, I noticed that with each stone I touched, the feeling of feet and earth merging became even stronger. My sense of connection to the earth, and with this ring of stones, grew stronger and stronger as the minutes ticked by. I did encounter several stones that seemed to be "slumbering," but the overall effect was very strong and positive. As with several of the stone sites I had visited on my last "stone journey," there was a good energy flow here. I had noticed that many of the Apostles stones had inclusions of quartz in them, and I think that may have something to do with the energizing of the site. I really do think quartz serves as an energy conduit in these stones and here I found quite a lot of it.

I came to a massive stone lying on the ground in the southwest. It was over 10 feet long, seven feet wide, and about four feet thick. As it was a nice sunny day (yes, they do have them every once and awhile), I climbed up on the rock and lay on my back. Closing my eyes I could feel the warmth of the sun and the embrace of the stone. It really was wonderful how comforting it felt, and I was in no hurry to leave.

When I did move on to the next stone I had a little laugh when I saw that someone had somehow carved a date and some unreadable letters into the stone. Very clearly I could see 1900 in large numbers but the letters were, sadly, too worn.

While I am not a fan of graffiti, in this case I could not help but wonder about what else might have been carved there. Lover's initials perhaps?

The last stone I visited sat there like a large stone block, and I saw melted candle wax on its surface where someone had probably performed some kind of ritual. I closed my eyes, centered, and had an image of a couple standing by the stone burning a candle and saying a prayer. Whatever the case, I can understand why this rock would have been chosen. I could feel its strength. This stone is a true source of earth energy to those open to what it has to offer.

Walking back to Sharon and the car I was very energized, and quite content. I could "feel" the earth again and the stones of this grand circle had welcomed me and filled me with their joy.

It is sad to me that this amazing circle sits there alone and untended. Over the several days we stayed in Dumfries, I actually met several locals who had never been to the circle. Visually the Twelve Apostles Circle is not all that impressive, mostly because the stones do not stand all that tall and because of the missing or fallen stones which create large gaps between those still standing. Even so, those who ignore these stones have no idea what they are missing. Not only are the stones "aware," they are happy to be visited.

The next morning reality set in. Yesterday's glorious sunshine had been replaced by exactly the weather I had experienced in the south of England one year ago. As Sharon and I set out, it was cold, wet, and windy. Among our various activities planned for the day we were to begin by going to the Torhouse (or Torhouskie) Stone Circle and with some good directions from a postman in Wigtown we managed to find it. Located right next to the B733 west of Wigtown, it is set on a wide open plateau surrounded by low rolling hills. You can see quite a ways in all directions. But as lovely as the setting was my enthusiasm was quickly "dampened" as we stepped out into the elements. I am sorry to say that I let the weather get to me this day and any chance I may have had to connect with these stones was seriously hampered.

Then there was also the metal fence that formed a square around these unfortunate stones. I do understand protecting them but not like this. It was kind of like a graveyard for stones, or even worse a prison, and I found it kind of depressing.

All that said, Sharon and I did give it a try. Torhouse is a small but impressive circle some 70 feet in diameter, consisting of 19 rounded granite stones which range in size from around two feet to four feet high. Of interest, it appears that the circle was placed on a slightly raised earth platform and that the stones were placed graded in height, starting with the shortest stones in the the northwest, on around to the tallest in the southeast.

Another cool thing about this site is that this seems to be a variation on a recumbent stone circle. In a recumbent circle the builders have placed a stone flat (recumbent) on the earth with an erect stone standing on each side of it sort of like football goalposts sat on the ground rather than in the air. Usually this is done as part of the circle itself and is aligned with some celestial happening. There are many circles

of this design in the north of Scotland but I had never seen one myself. Here at Torhouse, in the middle of the circle sets a small recumbent stone with larger stones on each side. Unlike at a normal recumbent circle, here there is space between the stones. I sat on the recumbent and wondered what was in its sights?

Between wind gusts I was able to dowse two energy lines in the area. One, though off center, ran in a direct east/west line across the circle.

Wet and cold we returned to the car and drove to Wigtown to explore some of the bookstores for which it is known, and to get dry. I was feeling sad actually. This was a circle I had really wanted to visit.

After my wonderful experience at the Twelve Apostles my hopes had been high. In Cope's description of his visit to Torhouse in *The Modern Antiquarian,* he says, "We have been here for hours today and have no desire to leave." I am sorry that was not the case for us. I hope I can one day return to these stones in a better frame of mind.

In some travel information on the Dumfries area I had read about the Gem Rock Museum in Creetown. This looked interesting and as it was on our way back to Dumfries, we decided to stop. They have a wonderful collection of gems in the museum, and then there is a shop where one can purchase items. I found some three inch scottish marble spheres which I purchased as well as some nice jewelry pieces. There is also a great short film they show in an old library type of setting about how gems are formed. It was well done and quite educational. From there it was tea and scones in the cafeteria and we were back on the road. Fun stop, especially on a rainy day.

We were looking for the Glenquicken Stone Circle which was supposed to be located just a few miles east of Creetown. However, the mist had become so thick, it was hard to see very far at all, and after spending quite some time trying to find the circle, we gave up.

The next stop on our drive back on the A75 to Dumfries was an ancient chambered tomb called Cairnholy. This was a really cool place and the setting was perfect. A grassy slope shrouded in thick mist, this setting could have come right out of *The Hound Of The Baskervilles.* Through the mist we could see tall narrow standing stones looking like a row of gnarly old teeth erupting from the earth. Walking the site, Sharon and I were impressed with the "strength" of these tall, proud, and defiant stones. It was like we were gazing at the remains of the tomb of a once powerful Lord of the Rohirrim. It seemed the air was alive with magic. You could really "feel" the earth beneath your feet as you walked, and you could smell the rock, the grass, and the earth in the air. In fact you could even taste them in the moisture of the mist. It was a powerful place, but after a short visit we were already getting quite wet and cold and decided we would have to leave. Though we had not stayed long, I was really glad we had stopped.

After the very disappointing visit to Torhouse, the next day my expectations were once again high as crossing into Northern England we drove towards the Lake District to find the Castlerigg Stone Circle near Keswick. Even more than Torhouse, Castlerigg, also known as The Carles, was way up on my wish list of places to see. This circle may be the most beautifully located of any of the many stone monuments. The stones sit on a flat, grass covered hilltop that is surrounded on all sides by even taller majestic mountains. Someone, long ago, gave some really serious thought to this circle's placement. Standing in the middle of the circle and turning 360 degrees, the view of the lush green slopes reminded Sharon of a scene from *The Sound Of Music*. It is truly an awe-inspiring sight.

When we had first arrived I was disappointed to see a number of cars parked in the lay by. But the weather had vastly improved, and with the sun poking through broken clouds, and with only an occasional sprinkle, my spirits were up, and it looked like a good day for a stone visit.

The 38 stones of the ring have good bulk, are of random size and shape, range from three feet to the tallest at seven and a half feet, and the circle itself is 110 feet in diameter.

There is a real sense of "seriousness" about this place. It feels good, but serious. At the north of the circle sat two of the larger stones, each about five and a half feet tall, and there is a wide gap between them that seems to be an entrance. Later, when I dowsed the circle I found a strong energy line running directly north/south through the middle of the circle and through this gap.

Inside the circle, against the southeast side, 10 stones form a rectangle shaped enclosure. This is the only circle I have seen that has something like this in it, and I have no idea what it was there for.

Walking the exterior of the ring I did not get a lot of response from the stones. The exception was one stone to the east from which I picked up a touch of energy, though nothing dramatic. I think there were just too many folks having a good time for us to be able to get close to, and comfortable with, the stones. Sharon and I had hoped that the people who were there when we arrived would depart and leave us alone with the circle. But instead, busloads of folks from Keswick began to arrive as did quite a few backpackers. It seems that because of its location so close to one of the area's main resort/vacation spots this circle gets a lot of traffic during the summer. While one part of me was actually very happy to see all these people coming to see this wonder, it just made it too noisy and busy for me to really enjoy the experience. Accepting that, I was thankful to have had the opportunity to have seen this beautiful place and to meet these stones. In the end, Sharon and I found our joy in watching a cute little girl in a white dress, with pink and white stripped leggings, running in and out of the stones and climbing those she could. It was enough.

After a wonderful lunch in Keswick (and a visit to the James Bond Museum!), we went looking for Long Meg and Her Daughters Stone Circle. Located near Little Salkeld, it is the sixth largest circle in Britain. This circle is situated on grassy pasture land, and though most circles sit on fairly flat terrain, this one was built on quite a slope. There are a couple of other interesting things about this circle. The narrow farm road you take to Long Meg runs right across the middle of the bottom half. Also, in the lower portion of the circle are a couple fantastic large oak trees. Though there may be others, this is the only circle I have visited that has trees within its enclosure, that is, with the exception of Avebury which envelopes portions of an entire village. I really liked the presence of these trees as they added a whole different ambiance to the place. There is something very special about the melding of earth, tree, and stone at Long Meg.

As we approached the circle from the bottom of the slope we could see Meg standing alone well outside its perimeter and near the top. In fact she stands 82 feet to the southwest and is said to be in direct line with mid-winter sunset. Sharon and I felt we needed to visit Meg first, and so we walked up and took some time getting to know her. Meg is a tapering, three sided block of sandstone that stands about 12 feet tall, and on her east side, if you look closely, you can see several spirals carved into the rock. There are, in fact, many more carvings, but they are very hard to find due to years of weathering.

We sat with our backs against the stone and opened ourselves to the peace of this place. Meg was very comforting and made us welcome. After a while I got up and dowsed around the stone finding a mild energy line running underneath, and continuing on right toward what appeared to be an entrance into the stone circle, as it was marked by two portal stones. I also ran one dowsing rod up alongside the stone and at about six feet hit a strong energy field which pushed the rod away from the stone. I had read about this happening at some stones and was quite excited to experience it here. I have wondered if maybe stones like this one are releasing energies from the earth like a relief valve so that those energies do not result in some more violent release like earthquakes?

The day was really lovely with large, puffy white clouds rapidly advancing across a sky of turquoise blue. The sun played hide and seek behind the clouds, but when it was out, it was warm and embracing.

Deciding it was time to get acquainted with Meg's daughters, Sharon and I went our separate ways. Walking the circle, which is really a 305 foot by 359 foot oval, we each stopped here and there to visit with different stones. There are 68 of these massive rocks (one as much as 30 tons according to Burl) in this ring, along with two outliers, and they appear to have been rounded and shaped by glacier action rather than through human efforts.

Stone Journey

When I reached the east side of the circle I came to another entrance, though it did not have portal stones like in the southwest. I am pretty sure it was an entrance however, as when I dowsed it I found a strong energy line running right through it and on across the circle.

Every now and again I would sit on, or lie upon, a fallen daughter, closing my mind to outside distractions and just enjoying the peace of the moment.

At one point I walked into the circle's center and stood looking out the southwest exit, up the hill towards Long Meg. I had read that she was aligned with the midwinter sunset and I could imagine people gathered in the circle, staring up through the portal at Meg as the sun disappeared behind her, ending one cycle and beginning another, knowing that the days would once again begin getting longer and warmer.

I met up with Sharon at the bottom of the circle. Lying alongside of each other on a massive recumbent stone, gazing at the beautiful sky, we watched as the wind-blown clouds changed from one formation to the next. We saw a horse's head in one cloud and an eagle in another. It was great fun. No one else was around, and we reveled in those precious moments alone with Meg and her daughters.

At one point we sat looking up the hill at the full circle spread before us and talked about the road that crossed it. I read somewhere that some people feel the road degrades the circle, removing some of the magic from the place. To us the road was insignificant to the point that we hardly noticed it at all. This circle is so strong, so "present," that the road diminishes it in no way.

As you walk this circle you can feel that this ring of stone celebrates the earth mysteries. I heard no voices but I could sure sense a strong presence. Meg and her daughters would be a powerful energy place for any spiritual ceremony. This circle has one of the best overall vibes of any I have visited.

Stone Journals

We finished our stay with one last visit to Meg. We thanked her and placed two Herkimer diamonds at her base. My brother Mark and his wife Erin had given us a box with a number of small Herkimers in it and had asked us to place them near stones where we thought it felt right.

The idea is to establish a link with back home and this was definitely a good place to start. It was a great site, and we left feeling blessed and energized.

I told Sharon I had read in *The Modern Antiquarian* about a small circle called Little Meg said to be situated somewhere nearby and she said, "Go for it." As we drove around, we were having little luck finding the site. The directions were not working for us and as the day was getting on, I decided to head back to Dumfries. It was just then that Sharon said, "There it is!" I backed up, and sure enough, looking through a large gate in a stone wall, I could see it. Really, it just looked like a small group of stones piled alongside a stone wall on the edge of a pasture, but there was no doubt that this was Little Meg. Having parked by the gate, Sharon said she would wait in the

car, and so jumping yet another fence, I walked the 100 yards or so to see what I would find.

Approaching the circle I could see it was quite small, not more that 15 feet across. Definitely the smallest I had encountered so far. The stones, too, were small with the largest being Little Meg which was still only about four feet tall. This stone was also quite bulky compared with the others and shaped rather like a round edged cube.

Next to Little Meg was a much smaller rock that had two rather extensive spirals carved into it. They pretty much cover the surface of one side of the stone and are

really impressive. These carvings are much more dramatic than those carved in Long Meg. Once again we have a puzzle. Why were they carved here on this one small rock in this seemingly insignificant circle of stones? Might this have originally been a cairn?

Running my hand over the spirals I closed my eyes, centered, and visualized a brown clothed man from ages long ago bent over the stone. He had a rock in each

Stone Journey

hand, one about the size and shape of a softball and the other sort of cone shaped, flat on the large end and maybe seven inches long. The cone shaped rock appeared to be his chisel, and he was striking it with the other stone, patiently etching a pattern into the stone's surface. I am not saying this was an actual vision from the past, but it seemed very real and I could sense the craftsman's presence with this stone. How many hours, how many days did he spend, rock against rock, carving the stone? And once again, why?

I dowsed the ring and found a good east/west energy line running across the circle and right under Little Meg.

With the afternoon sun shining down upon me, I climbed up on Little Meg and settled in. Sitting there, legs crossed and back erect, the warmth of the sun flooded through me and I began entering a state of deep relaxation. I had the feeling I was on a large, soft cushioned throne, and I laughed to myself as I opened my eyes to look upon my advisors gathered before me. I thanked them, and said I was open to any guidance they might have to offer.

At this point I had that same feeling I have experienced with some other stones, like The Blind Fiddler, of being absorbed into the stone with a warm welcome. I cannot overstate just how powerful and emotional this is. I also cannot explain it. I simply opened to the stone and like the Dave Clark Five song, I was "Glad All Over."

After a short time I heard the bellow of a cow. Opening my eyes I turned and saw a huge heifer entering the pasture some 75 yards away. She was followed by about 15 others including a couple of young bulls who kept annoying her with their lustful intentions. She would have none of it and kept kicking them when they got too close.

She suddenly stopped and looked right at me sitting on my throne. Turning she walked straight towards me followed by her entourage and in short order they had formed a semi-circle around me. They just stood there looking at me, as if waiting for me to enlighten them. So, in my own little "sermon on the rock" moment, I stood and began talking to them about what a wonderful day it was and how nice it was to be there with them. I explained that life was short but good, and they should enjoy it as much as possible. I then told them that when troubled they could always find peace in the company of the stones. Thanking them for their attention I hopped down from Little Meg and chuckling, walked back to the car.

Sharon, who had been watching this exchange from the car said that as I was walking back, the humping began in earnest with several of the heifers being much more open to the young bulls' advances. I was pleased that they took my words to heart.

A few days later on July 4th, the day in 1776 when the US declared its indepen- dence from Great Britain, we flew to the Isle of Lewis. We were making this journey for one reason only, to go to the Callanish Stones. It was another site I had dreamed of visiting for many years, though, in fact, I had come very close to canceling this part of our trip.

About five months earlier the Eyjafjallajokull volcano on Iceland had erupted causing chaos all over Europe. Months after the eruption flights were still being cancelled due to the smoke and ash cloud the volcano continued to give off. There was also the news that each time this volcano had erupted in the past, it was followed within six months by the eruption of an even bigger volcano named Katla. One could only imagine what the results of that might be. As our trip was planned to occur right in this six month time period, we at one point gave thought to canceling our whole trip, but in the end decided against it. However, the islands to the north of Scotland were right in the cloud and ash path should such a disaster occur and that seemed very risky. The expensive nonrefundable flight tickets were also a concern. This was a real dilemma. Visiting the Isle of Lewis and the Orkney Islands was for me probably the most anticipated part of this trip.

To resolve my concerns I had turned to our stone circle at home. Dowsing rod in hand, I entered the circle of stones, voiced my concerns to the spirits of the circle, and asked simply if this was the right time to take this trip? I asked the question five different times as I walked the circle, each time rewording the question to some degree. The answer I received to each inquiry was a strong "Yes, we should go." I then asked if we should be concerned about the volcanos and this time the answers came back a strong "No." With that, I had gone straight into the house and finished booking our rooms.

Arriving safely (no volcanic activity) at the Stornoway airport on the Isle of Lewis we found that it was a cold, blustery day with occasional showers. Every now and then the strong winds would blow gaps in the clouds and the sun would shine through, offering hope that it might get better.

Picking up our rental car we got on the A858 and headed out for the Callanish Stone Circle, about 40 minutes away. There are actually several stone sites by this name in the area, but we were going to the main one. As it was Sunday everything on Lewis was closed (actually there was one gas station open half day) including the information center at Callanish. So, having parked the car we followed the posted path up the slope. Cresting the hill we saw there below us on the ridge line the most impressive gathering of stone sentinels one could imagine. Completely unlike Stonehenge but just as magnificent. With East Loch Roag on the west side and the peat moor stretching out before us in all other directions, it really is a bleak environment. Add to that the cold, windy, "looks like it will rain any minute" weather and this location challenges you with the question, "Do you really want to be here?" The answer was of course an emphatic, "Yes!"

We approached the stones from the south. Before us ran a straight row of five tall, narrow standing stones leading to a small circle some 40 feet across. The circle was made up of 13 very tall, narrow, and thin stones shaped like deformed dominoes. In the very center of the circle stands a 15 and a half foot tall stone that is about five feet wide and only one foot thick, with the remains of a cairn at its base.

Leading off to the east was a row of four or five stones, to the west a row of four stones, and to the north ran two parallel rows of stones forming an avenue. The row due north was made up of 10 stones and the one slightly to the west of nine. All in all, the site, which is about 400 feet long by 150 feet wide, sort of resembles an Irish cross and consists of 47 of the most unique megaliths I have ever seen.

Another really cool thing about these stones is their actual physical composition and their resulting appearance. They are made up of local gneiss. Looking at them I was reminded of the marble cakes my mom used to bake for us as kids. She would first put a chocolate batter into a round or rectangular baking dish. Then she would pour in a vanilla batter, moving her spatula around in such a way as to mix the two batters together forming swirls of brown and white. Once baked it made a wonderful cake which looked a bit like marble and thus the name.

The surface of these Callanish stones also had similar swirls. In some there were combinations of pink and orange. Others displayed swirls of black, gray, and a brilliant white. Unlike the cakes from the baking dishes my mom had used, these stones were far from perfect rounds or rectangles. The molds for these creations were all quite individual, and unique in shape and size, though most did have a common theme of tall and thin.

For an even more dramatic effect, in some of the stones you find large chunks of white, clear, or lavender quartz looking like randomly placed gemstones tossed into the batter right before baking. These Callanish stones really are beautiful and quite different.

Walking among the stones I picked up on both masculine and feminine energies coming from different rocks. They were quite subdued but they were there. Where in the past I have just picked up on earth energies, more and more I am beginning to find that some stones give me a real male energy vibe and others female. The male energy is often strong and energizing while the female energy is usually quite calming.

At one point as I stood looking up the avenue towards the circle It seemed like I was witnessing a gathering of wise men and women who were actually conversing on some different level to which I was not privy. I know, crazy stuff, but fun.

Moving from stone to stone, some I touched, some I caressed, and some I spent more time with than others. It was fun to see Sharon, too, slowly moving from one stone to another enjoying the peace and solitude of this place. Despite the weather, we were in no hurry.

During all the time we were there the weather did not improve but at least it wasn't raining. The cold winds were at times so strong that even when I crouched with my back against a large stone, it serving as a wind break, I was still being rocked back and forth by the gusts. That said, I in no way let the weather interfere with, or dampen, my enthusiasm for this experience at Callanish. As I crouched with my back to one of the stones in the line going off to the west, I opened myself and received a warm sense of welcome and I forgot all about the cold wind. I also noticed a sense of seriousness here like I had experienced at Castlerigg, but in this instance it was much more dramatic. This was no party place. This was a place to come for personal growth, for inner answers, and as at The Bowl Rock, here you needed patience. You needed to be still. Sitting there as still as my mind gets I thought I could hear voices, actually more like murmurs, but I could not make out what was being said. I kept trying to quiet my mind but to no avail. Though I had no success understanding the stones, I said to them, "Thanks for trying."

There are said to be significant astronomical functions to this site. Equinox and Solstice sunrises and sunsets are quite obvious and having done some study on the subject I find the astronomical information both fascinating and often believable.

Later, when looking at aerial photos and at drawings done of the layout of the stones, I was struck by a thought. The stones look like a representation of a star constellation of the human body laid out on the ground. From the stone circle, or body, there are two lines going to the north like legs, one line going east and one west like arms, and one going south for neck and head. Kind of cool. Might it have something to do with the astronomical uses of this place?

All that said, for me the wonder of this site is just Callanish Itself. It is just an awesome display of the interaction of man, earth, sky, and stone.

We left two Herkimer diamonds at the base of the center stone, right below a place where the swirls formed a large heart. It seemed right somehow that there was a heart on the stone at the heart of this amazing complex. Our time at Callanish had been precious. The stones had blessed us and we walked back up the ridge line with our own hearts feeling happy and satisfied.

I should mention that while at Callanish we had encountered quite a few people of all ages. They all seemed to be very appreciative of the place and as a result really did not interfere with our enjoyment of being there. This is not a place you get to easily, so maybe that weeds out those who do not have a real desire to visit and experience these stones. It was actually quite nice to see them being treated with such respect.

Two days later Sharon and I flew into Kirkwall on the Orkney Islands, and once again, no volcano troubles. Having picked up our rental car we then checked into the St Ola Hotel where we had a pleasant room overlooking the harbor. The nice lady who took us to our room informed us that a cruise ship had come into the port and that there would probably be loads of tourists going to the main stone sites of Stenness, Maeshowe, and the Ring Of Brodgar. We were also told that they would be gone by early afternoon. We thanked her for this advice and with that in mind we chose to start elsewhere and drove south to South Ronaldsay Island to visit the Tomb Of The Eagles.

The weather was all over the place. The sky was mostly overcast but every now and then the sun would force its way through. One minute strong winds would blow, and the next it was calm. It would rain quite hard for a short spell and then suddenly stop. Nonetheless, Sharon and I were excited as we began our exploration of the Orkneys.

Arriving at the Tomb Of The Eagles (a burial chamber), we began with a very informative tour of the museum. The two gals who guided us through the small but excellent museum were quite knowledgeable, and we really enjoyed our time with them. Then, borrowing rain coats that the museum had available, we took the beautiful one mile walk across the headlands to the tomb. I must say I was really not impacted on any level by this site, but the location is impressive, the little dolly cart you pull yourself in and out on was fun, and the views along the sea cliffs were spectacular.

Later in the day we made our way to the Stones of Stenness, also referred to as "The Temple Of The Moon." I had seen many wonderful photos of these giant megaliths and had high expectations. But even after having been to Stonehenge, Avebury, and now Callanish, I was still not prepared for the reality of Stenness. As we approached on the A965, even from quite a distance away we could see three of the remaining stones standing like giant sentinels towering over the flat terrain around them. I was so taken aback when I first saw them that I almost stopped right in the road.

Getting even closer we could see there was actually a fourth stone in what remained of the circle. It was much shorter but it is in fact only what remains of what was once a tall stone like the others. The sad truth is that originally the circle had 11 or 12 of these majestic giants.

I was really glad we had waited until the tours had left before visiting this site. Even though it was overcast and very cold, I was once again seized with that joy of youth as I parked the car and hurried to stand with the stones. This is a place one really must see and "feel" first hand as no words can really describe its "presence," its "strength," its ....., well like I said, there are no words.

Walking among the three giants, I was struck by their shapes. They resemble long, narrow, X-Acto knife blades rising from the earth, threatening the sky. The tallest is almost 19 feet high, four and a half feet wide, and less than a foot thick. You can sense a real strength in these stones and standing next to them you feel quite insignificant.

The fourth stone, though much smaller, is still about six feet tall and has a unique "one way arrow sign" kind of shape. Sharon and I referred to it as the "arrow stone." I kept feeling drawn towards it, so I walked over and settled into a crouch, flat footed with my back to the stone. Closing my eyes and opening to the spirit of the stone, I began to have that sensation of my feet sinking into the ground. In no time I really felt as if my feet were completely submerged up to my ankles in the earth and I was rooted there. It was then that I heard, "Welcome!" One word, but it put a broad smile on my face as I relaxed and felt the stone's embrace.

As I sat there quiet and still, I asked, "Can you help me? What can I learn here from the stones?" I sat and I listened and shortly came this reply. "This is a place to touch the earth, to ground yourself. Once rooted you have the strength of the earth itself." This was the very message I received as I sat there, feet in the earth, joy in my heart.

Pondering these words, I imagined a tree. A tree needs deep, or long roots to then grow tall and healthy, and the soil in some locations is better for that growth then in others. Just as roots soak up the nutrients for a healthy tree, by being grounded, or rooted, we can soak up the knowledge needed for a spiritually healthy human, and this location was very supportive of that growth.

Standing, I thanked the stone and walked over to what appeared to be the remains of a cairn, sitting in the center of the circle. These remaining stones seem to create a doorway, but to where I have no idea. The cairn itself has mostly disappeared.

Turning to the three taller stones I felt a strong desire to walk over to the one closest to me. Running my hands over its surface I was surprised to find considerable energy coursing through the rock, just under the surface. I flushed as I realized that it was a definite masculine energy, not as powerful, but not unlike the one I had felt years before at Erdeven in France. My reaction to this stone was not nearly as dramatic but it was there nonetheless, and I thoroughly enjoyed it. Unlike the shorter stone which drew energy in, and grounded, this stone was a conduit for the release of energies. It is my experience that some stone circles are very uplifting and others are very grounding. The Stones of Stenness seemed to offer both. A complete balance.

Though only a portion of the original circle remains these stones are very proud and have a real "sense of place." While this ring would have been absolutely magnificent in its full glory, these remaining stones have lost none of their significance.

It was getting late, and before it got dark we wanted to visit the Ring of Brodgar, "The Temple Of The Sun," which we could see poised on a ridge off in the distance. Knowing we would return to Stenness the next day, we thanked the stones, returned to the car, and drove across a short bridge that separates two lochs and connects these two impressive sites.

What a joy! The wonders just kept coming! Approaching the Ring on the B9055 you could see many stones standing tall and proud against a seemingly endless sky line. That it was late and the sky was darkening with the promise of a cold rain only added to the atmosphere, the mystery of this moody place.

Brodgar is the northern most of all the UK stone circles. It is a near perfect circle and it has a henge with two entrances. The ditch is still there but the outer bank has disappeared. The circle itself is huge, some 340 feet across with 29 stones remaining of what once may have been 60. Though not as tall as the Stenness stones they are none the less very impressive. Most are seven feet or more in height with the South stone being over 12 feet and the West stone over 15. Like Stenness many of these stones have that same knife blade shape.

Walking the circle I was once again struck by the uniqueness of each stone. There just seemed to be a real purpose to each selection. If these stones were not shaped to some degree by the builders then definitely each was carefully chosen for its natural shape. Along with the X-Acto shaped stones, there were many whose shapes provided images easily named. Among those were "the embracing couple," "the clapping hands," "thumbs up," "the boss," and "the pyramid."

As we continued to walk the ring, I became aware of the "voice" of the stones speaking to me in the most subtle way. "Though each stone brings something very special to the circle, as a whole we are of one purpose." Moving from stone to stone I wondered what that purpose might be, but it was like I had lost the channel on the radio. There was only silence.

By this point in the evening the cold was doing its best to work its way through our clothing and we knew we should be getting ready to leave. We came across a stone lying flat on the ground with a sign posted next to it saying it had been broken and toppled by lightening. If standing stones are in fact a place where energies are released, as well as drawn in, one can see where lightning would be attracted to such a location.

The Ring of Brodgar is surrounded by fields of heather, with the inside of the ring one large patch of heather as well. On the inside of the circle there is a pathway which runs alongside of the stones providing easy access to them. The heather inside the pathway however prevents easy access to the circle's center, and there are signs posted not to walk there. I doubt this is how the ring's creators would have used it. I would assume it was a place to meet and worship, with the center being of great importance.

I cannot understand why the caretakers of this wonderful ring do not keep the inside cleared of brush? This is the only circle I have been to where such was the case. Still, we were thankful for the access to the stones, as Sharon and I really enjoyed this circle.

Preparing to leave we placed Mark and Erin's Herkimers at the base of two stones which stood side by side, one having a strong male energy and the

Stone Journals

other female. It just seemed right. The Ring of Brodgar reminds me a bit of Avebury. The spirits live deep here, and though I did have a brief interaction with them, like Avebury, I know I must return and I must be willing to spend time. Time to just stand, or sit, and wait.

On July 7th Sharon and I returned to the Stones of Stenness. I love this place! The sun was out and there was a beautiful blue sky with large white cumulus clouds rapidly marching across it from west to east. And there before us stood those most magnificent of megaliths, as if posing for a portrait. Happily, we had them all to ourselves.

Having been so overcome by the stones the day before I had not noticed that in fact, this too was a stone circle/henge with an entrance in the northwest. Though both ditch and bank have been diminished over time, they are still there.

As we moved among the stones I thought to check my compass, having forgotten it the day before. I found that the cairn remains sit in an east/west alignment, and looking through the two "entry" stones I was looking right at yesterday's "male stone." That very special stone was the west point of the circle. The tall stone standing furthest to its left (looking at them from inside the circle) was in fact the South stone.

While I was checking the circle for compass points, Sharon had been visiting the "arrow stone," the shorter stone which the day before had made me welcome. She suddenly came hurrying towards me and asked enthusiastically, "Have you heard any messages?" When I said "No," she began telling me of her experience. When she had gone to stand by the "arrow stone," she surprisingly heard a voice say to her, "You must show respect to the most insignificant stone first." That was it.

Now, I should explain that my wife, has for 46 years, put up with my being a little bit "different." Sharon does not hear voices from rocks. And yet here she was bubbling with excitement about just that. And what a perfect message. In life we are so often most impressed by the person, place, or thing that is physically most attractive or most powerful, completely ignoring the magnificence of that which makes no effort to impress. There at Stenness the "arrow stone" stands dwarfed by the other three towering megaliths and yet you can sense that this stone is maybe the heart of the complex. It was to this stone that we were both drawn. It had welcomed me the day before and now and it had "spoken" to Sharon. I was so happy for her that she was blessed with this experience.

Filled with Sharon's joy I crossed over to the "male stone" to spend some time with it. Running my hand over its surface, I was again flooded with the pulsating energies of this wondrous "being," and I use this word very seriously. The stone then spoke to me. He spoke to my inner self in a voice so slow, so deep, so calm, so quiet, and yet so passionate. It was like listening to a recording of a Buddhist chant being played back at a slower speed than that at which it had been recorded. The message was clear and simple. "Respect the earth. She is the mother of us all." It came almost as a mantra and pulsed with the energy of the stone. Wonderful as this was, there was also a sense of sadness about this stone, and my heart ached when I removed my hand. This stone missed the companions long gone and missed the role that they once played in the lives of humans.

I remember talking with Sharon later on about how wonderful it would be to be able to visit the same stone site day after day, for weeks, or months, or years. What then might one learn?

Though it was time to go, I knew, that in fact, this place would always be with me. Thanking the stones, I then buried a Herkimer at the base of the "male stone." Placing both hands on the stone I then thanked him for opening to me, and was blessed with a strong surge of controlled energy flooding my body. I felt the luckiest of people as Sharon and I returned to the car.

The next destination was a chambered tomb called Maeshowe. But first I wanted to stop at a lone megalith I had noticed standing right alongside the road that ran between the Stenness Stones and the Ring of Brodgar. In a booklet I had picked up I saw that it was called the "Watchstone." When I had seen it the day before, I felt a strong pull from it, and knew I must visit it before leaving.

So, there it stood on the water's edge between the circle stones and the bridge. More than 18 feet tall, one side covered with lichen, it is alone, and satisfied with

itself. I assumed this growth was the result of it being so close to the loch as I have never seen this heavy an effect before. Having parked the car, I walked up and was impressed with the strong energy of this stone. Reaching out to touch it, I found it had the same energy as the "male stone" at Stenness, and it coursed through me filling me with a much appreciated warmth. I also felt a kind of familiarity with this stone similar to what I had felt with The Blind Fiddler in Cornwall. I wanted to sit with my back to it and see what might develop, but time was short and its location, with water on one side and the road on the other, made it a difficult place to get acquainted. Also, Sharon was patiently waiting in the car. Still, I left happy and satisfied, thanking the stone, and hoping to return one day.

We had scheduled a tour of Maeshowe and arrived just in time to join our group. This chambered tomb is considered to be the finest Neolithic period building in Northern Europe and to actually see it one can understand why. Approaching it via a trail across open pastureland, we saw a group of 10 or 15 cows lying in a perfect large circle right alongside of the tall earth mound that is Maeshowe. What is it with cows and these ancient sites?

First you come to an earth wall followed by a deep ditch, both encircling the mound. Crossing them, you follow the path to a narrow slit cut in the side of the mound and enter a long passage leading to a square shaped chamber. Off of this main chamber, there are three smaller chambers. As soon as you enter, it is the stonework here that amazes. The walls, the floor, and the ceiling of the entrance passage are each made of one solid thirty foot long stone slab. It is incredible! In each corner of the main chamber is one of the same X-Acto knife blade stones you find at Stenness or Brodgar. The remainder of the walls and ceiling are a construction of very impressive stacked flagstones. There is great history here with wonderful stories about Vikings and the runes they carved in the walls. It is also very cool because like at New

Grange, in Ireland, the sun lines up perfectly on Winter Solstice to shine down the entrance and light up the inner chamber. This is an amazing site.

Another wonderful place to visit was Scara Brae. This is a marvelously preserved prehistoric farming settlement located on the west coast of Mainland Island, Orkney. Built some 5000 years ago, this site has survived because in the centuries after it was abandoned, the winds and sea backfilled and covered it with sand creating a natural protection for what was buried underneath.

Today, thanks to some severe storms, it has once again been revealed, and to walk this site is to see back into the times and lives of the people who built the magnificent stone monuments on the Orkneys. These were a people who really did have a sense of community and whose construction skills were way beyond what one might imagine possible of the people of that time period.

Both Scara Brae and Maeshowe provide a real world insight into the lives and skills of these people. Some of the stone monuments they constructed were simple, others intricate. Some were small and some large. But in every case, as with other people who made similar constructions throughout the British Isles, much thought had gone into the design and location. They had to choose each location carefully, paying attention to both the practical as well as the aesthetic and or spiritual concerns.

Did they pick a site because it was close to the needed stones or did they choose the location for other reasons and then figure out how to get the stones they needed? Choosing which stones to use and the distance over which they had to transport them, along with the number of people and the technologies that would be required, would all have been of major concern. Some of these monuments would have taken generations of people to build. Then there were the astronomical alignments and earth energy lines to be considered.

As to the individual stones chosen for circles, avenues, etc. it appears in most cases that I have observed, that each stone seems to have been intentionally selected. There was nothing haphazard about which stone went where. Sometimes they used a stone just as it came from the earth but in other instances the stones were carved to one degree or another to create a desired effect. All in all, their skills as well as their concerns for, and devotion to, these stone monuments are quite evident even today.

These were not some race of ignorant, unimaginative, hunter/farmers. When Sharon and I walked through Scara Brae, I definitely got the feeling of "community." These were a people who looked after each other. They were a people who lived life, they did not just endure it. Looking in the empty homes I could imagine families living quite happily there in some age long gone by. Comfortable and content. As I left this place I did so with a great respect for these masters of stone and a sense of connectedness with, and an admiration for, a people who obviously listened to and followed the advice that I had received at Stenness. "Respect the earth. She is the mother of us all."

Over a period of several days, we had visited many different stone sites on the Isle of Lewis and the Orkney Islands. Callanish and Stenness had completely "rocked" my world. Though we were about to leave for Italy, a very different place altogether, there was still one last stone-stop on this leg of our journey.

We flew back to England to once again visit Stonehenge. This time, however, we were actually going to walk among the stones. After all the years of wishing and hoping, I was able to get Sharon and I booked on a Stonehenge tour with the Wiltshire Heritage Society. At a little after 7:00 PM on July 9th, we were with a small group of just 25 people who crossed the fence line and approached the stones. The whole site had been closed off to the public. Dreams can come true! For about half an hour

our guide provided us with information which I am sure was great, but honestly, I was paying very little attention and soon had wandered away from the group. I was standing in one of the greatest megalithic monuments on the earth! I was actually walking among the stones of Stonehenge!

There was only one problem. Before we entered the circle we had been told very clearly that we were not allowed to touch the stones. Our guide said this was because of some endangered species that grows on the rocks which can be harmed in some way by the skin oils from human hands. They were very serious about this and in fact there were several guards who watched us very closely to make sure we kept hands off. For me this was a bit of a bummer as I get my best interactions with the stones by contact, even if it is just sitting up against them. Still, how could one not be happy standing in this most amazing stone temple?

When the lecture finished and everyone was free to wander the site, I was glad I had taken those moments to myself. Sharon rejoined me, and we began exploring, taking in all we could in the 45 minutes left to us. It really is hard to find the right words to describe just what an impressive place Stonehenge is. This is a one of a kind place on this entire planet, and it was good fun for Sharon and I to be sharing the experience together.

While I had no deep "spiritual" connect with Stonehenge, the experience was powerful and moving nonetheless. Some other circles are just as impressive in their own way, but it must be said that there is no other circle like Stonehenge. The sheer size of these stones is breathtaking in both height and mass, and the legendary arches can be found nowhere else in the world. The mind boggles trying to imagine some characters 3000 to 5000 years ago coming up with this plan, let alone figuring out how to construct it. The lintels alone weighed more than six tons each and had to be raised up to 24 feet in the air. And then, how did they sell the idea to the hundreds, probably thousands, of people that were needed to build it, and to keep them at it for many generations?

Finally, add into the mix the transportation of these massive stones over long distances. It is said that the blue stones came from about 150 miles away in Wales. It really is unimaginable, and yet there it stands.

Realizing we were just about out of time I waited for an opportune moment when the guards were in a position so as not to see me, and I placed the last two Herkimers at the base of one of the big columns. That done I rejoined Sharon as we were being ushered out of the circle.

It had been a beautiful evening, with blue skies and big puffy white cumulus clouds. The sun sat low on the horizon creating a wonderful color display of reds, oranges, and purples. Looking back on the circle I snapped one last mental picture that I hope stays with me always. I did not get to touch the stones physically, or to connect with them on any deeper level, but this was an experience I shall never forget. What an incredible way to finish this "Journey to the Stones."

Later, as I sat thinking about our Stonehenge experience, I wondered if maybe the spirits of those stones have been suppressed by the constant invasion of the circle by hundreds of thousands of people, most of whom are in no way interested in what the stones might have to offer them. Pondering this idea I remembered something similar I had read in Richardson's book *Spirits of the Stones*. He relates a story told by an Australian woman about her Stonehenge visit. "Her own feeling is that the energies have been so mucked about with over the centuries that the circle has gone into sulk mode." Whatever the case might be, I would love to go back and try again.

78 | Stone Journey

"The ancients, said Socrates, were uncomplicated, and if a certain rock was known for telling the truth, they would listen to it."
John Mitchell
Simulacra

Stone Journey 3

SCOTLAND

STONE JOURNEY 3 - July 21, 2011

Sharon and I have returned to Scotland, and it is so good to be back. This trip sort of came together on short notice. I was going to be on tour in Europe for a few weeks, so I said to Sharon why not join up with me in Scotland when the tour ended? She was wanting to get back to do some more serious ancestry search in the Dumfries region so her flight was booked and a few months later we arrived in Edinburgh.

After a few days in that wonderful city, we rented a car and headed south for Dumfries with a stop at Rosslyn Chapel. What a magical place it is. A year ago the whole outside had been covered with scaffolding and was partially enclosed due to a major restoration project that was being done. This time the front half was fully exposed, and it looked great. The interior of this charming structure is beyond imagining and as with our visit last year, we were completely bowled over by the stone craftsmanship. We spent a joyful hour wandering around looking at one intriguing carving after another. This is another one of those places that has to be seen as words just cannot do it justice.

I should also note that the area around the chapel is wonderful as well, and is definitely worth the walk. Of special interest are the castle ruins at the end of the road and the "tree spirit" who lives alongside the road. Should you take the walk to the castle keep your eyes open on your left and you may see it peeking out from the roots where there is a bench on which to sit.

Driving south we stopped for tea and scones in Moffat and then went in search of a circle south of Eskdalemuir called the Loupin Stains Stone Circle. It was pretty easy to locate, sitting just off the B709. We found a parking area with a large sign posting information about both the Loupin Stains (pronounced like cow pen) and Girdle Stains which is another stone circle close by. Looking across the road from the parking space and about one hundred yards down the grassy slope we could see a small, humble, stone circle. I was back!.

Now, Sharon had not really dressed for this situation. Her dress, leggings, and nice leather loafers were not really the best items for climbing fences, walking over wet boggy ground, and jumping over pools of water. So, she decided to stay behind.

As I approached the circle, the first thought to come to mind was "What a sweet place this is." There really are no better words to describe this circle. As I moved among my newly found friends, I felt a rush of joy come up from the cushy green carpet over which I was walking. These stones were happy I was there. Though their voices were quite muted, it seemed I could hear them chuckling, like children under the covers at night trying not to be heard by their parents. I had to laugh and was happy to do so.

The circle consists of twelve irregular shaped stones. Though most of the stones are small, being only between one or two feet in height, there are two good sized stones about five and a half feet tall each that form an entry to the southwest. One is thinner and tapered downward somewhat while the other sits like a huge flat topped block. The ring itself is far from perfect. It is actually more of an oval 34 feet by 37 feet and even at that a few of the stones do not fall right in line. These factors, however, enhance rather than diminish the charm of this ring.

Adding to the uniqueness of the site, this circle is built up on a raised platform of earth that rises several feet above the surrounding landscape. The only other circle I have encountered built in such a way is Torhouse, but to me the effect here is even more pleasing.

Having felt the circle's welcome when I first walked among the stones, I decided to sit on one of the small rocks and try opening myself to them. Immediately my feet "sank" into the earth and the tension from the drive flowed down my legs and out. I quickly became quite relaxed.

Sitting there, feeling wonderful and grounded, I began looking closely at the two big stones. Placed across from each other as they are, I was sensing a strong bond between them, but of very different energies. Examining each of them separately, I found the thinner of the two had a strong male energy while the larger, block shaped rock was definitely feminine. As I was pondering this, my thoughts shifted to Sharon sitting by herself up in the car. I was actually glad she had not come with me as she probably would have ruined her shoes if not her dress and leggings. I turned to look back up towards the car and was quite surprised to see Sharon approaching the circle. I was happy to see her, but her shoes looked soaked, and it was beginning to sprinkle. Not a good starting point for her. I could see she was not too happy.

I had her sit on one of the rocks to let some of the frustration go and made one more quick visit to each of the stones. I got a strong pull from the big rocks and promised them I would return. This is something I never do for obvious reasons, but on this day, in this place, it seemed right. Though in the distance I could see a sign pointing the way to the Girdle Staines Circle, I knew this was not the time. Before leaving I asked Sharon to take a couple of pictures of me in the circle. I have few photos of me with stones as I am usually the photographer. She took a couple of shots and then saying farewell to this most sweet circle of stones we went back to the car. I was quite happy to have found this location and left feeling great.

After we had returned to our home in the U.S. I was reading about the Loupin Staines in *A Guide to the Stone Circles of Britain, Ireland, and Brittany* by Burl and saw that the name actually means the Leaping Stones. It seems it was a tradition long ago for young men to jump from one of the big entry stones to the other. I found it quite interesting that when I had Sharon take my photo there, I chose that occasion to climb up on one of the big stones and act like I was getting ready to leap towards the other. I had definitely been "feeling" the stones and had been connecting on a deeper level. I cannot wait to go back.

We next went to visit Kagyu Samye Ling Monastery and Buddhist Temple. This was the first Buddhist temple established in the West and it says a lot about the country and its people that this remote location in Scotland is where they chose to build it. I am not a Buddhist but I cannot recommend this place enough if you are ever in the area. Visually it is stunning, and the sense of peace that you feel is both healing and inspiring.

As the day was getting on (and wet) we headed for Dumfries and back to the Dumfries Villa B&B where we had enjoyed our stay the previous year. In route, we drove through Lockerbie and on the west side of town, in a portion of the local cemetery, there was a memorial called the Garden of Remembrance, built in the memory of the passengers who died on Pan Am Flight 103. Remembering that whole awful episode we felt drawn to stop and pay our respects. I am so thankful that we did. It is wonderful what the people of Scotland have created there to honor those lost in this terrorist airplane bombing. It is grand in its simplicity. A garden that celebrates the lives lived as well as the lives abruptly ended. Sharon and I were deeply moved by the experience.

As Sharon had plans to spend most of this day exploring the Dumfries ancestry archives in her continuing search for information about her Kirkpatrick roots, I was left free to do whatever I chose. So, I headed for the Twelve Apostles Stone Circle. It is only a few miles out of town and my visit there last year had been wonderful. Pulling into the parking area alongside the field in which this circle sits, I had that feeling you get when stopping in to see good friends you haven't seen in sometime. Both excited and a bit apprehensive.

Looking across the field, there were the stones, and there were the cows. Of course, there were cows. Jumping the fence I crossed the field and approached the large stone that I had lain on when visiting this circle last year. The whole herd of cows began walking towards me. Mounting the prone giant I was soon surrounded on all sides by a large congregation of black and white bovines. They just stood there staring at me, packed tightly together, some with their heads resting on the rock. Standing on my

stone platform I took the occasion, as I had at Little Meg the year before, to give them a rousing sermon on the peace and joy to be found in the presence of the stones.

Stone Journals

They did not seem overly impressed. Asking them to please allow me to continue my walk among the stones, I went to jump down from my rock and was happy to see a parting of the "Black Sea" as an opening appeared. They let me pass.

Just as when I visited these stones a year ago, I felt very comfortable. However, this time the stones of this ring seemed quite subdued compared to last year. In fact, several felt sort of like they were in a deep slumber, even more so than on my previous visit. Still, as I walked from stone to stone there were a number of them from which I received a welcome, or at least a recognition, and for that I was thankful.

When visiting stones this individual welcome/recognition can happen in many ways. Often I am just drawn to a rock. I just "know" I must get acquainted with this rock. Then in some cases this recognition will happen when I touch the stone. It might be a warmth in my hand (and there is a difference between the warmth from the sun and the warmth released by the stone) or a flow of energy from the rock. Sometimes just walking into a circle I get that sense of energy coming up through my feet. On an occasion there can also be a very earthy smell or taste that I might experience when in contact with a stone. As for any actual communication, the "voices" I hear are inner, but very real nonetheless. I make no effort to create these conversations, I just happily accept them.

Last year when visiting the Twelve Apostles, I had forgotten my dowsing rods and compass but not this time. Walking the perimeter I came across strong energy lines running both north/south and east/west. They crossed right in the center of the circle just like with my circle back home. This kind of discovery always excites me.

After a while I was drawn back to the massive prone stone laying in the southwest. Climbing back up on it, this time I lay down on my back and began absorbing the energy it had to offer. It was so good to be plugged back into the earth's power supply, and soon I was full up.

I had been laying there for some time when I had the feeling I was being watched. Opening my eyes I found I was looking right into the big, glassy, black eyes of one huge cow head, just a foot or so away. I must say it gave me quite a fright. The two large onyx orbs just stared at me, as if waiting for some purpose to be revealed. I jumped up, hopped down, made my apologies, and quickly walked away leaving the cow to come to its own conclusions.

Noticing a bicyclist watching me from outside the fence, I walked over and introduced myself. He told me that as a "wee boy" he had been brought to this circle several times, but in the years since he had not been back, and had completely forgotten about it. He had just rediscovered the stones on a bike ride a few months past. Now in his 50's he was enjoying revisiting the circle on a regular basis, but told me that he had not yet climbed the fence to walk among the stones. He said he just liked looking at them and that he always left feeling better than when he had arrived. I was the first person he had seen actually out in the circle and now he was thinking that on his next visit he would get out in the field with the stones. I did of course encourage him in this. If more people would spend time with the stones, I am sure that many of those that seemed to be sleeping would awaken.

As I walked the circle one last time I thought how sad it was that sites like this are not maintained. It would be nice if there was a solid path leading across the field and to the circle. It would also be great to be able to walk among the stones and not have to worry about where you place your feet. Cows, like sheep, really do not care where they leave their deposits. But I would not like to see it fenced in like at Torhouse, creating that sad prison effect.

What a fun day. Driving west we had a wonderful time, making stops as the mood would hit us to explore castles, stone monuments, abandoned abbeys, and more. We decided to make a return visit to Cairnholy as we had enjoyed it last year, and this time we had a perfect sunny day. Arriving at the site it all looked so different. Last year the stones were enveloped in mist, and you could not see much more than fifteen yards in any direction. This time with clear blue skies overhead, the stones stood proudly in front of a mound of bright green, as if on guard, protecting the ancient tomb entrance. Looking to the south we had a spectacular view of a lush wooded hillside falling off to the sea far below. It was glorious.

Not having done so last year, the first thing I did was get out the dowsing rods and began walking the site to see what I might find. The result was nothing at all. Not a twitch. I had never checked a burial site like this before but was really quite surprised to find that such a beautifully placed cairn had no energy lines running through it. Maybe they did not see a need for life giving energy in such a place. What would be the point?

When we arrived at this site, there was a fellow already there who was doing measurements and calculations having to do with shadow lines cast by the stones. He was quite secretive about his actions, and though he was pleasant enough we just left him to himself.

We then walked on up the road a short distance to Carinholy II. We had not visited this cairn the previous year. It was much smaller in size, but it did have a capstone in place, and it really was charming. Though the 360 degree view was great the location of this site, on top of a hill, overlooking Wigtown Bay, was well chosen no matter what the reason.

As we walked around these stones there was a wonderful sense of comfort here, and I found myself thinking how nice it would be to climb up on the capstone and take a nap. But we had a long day ahead of us and needed to keep moving.

Before leaving I decided to check the site for energy lines, and just like Cairnholy I, I found nothing. I really am puzzled by this. We then walked back down the hill for a last visit to the larger site.

Sharon and I really enjoyed our visit to these ancient cairns. The day was sunny and bright, the weather was near perfect. Oddly enough, however, we were actually kind of missing the moody wet mist that so completely enveloped these stones on our visit last year. There was something very "other worldly" about that experience. You could really feel the earth and rock that day.

Next was a short stop at the Gem Rock Museum in Creetown. We enjoyed it so much last time, we wanted to go back. While Sharon was looking to purchase an

agate necklace with earrings, I was asking around to see if anyone could help me find the Glenquicken Stone Circle. Our efforts last year were unsuccessful, and today I had high hopes. Sure enough one of the fellows in the shop knew the way and gave me what proved to be quite accurate directions.

Two miles out of town on a small country road, we found the parking space we were told to look for and parked the car. We quickly were out of the car, across the road, had climbed over a stone wall, and started across a large field. In the distance we could see a wire fence. We also spotted two people walking along the other side of it, heading away from where I thought the circle might be. This circle was said to be made up of a ring of smaller stones with a large center stone. I could just see what I thought was the top of this center stone standing above some brush growing along the fence, and we headed right toward it.

About half way across the field, I said to Sharon, "This is going to be a good one." I could feel the circle's energy, subtle, but there, and the closer we got the wider became my smile.

Arriving at the barbed wire fence we could see Glenquicken there before us. It is not all that large, but what an impressive circle it is. Aubry Burl describes this as "The finest of all the center stone circles."

As Sharon followed the fence down a ways to cross through a gate, I climbed over and introduced myself to the stones. The energy here remained subtle, but I soon felt it slowly working its way up through my feet and I was most thankful.

Sharon arrived, and we began a closer examination of the stones. The ring is made up of 29 rather rounded stones between one and almost three feet high. Many appear to be set on edge rather than standing tall. In the center stands a grand, squarish stone column a little over six feet in height and three feet by two plus feet wide. Small in size when compared with stones at places like Stenness or Avebury, this stone was in no way small in stature. I'd felt a welcome from the circle as I had approached it but standing inside the circle I felt an even stronger more personal embrace emanating from this center stone.

Walking the circle with my dowsing rods, I was not at all surprised to find strong energy lines here. In fact, I found strong north/south and east/west lines crossing right under the center stone, once again, like our stone circle back home.

It really was great just wandering around in and out of the stones on this beautiful summer day. One must take full advantage of these days when they happen in Scotland. But the wonderful weather also brought out all kinds of flies, mosquitos, and other strange, large flying critters. Sharon had chosen to wear shorts that day and the insects were becoming quite an annoyance. So, she decided to go back to the car to wait. "No hurry," she said.

I stayed on and spent a little time walking the ring going from stone to stone. In an ancient place like this, in the company of stones, you realize that they have been here for centuries just "being" while the world continued on around them. Our visit to these stones was but a brief moment in time for them. It can, however, be a valuable moment for us. If you are lucky enough to spend time with stones like those at Glenquicken, and if you slow down and open yourself you will find a sense of peace, a calm, and even a joy. And, if you listen, you may also hear the stones' message. Here at Glenquicken the message was quite clear. "Everything that we love and hold dear is dependent upon our relationship with the Earth." Like the tide rolling in and out on a beach this mantra kept flowing in and out of my head.

If you care for the earth, then the earth will take care of you. When I am in the company of stones, in one way or another, this is their constant reminder, whether it comes as a voice loud and clear in my head or just as a comforting embrace while laying on some large fallen slab.

I walked to the center stone and placed my hands on it. It took a minute or two but I soon began to recognize that strong male energy flowing into me. What a wonderful, powerful, feeling. This stone was wide awake and happy to share, and I was soon overflowing with energy and a strong desire to use it. The whole circle of stones seemed to come alive around me, and I felt embraced by them all. Though I knew it was time for me to be going, it was actually kind of hard for me to leave.

Walking away, there was only joy as I turned and called my sincere thanks to the stones that had so freely shared with me. I climbed the fence and started back across the field still feeling the energy flow radiating from the ring. Climbing over the rock wall, I hurried to embrace Sharon who stood by the car watching my approach. She could feel the energy radiating from me, and she knew its portent. "Now, Pat, take it easy" were her words, spoken softly but firmly. Once again she was in control of the situation, which was a good thing, as right at that moment another couple came walking over the bridge alongside which we had parked. Having seen us, they approached. They, too, were looking for the stone circle, and we were happy to be able to point the way.

As we prepared to leave, we saw yet another couple coming down the road from the other direction, and they were also searching for the Glenquicken Circle. It was wonderful to meet other people out looking for this precious ring of stones. I hope that they also found its joy and experienced its welcome.

These were the last stones I visited on this trip and what a glorious way to finish this "stone journey." I was sad to have to leave Scotland. There were still so many sites I would like to visit. I love this land and its people. And, I love its stones.

> "Seeing for the first time the massive ditch and hulking tonnage of stone that is Avebury Circle is an experience never forgotten."
> Catherine Tuck
> *Landscapes And Desire*

Stone Journey 4

SOUTHERN ENGLAND, SCOTLAND, NORTHERN ENGLAND

STONE JOURNEY 4 - April 29, 2012

Today, Sharon and I returned to the UK. Flying into Heathrow we rented a car and in rainy, windy, weather (what else) we drove straight to Avebury. I could think of no better place to begin our journey. I have always wanted to spend several days at this site in the hope of making some kind of connection with the stones. Each time I had been to Avebury in the past my visits were brief, and though with each visit I had felt something going on, I had not been able to tap into whatever it was. Just maybe, with this visit I might have better success.

Checking into the Avebury B&B early in the afternoon, we were met by Antoinette who owns and runs the business. We found her to be a wonderful spirited person, and I knew this was going to be good.

Once we were settled in we decided to take the 10 minute walk into the village with its famous circle/henge. It was a beautiful walk down country lanes and well maintained walking paths that led us right into the heart of the village. At one point along the way we could see Silbury Hill off in the distance. What a great surprise!

After a visit to Avebury Manor and gardens, both being good fun, we exited and began walking along the inside of the henge, stopping to visit various stones as we went. It being cold, windy, and somewhat rainy, we soon felt a need for warmth and food, and so landed at the Red Lion Pub, located inside of the circle. The meal was quite good and we left there feeling content. Still, after visiting a few shops, the fatigue of the flight and drive set in and we decided to call it a day. I had yet to feel "plugged in" to the energies of Avebury. I knew they were there but they continued to allude me.

The next morning began with a nice breakfast and a visit with Antoinette. Then we were off to make a complete tour of both henge and circle, no hurries, no worries. As often as I have been to this place, it still impresses, and I was ready for whatever was in store for us.

We began at the stone circle. We walked from stone to stone examining each as we went and, on several occasions, found a face or two hiding in the rocks. It soon became fun looking for these stone faces, and we were quite surprised over the course of the morning at just how many we were finding. It

seemed like more than coincidence to find so many. I was beginning to think that the planners of this site really may have picked these stones because of the faces, or that maybe they had done a little touch up to make a hidden face even more obvious. Whatever the case may be, it does open up another area of consideration.

In fact, after having made this journey I purchased several books on this very subject. *The Secrets of The Avebury Stones* by Terence Meaden and *Pictures From The Past* by Martin Ringer are good examples of such books. The more I think about it I cannot help but wonder how much of an affect weathering has had on these stones over the last 4000 to 5000 years? Even in hard stone like this there must have been some degrading of the stone. So, maybe originally there were many faces, symbols, characters, etc. that were carved into the stones that are no longer visible or hard to find because of this weathering. The carvings in Long Meg for example were in a softer stone and almost impossible to see today.

Along with walking the inside perimeter of the henge, examining the stones, we also walked the top of the mound where possible. On this visit they had sections of the mound blocked off so that you could not go up on top. This was evidently to prevent erosion damage. I hope they figure this out as walking the entire circle from the top of the mound is quite special. It is only from up on top that you can see just how large this monument really is. So, when it was permitted to do so, we followed the path along the mound top. At one point I had stopped to take a few pictures and when done I noticed Sharon standing quite still, looking into the circle below. She stood like this for several minutes before resuming her walk. She seemed in a reflective mood, so I did not bother her.

After a bit Sharon stopped to inform me of the experience she had just had. She explained that while she had been standing there she became aware of a pulsing sensation emitting from her female organs. The pulse was at a slow, steady pace and strong enough to be very noticeable. As she had never experienced anything like this before, she was puzzled. Thinking about it, I told her it kind of made sense to me as tomorrow would be Beltane, a very important ritual day celebrating life and the life force and that maybe she was being impacted by those energies?

As we continued on it seemed as though I could feel the energy under my feet, subtle but there. Was Avebury opening to us?

Exiting the henge from the southern entrance, we crossed the road and began the walk along what is called West Kennet Avenue. Here stand the

94

Stone Journey

remaining stones of what was once a long stone lined avenue winding off to the south. Most of the stones that do remain are quite large and in a variety of shapes. Though there does seem to have been some attempt to place taller, narrower stones across from, or next to, stones which are wider and more diamond shaped, this was not always apparent. It is thought that the tall narrow stones represent the male energy and the wider diamond shaped stones represent the female. I did not pick up on any of that but that is just me.

It was as Sharon and I were walking up the avenue that I had my first real experience with Avebury. Having exited the henge we entered the stone lined avenue and began walking up the slope. I was telling Sharon about how in ages long gone by people would follow this route down into the henge-hidden circle to participate in rituals and ceremonies, for the temples lay within. While I was talking, I suddenly caught my breath, as I began "seeing" hundreds of people walking down the avenue towards us. They were dressed in very simple clothing, browns and whites, and seemed very intent on their procession into the circle below. Shortly, we met up with those coming towards us, and I could "feel" them passing through me like a light

breeze blowing through my body. It was a very strange affect and though I was startled by it, it did not distress me, and in a way I welcomed the moment. Turning to look back down the slope, I saw no one. Though Sharon saw none of this, she knew something had happened and when I told her what happened she accepted it as if it was really not all that surprising. She, too, was feeling the magic of this place. The moment had passed, and I was thankful for it. Avebury really was opening to us this time around.

Thinking back on this later that day I remembered my experience at Stanton Drew a few years back. That too had involved an avenue and though the experience was somewhat different, they both had seemed so real.

Continuing up the avenue we once again began seeing faces in the rocks lining the way. In some cases there were animal heads or giant stone birds, and one stone looked like a shark head rising from a sea of green. At the end of the line was a stone that looked just like a knight chess piece, being in the shape of a horse head. Nearby, frozen in stone stood a monk, or better yet a druid in his robe with the hood pulled up over his head. It was all good fun for us, but once again I could not help but think this was not just coincidence or imagination. Surely these stones were picked because of the characters imprisoned within them. Once again, there was a purpose.

Walking back to the henge, we entered, and walked to, the devil's chair. This is one of two huge stones which mark the entrance to the circle from the south. It measures 14 feet wide by 13 feet tall and weighs 60 tons. Massive indeed. This stone has a seat carved into it (whether natural or not, I cannot say) which is thought to be where the priests would have sat to watch the rising of the sun on the morning of the winter solstice. The stone was, in fact, placed in just the right location to have allowed one to see the sun as it rose and shone down through the southern entrance on mid-winter day all those years ago. Sharon and I both took our turn sitting in the seat, and I must say, it did feel like a sacred place. Sitting there, I began to draw energy from the earth up through my feet. This was a first for me at Avebury, and along with the energy came an "awareness" of a need to get my own house in order. A need to be even more serious about caring for this earth as did those who sat on this stone seat so long ago. For a lot of people, this is just a place for a photo op. For me it was a place to awaken, with a call to action.

I noticed a couple of other people waiting for us to move on so they could take that photo, so I thanked the rock for giving me the "call" and promised to act. We finished walking the remainder of the circle and headed back to the B&B. It had been a wonderful day so far. Both Sharon and I had been blessed with very personal experiences in this most amazing place. But, there was much more I wanted to see in the surrounding area and time was running out.

Back in the car and in route to get our afternoon tea and scones, we stopped to look at the Cherhill White Horse. There are actually quite a few of these figures carved in hillsides in the south of England. They were created by scraping off the top layer of earth and revealing the white chalk below. In this case you have a large white horse. In other places there might be a human figure or maybe just a hand. The figures are very large, can be seen from a long distance, and are great fun.

After tea we went to have a look at Silbury Hill. It sits there, a giant cone shaped earth mound dressed all in green, silently waiting for what? This place really is a mystery to me. With the stones I can understand their possible uses and even feel their energies. With Silbury, I am at a loss on all levels. All levels that is but one, it is a marvel. But as impressive as Silbury is today, it would have been even more amazing when it was built. Back then it was said to have been completely covered with chalk. The bright white hill would have stood out like a beacon in this lush green environment.

Just a little further up the A4 we parked and hiked up to visit the West Kennet Long Barrow. It was actually a nice afternoon, with partially sunny skies and little wind. There were vast fields of rape in full bloom and these brilliant yellow flowers, along with their bright green leafy stalks, were enhanced by the glorious sunshine. We were both in good spirits as we arrived at the barrow, sitting on the top of the hill, seemingly unconcerned with the world around it.

Sadly, another fellow had arrived there before us. He was inside in the back chamber and stood staring at us as we entered. We both felt a strange, even malevolent energy coming from him. He talked to us about the barrow and wanted us to know that he knew all about it. Sharon and I just wanted him to leave. In time he walked to the entrance explaining that he was going to go to a sacred well located nearby and said that we should go with him. When I politely said we might come along a little later, he explained the directions and said we should not miss this place. Then, off he went. It almost seemed as if he had been an apparition, as he vanished so quickly from the front of the passageway.

Sharon then went back outside and waited for me as I took a couple of photos. When I came out, she said that the man had really creeped her out and she did not want to stay inside. The whole experience had been polluted by this fellow's presence. I had to admit to her that I too had a bad vibe from the guy and was unable to shake it. Walking back down the hill we saw his form disappear over a ridge line to the west. Very weird. No enlightening West Kennet experiences for us on this day.

I returned Sharon to our B&B and then drove to meet Adam and Eve, two massive stones, also known as The Longstones, which were located nearby on a ridge overlooking Avebury. Once there I hoped to settle and ground myself after the negativity of West Kennet.

The two stones sat in a field not far from where I parked the car. Separated by a distance they are both large Avebury type stones, one being tall and narrow and the other much broader. A repeat of the male/female theme?

After the fun Sharon and I had had looking for faces in the stones earlier in the day, it seemed natural to do the same now. As I approached the first and larger stone, I saw a Jimmy Durante face staring at me, huge nose and all. Not very feminine I must say. Walking around and looking at it from the side, I was quite surprised to see a large bird head. Then, turning to look across at the other stone I saw a bust of Thomas Jefferson. I say again, I cannot help but think that many of the Avebury stones were specially picked for the characters found within them. Obviously not T.J. in this case but a male bust nonetheless.

Dowsing the stones I found that each had an energy line running under it going pretty much north/south. I also found a connecting line running between them. Starting at the larger stone, I followed the line and about half way between the rocks the line made a tight loop and then carried right on to the T.J. stone. I also tested each stone for energy fields and found that they both had a strong field pushing the rod away from the stone about 7 feet up. Even though my skills have become better at finding these energies, I am still in the dark as to what they really mean. I've read the books, but still they are a question mark. In any case, very cool, and I was once again feeling good and grounded. I had my center back.

    I was feeling so good, I decided to go back and get Sharon. When we returned, Sharon had no trouble seeing the faces in the rocks and was soon moving between them, feeling the joy of these wonderful stones. She called me over to the T.J. rock and told me it was "breathing!" I have on many occasions felt the pulse of a rock (which I attribute to the energy flowing through the stone) but I have never seen it breathe. She had me stand in a certain place close to the rock and watch its surface, explaining that she could see it breathing in and out, slow but steady. I tried, but sadly my eyes failed the test. I have no idea what that was all about.

    When we left this magical place, we decided to get some dinner and found a restaurant in Marlborough. I had gone to wash my hands, and as I returned to our table Sharon looked up at me and smiled, saying, "You're really in your element here aren't you Pat. You are just so happy and full of energy." "The stones do bring me joy," I replied.

    It was 4:00 AM, May 1, when our host knocked on our door to wake us saying it was time to go. We were going to celebrate Beltane in the Avebury Circle. After getting bundled up in our warmest clothes and rain gear, Antoinette drove us into the village. It was dark, cold, windy, and there was light rain. Parking, we went to the home of one of the locals who lived inside the circle. After a few introductions to others who were already there, we were told that the fellas went out into a tent in the garden while the ladies went inside the house. Though Sharon and I did not expect this, we just went with the flow. This was our first Beltane ritual and we were looking forward to the experience. In the tent most of the men were getting their faces painted green with varying embellishments in black. Many were also making wreaths of ivy and placing them on their heads or around their necks. Though I was not up for the face paint, I was happy to add the ivy adornment to my head.

It was still dark and the weather conditions had not improved when the men went out into what remained of what had once been the northern of the two inner circles. We gathered together behind the 201 stone (there is an established numbering system for the Avebury stones), where we were hidden from view. Most were dressed in warm casual clothing but there were also a few druids in robes, and then there was the Stag. Clothed in a long fur cloak, full face paint, and with a large stag skull with horns mounted to his head, Steve was the leader of the ceremony, and he was quite an impressive presence.

They began singing an enchanting song about the Stag while drums were being beaten, and standing there in the cold and wet I found myself drawn into the energy of the moment. Many of the voices were actually quite good and resonated strongly through the night air. It was still dark but as we stood there next to this giant stone you could sense the presence of the other Avebury stones watching and joining in with their thanks and blessings. I find the more I visit the stones the more I can feel the reality of this interconnectedness.

With the drums beating, and the voices calling out to Cernnunos, the horned god, I closed my eyes as the earth energy began flowing up through my body. I could "see" around me all the stones of the circle and I was in the center, and I was content.

After a while, someone said he could see the ladies entering the northern circle. The singing came to a crescendo and with a cheer from the Stag there was a moment of complete frolic as the men ran from behind the stone to chase after the women, giving a kiss to those they caught up to. I knew I would need to hurry to get to Sharon as I was sure she would find this uncomfortable. But the Stag was too fleet of foot and before I could find her in the dark he had planted a kiss on her cheek and was off again. As I ran up to her she stood there with an ivy wreath around her head, a bit of green face paint on her nose, and a puzzled look on her face. We both laughed, and as we embraced, standing there in the middle of the Avebury Circle, I felt huge content.

Once the chase was over, Steve led the group over to the remains of the southern inner circle to celebrate Beltane. As we gathered together the rain became a little heavier, but it did not seem to dampen anyone's spirits. Though it was becoming light enough to make out the inside of the henge and some of the giant stones, you could not really see the sun through the dark, overcast sky. Still, everyone stood facing in the direction of the sunrise while the local Archdruid led us in the welcoming of the sun ritual.

Next came the wrapping of the Maypole. There were a large number of colored streamers coming off the pole and Steve began organizing a circle of people around the pole, all holding a streamer. Half the people were facing one direction and in between each of them the other half were set up to go the opposite. Soon people were winding their way in and out of each other wrapping around the pole. This was all done to the sound of constant drum beats. Sharon was given one of the streamers, and I had quite a laugh watching as she tried to work her way in and out, over and under. It was very enjoyable and uplifting for all present.

By the time all was said and done several hours had past. We had dressed for foul weather, and yet still our exterior clothing was soaked, and the cold had worked its way into our bones. With the closing of the ritual, Antoinette took us back to our B&B. We were happy and thankful for having been blessed with this experience. The setting could not have been more dramatic or more pleasing.

Our stay in Avebury was coming to an end, but what a memorable couple of days it had been. Before leaving, we asked Antoinette to call a photographer friend who had taken a wonderful aerial view photo of Avebury which she had displayed in her dining area to see if we might be able to obtain a copy. He was happy to accommodate us, and so on our way to Bath we stopped by his home to purchase it. The photo is quite large, and we have it framed and hanging in our living room. I often find myself standing in front of the photo, staring at the scene, and remembering our wonderful experiences there.

After two grand days relaxing in Bath, we were headed for Glastonbury. Though it was a rainy day, in route, I went in search of a long barrow called Stoney Littleton. Driving down seriously flooded, narrow country lanes (the rain had poured all night), we were relieved when we arrived at a sign posted parking area. Rain gear on, we walked a nice old wooden foot bridge over a rapidly flowing creek and set out across lush green pasture land, following a trail leading up towards the hilltop. Luckily it was not a long walk, as the ground was saturated and very mushy. Though there was still a light rain, our Keen boots and waterproof outer garments kept us dry, if not warm.

From the outside this barrow is quite simple in its appearance. There is a ring of rocks stacked a couple of feet high which form the perimeter wall at the base of a large grass covered, oval shaped, earth mound about 100 feet long. Approaching the entrance the rock walls on both sides rise up to about four feet at the actual entryway, which though small and low, is

impressive nonetheless. On the left side of the opening there is a squared off stone pillar about two feet across. At the base of this column there is the imprint of a large, coiled, ammonite fossil. This took me quite by surprise as I have not seen anything like this at a stone site before. The builders obviously placed this stone at the entrance for a reason, but who knows what that reason might have been. Still, it is very special.

I had to duck down to get inside. It was dark, and I was glad I had brought my flashlight. The interior is lined with stacked flat rocks, both walls and ceiling. Hunched over I walked down a straight central passage about 50 feet long. I found three junctions along the way which opened to small rooms on each side. At one of these junctions I was almost able to stand erect as the ceiling rose a bit higher at that point. At the end of the passageway there was another room that though a little larger, was still a small space. I was able to stand completely erect in this room, however, which was quite a relief.

Settling into a crouch I turned off my flashlight, leaned up against the back wall, and sat looking down the passage to the light of the entrance at the other end. I knew Sharon was outside waiting, but I wanted a few moments. I tried to open myself to this place, but the cold and wet were getting to me. Drops of water from the waterlogged soil above were dripping down through the rocks and onto my head. I just could not center. Time to go. This is a really cool spot and once again, had it been a nice sunny day I would have been in no hurry to leave.

Next it was on to Glastonbury. Some might think this town a bit over the top with all of the New Age/Mystical/Spiritual/Pagan shops, tours, workshops, etc. but I find it

an inspirational place to be. Once we arrived we went straight to the garden of the Chalice Well which is a sanctuary of peace. Each time I go there I feel better about the world. I have hope. Few places I have been to "feel" so good. The Chalice Well itself is very special and one legend has it that the Holy Grail is at its bottom. It is considered to be a sacred place and the waters from the well are said to have restorative powers. Though you cannot get water directly from the well, it does surface down below the well where it is funneled through a

channel and then flows out from the mouth of a lion's head and on to a "contemplation" pool. From the pool the spring continues on down through the garden. It is from the lion's mouth that you can drink from the spring. The water is cool, tastes of rocks, and feels smooth and comforting as you swallow. For this trip I had purchased a metal flask and brought it along for this very reason. I filled it with the cool waters from the spring and carried it with me. Every so often over the next week or two, I would take it out and have a sip, feeling that sense of peace flush through my body.

We next made the climb up onto the Glastonbury Tor. Rising majestically above the surrounding town and countryside, it can be seen from quite a distance away and from all directions. Standing on the top of the tor, defying weather, time, and the ravages of man, is the tower from the old Saint Michaels church, all that remains of what was once a thriving Christian community.

As Sharon and I were walking up the path, we came to a bench behind which sat two rather unremarkable low boulders. I pointed them out to Sharon and stopped to feel one. It just seemed I should acknowledge it for some reason. The next day before leaving town, we purchased a book about everything Glastonbury. In it was a photo of those rocks and the description referred to them as the Druid Stones!

At the top of the Tor we stood in the center of the tower looking out over the land below. I felt a strong energy emitting from the earth under us and as that familiar tingling sensation ran up through my legs I was soon feeling quite grounded and content. Even with all the hype one hears about Glastonbury and its Tor there is really something special about this place. There is real power here.

We spent the remainder of the day walking the town, in and out of the many fun shops. In one shop I was drawn to a nice pendant necklace of Healers Gold and in another, a copy of *In The Grove Of The Druids* by Phillip Carr-Gomm, which I was quite happy to find.

Before leaving town on the 4th, we went to walk the Abbey grounds. The ruins are very impressive. According to local history this is where the remains of Arthur and Guinevere were found back in the 10th century. It is also said to have been founded by Joseph of Arimathea, the Uncle of Jesus. Not a bad story.

While walking through the remains of St. Mary's chapel, I decided to go down through an archway leading to the abbey well. I found the well locked off and as I walked back out into the open I was startled to see a large Templar knight standing just to my right, up against the wall, with a large sword in hand, point to the ground, and he was looking right at me. It gave me quite a fright. The apparition was gone in a flash but for that moment, it had been quite real. As in the words of the Buffalo Springfield song, "There's something happening here but what it is ain't exactly clear."

Driving back towards London on the A3, suddenly like in a popup book, Stonehenge appeared just off the highway to our left. What a wonderful surprise. I had never seen it from this vantage point before and even from in the car, passing at 65 miles an hour, I could feel the rich energy of those glorious rocks beckoning. Not this time, however.

The 5th was a travel day. After a plane flight to Glasgow, we rented a car and drove to Ardrossan on the West Coast, where we caught the last ferry to the Island of Arran. This is just one more in a long list of magical places in Scotland.

The next morning, having spent a comfortable night at the Rosaburn Lodge Guest House B&B in Brodick, we were up for an early breakfast and off to see a megalithic site that was the main reason for our visit to the Isle of Arran. After a nice drive across the island, we drove north on the A841 until we found the parking area for the Machrie Moor Stone Circles. The weather was actually decent, with occasional sun and periods of fairly clear skies. It was cold, but we were dressed properly.

Across the road from the parking area is a gated dirt road which leads off to the east. Walking about one mile down that road, we came to a stone ringed, flat burial mound just off to the right. After a quick stop we headed on, and I soon saw off to our left a lone stone standing up on the hill above us. Leaving the road, it was just a short walk up to a wonderful sandstone sentinel maybe five feet tall, standing all by itself, and overlooking the wide valley below in which I could just make out more standing stones. My heart began beating a little harder. I could feel energy coming from this stone, and dowsing it I found a strong energy line running northeast/southwest under the stone.

The stone itself had been dramatically weathered over the years creating deep scars which ran from the top down. It also had a dense lichen of some type growing on it. Standing there looking at this stone I had the feeling that, like several other stones I have met, it accepted its situation rather than liked it. I then noticed just a little ways away another lone rock that had been completely fenced in. Wondering why, I walked over for a look and found it was engraved with a wonderful poem in memory of someone who had once lived in the area, who had loved it there, and was now buried there. It was quite moving.

Looking down on the moor below I saw what appeared to be a circle of stones right off the road and so hurrying on we soon came to a

Stone Journals

striking, double stone circle. These stones were a more rounded boulder type of granite, with the interior circle made up of the larger stones. This was a compact double circle about 60 feet across with most, if not all, of its stones still in place. Looking at a map of the site later on, I found that this is called Circle 5 or Fingal's Cauldron Seat.

Entering the double circle Sharon and I were both greeted with a very satisfying sense of comfort. While Sharon sat on a stone and watched some lambs playing nearby I decided to do some dowsing and soon picked up a strong energy line entering from the south and exiting from directly under a large stone to the northeast. I also found that the stones on each side of this northeast stone had energy lines running out from them about three feet which then looped back to the stone like large flower petals. When Sharon saw this flower petal effect, she commented on what a sweet and comforting circle it was, and coupled with the sweet perfume of gorse in the air it was indeed like we had found a circle of beautiful stone flowers on the moor.

Leaving Fingal's Cauldron Seat we walked down the hill at least a hundred yards to a grand four poster circle (Circle 4) that sat unobtrusively on the moor. Four large hunks of granite, each about 3 feet tall, form a circle about 29 feet across. One looked rather like a large marshmallow. I walked to the center of the circle and taking out a dowsing rod decided to see what would happen. As I began to move, it immediately began turning back on its self. I was soon walking around and around in a tight circle in the center. I then asked to exit the circle and was taken out on a strong northeast line heading further down the hill towards a tall lone stone standing resolutely on the flattening moor below.

The line wandered some, though still heading in the general direction of the tall stone. About a third of the way along I found myself walking in an elongated figure eight pattern and then continuing on. Then about two thirds of the way between sites the line made a small loop before heading straight on to the stone. I must say I found this all quite amusing. The line went right up to and under this impressive stone. Approximately 14 feet high, this is a spectacular piece of eroded sandstone. Looking around I saw protruding from the earth the remains of several other stones which, along with this tall megalith, once formed a circle about 50 feet in diameter. This is Circle 3. Over the years the stones of this circle have been broken off or buried while others were probably hauled away. Why has this one lone megalith survived?

Moving into the circle I had that wonderful feeling of being plugged into the earth again. While Sharon stood leaning against the remaining standing stone, I stood in the center of the circle soaking up the energy. It was great!

After a while I pulled out my dowsing rod and quickly found a line leading off to the east. Following this line we went straight on for well over a hundred yards to three more large standing stones which were once part of yet another stone circle. This made the fourth circle we had encountered and all within sight of each other. Incredible!

There was something very familiar and comfortable about these three stones and this circle. Walking around the site (this being Circle 2), I soon realized what it was. They reminded me of a smaller version of the Stones of Stenness. This circle would have been only 42 feet in diameter but the tallest of the three remaining sandstone giants was over 17 feet. I was getting none of the strong energy experiences I had while at Stenness, but I had the feeling something was there, buried deep.

Also of interest at this circle we found two circular shaped stone slabs lying on the ground that someone, long ago, had obviously tried making into millstones. A lot of work had gone into taking a couple of the circle stones and working them down into these large, round disks. It seems that at some point they must have given up on this task as one disk had broken in two and both just lie there on the ground.

Sadly, by this time the weather was changing, as it is wont to do. It was getting colder, and the clouds were getting darker. Sharon had been great, but I knew she

Stone Journals

would not last a lot longer and there was still more to see. I recall saying to Sharon, "I will need to come back to these stones. I cannot remember ever having had more fun."

Looking further to the east I saw two smaller circles, and following the rod I was taken to the circle farthest away first. This circle sets at the perimeter of all that has been discovered so far at this amazing complex of wondrous circles. Mapped as Circle 11, or 1a, it is a circle about 46 feet across and is made up of 10 small stones of granite and sandstone which are placed so as to alternate from one type of stone to the other. Was this just an esthetic choice or was there some deeper purpose?

The line I had followed into this fifth circle then turned north and led me back to Circle 1 which I had bypassed. The stones in this circle, the last we were to visit, were a bit larger than those in Circle 11 but still much smaller compared with those in the first four circles visited.

Sharon and I were having a wonderful time walking from circle to circle, laughing and feeling the joy of the Machrie Moor stones, but it was time to go. Six great circles in one location. It really was amazing. As Sharon and I walked away I told her this was "one of my very most favorite places I had ever been." I loved this site, and I loved these stones.

Walking back to the car we made a brief stop to see the remains of a burial chamber which sat a short ways off the road. All in all this is a most incredible megalithic complex. A stone age Wonderland.

Driving along the west coast we came upon a lovely stretch of stone beach. As I like to bring home rocks from places I visit, I pulled over. I decided to try something I had never done before and walked down to the beach with one dowsing rod in hand. Centering, I asked which rock I should take home with me. After walking along the beach a ways the rod turned back on itself and kept me going round in a tight circle maybe two feet across. I then took off my opal pendant necklace and using it as a dowsing tool I began moving it back and forth across the circle, from one side to the other. The whole time I was centered on finding the stone I was to take home. About half way across the area it began swinging dramatically and then stopped. I decided it must be one of four rocks. Once again concentrating on which rock I was to take, I started moving the pendant over the four rocks one at a time. As I crossed the third rock, a rather flat plain green stone maybe two inches wide by four inches long, the pendant began swinging in a circle. It is a real fun to feel and see these responses to my queries. I picked up the green stone along with a small purple rock setting alongside of it (I just liked its color). Why I was led to this particular green stone I do not know. The two sit on a windowsill near my bed.

After our stay on Arran we spent two days and nights in Ayr and then a night in Stranraer. Our next stop was to be Dumfries. First I decided to take a side trip about twenty minutes south of Stranraer to a site I noticed on my map called Kirkmadrine Stones. Though there initially were several Scottish Heritage signs showing the way, driving what should have been the last mile we saw nothing. Going back over that last mile a second time, I did see a sign pointing up a narrow path through some farm fields, but it said something about a cairn. I decided to walk it just in case.

Sharon remained in the car as it was quite windy and sprinkling. Going about a third of a mile I saw in a field, just on the other side of the stone wall alongside which I had been walking, a single standing stone about seven feet tall. On up the path a ways I could see a ladder crossing over the wall so I climbed over and was soon getting acquainted with my new friend. Placing my hands on the stone I could feel warmth and welcome.

There was also a sense of strength and comfort emanating from this rock as my feet settled into the earth. But it had started to really rain, so I did not stay very long. I thanked the stone and returned to the car. Though this stone stands there by itself it seemed quite content with its situation.

Back at the car I told Sharon what had happened and said I did not think this was the right path, and that we should try again to find the Kirkmadrine Stones. Heading back down the narrow road we soon saw a small sign on the right by a gate that we had not noticed on the previous passes. As the rain had let up and as there was a nice old rocky country road to walk instead of a muddy footpath, Sharon decided to join me. Passing through the gate we followed the road up a hill. It was lined on both sides by beautiful trees of some type and the ground was covered with a carpet of bluebells. This was a most lovely setting no matter what else might lie ahead. After a short walk we came out from under the trees onto an open hilltop on which sat an old stone church and graveyard.

Covering the front entrance to the church was a large closed-in glass display case in which we saw two large flat stones and one smaller one on which Christian symbols had been carved. Were these the stones we had been in search of? Not what I was expecting. So, were these old pagan stones that the Christians turned into gravestones as a means of showing the "power of Christ" over the old ways? Or, were they may be crafted as a way of showing respect for and honoring the old customs? I doubt it was the latter, but one can hope. Standing there looking at these three stones we both felt sad. Sharon remarked that it reminded her of seeing an animal on display in a cage at a zoo. I too felt like they were imprisoned there. There was no joy in these stones. I wanted to free them and place them back out in the open.

Deciding to dowse the place I walked around the exterior of the church and found that there was, in fact, a strong energy line running east/west right through the building, entering the left front and out the right back side. The church had been built facing the east rising sun. I find it interesting that this is often the case. I wondered if the church had been built on this location to take advantage of the energy flow or to cover over and try to replace an older pagan site?

This morning while Sharon was doing family research at the Dumfries library I was off to be with the stones. When in the Dumfries area last year we had visited the Loupin Stanes Stone Circle and I had known then that I would want to get back. This was my chance.

As I passed through Lockerbie I thought of the memorial to the passengers of Pan Am flight 103 that Sharon and I had visited last year. It had been an emotional experience I must say. I continued north and as I was approaching Eskdalemuir I started to feel the pull of the stones. I began singing a chant based on the song the men had sung at the Beltane ceremony in Avebury.

"The Loupin Stanes are calling out, calling cross the land
The Loupin Stanes are calling out, calling out to me
Oh Loupin Stanes they're calling out, calling out
Oh Loupin Stanes they're calling out to me"

I know, kind of silly, but it felt really good to me at the time.

Pulling into the parking area I could see the Loupin Stanes in the field below and could not wait to get down to, and walk among, those charming stones. It was cloudy and cold but there was no rain as I started down the slope to the circle. My last visit had been hurried but this time I could take as long as I needed. Approaching the stones I was paying more attention to the surrounding area then on my last visit, as I had read in Burl's *Guide* that there were actually three circles located at this site. Sure enough, just southeast of the Loupin Stanes were a number of small rocks protruding from the earth forming a slightly smaller circle about 70 feet across, and just to the northwest was another even smaller stone circle of which only four stones were visible. Both circles were overgrown with grasses and easy to miss.

Deciding to check for energy lines I dowsed the smallest circle first and found nothing. Then going to the circle to the southeast I picked up a line which I followed straight down into the Loupin Stanes. Near the center the line began going in a circle much like my experience at Circle 4 on Machrie Moor. Centering on how to leave the circle I picked up on a line which took me south up a hill to a small lone stone that sat at the top. The line led on from there but I decided to go back down the hill and spend more time with the Loupin Stanes Circle, which seemed quite content sitting on its raised earth platform.

I began walking this pleasant circle, talking as if to old friends, and though none responded in

Stone Journals

kind, I sensed their welcome. I stopped to sit down on two different rocks for short periods of time and both blessed me with a flood of warm energy flowing up through my feet and legs. There are 10 stones in this circle, most only one to two feet high though the two taller entry stones are more than five feet tall. I climbed up on one of the two large entry stones (the one opposite of the stone Sharon had taken my picture on the previous year) and as I stood there gazing across the lush green landscape, I felt a strong tug to follow the energy line I had found earlier, back up the hill to the rock, and then to see where it went from there. I "understood" that this was a sacred path, that many had walked it before and I should follow. So, jumping down from the rock, I took out a rod and began the walk, anxious to see what I would find.

Arriving at the hilltop stone, I looked down the slope and off to the west was a sign reading "Girdle Stanes" with an arrow pointing in the same direction as the line I was following seem to be going, just at a lower elevation. I continued following the line on south to yet another partially buried stone at which point the line turned 90 degrees and took me downhill to the west, towards the Esk River which runs along the valley floor. The line did a bit of wandering back and forth until I reached a shelf on the hillside, at which point it once again turned south. I noticed I was now on the path that the Girdle Stanes sign had been pointing to.

Walking this line, I found it soon came to, and ran directly under, yet another small solitary stone maybe two feet by two feet and protruding from the earth a foot or so.

I had no doubt that these small stones marked the ancient pathway. I imagine that they were originally standing stones which had long ago fallen over and/or had begun to be swallowed up by the earth.

Sure enough the line carried on along this shelf until it came to another lone stone where the line made a circle around it before continuing on another 100 yards or so to a larger stone. Passing directly under this rock, the line did a little wandering before arriving at yet another of these individual path stones, none of which stood more than a few feet tall above the ground. As I followed the line around the east side of this stone the terrain dropped off, and down below I could see the Girdle Stanes Stone Circle. Spectacular! Placed on green grassy pasture land on the valley floor with the White Esk River running right alongside, there is a rugged edge to this pastoral setting. In fact the river has over the years eaten away some of the soil under the west side of the circle and about a third of the stones have fallen off into the river.

Nonetheless, it is a large circle, being about 130 feet in diameter. There are 26 stones remaining ranging is size from two to six feet in height and irregularly shaped. I could also see the remains of a henge along the outside.

I followed my rod on down the hill and into the center of the circle where it made one loop and then continued on to the south. There the line exited the circle. Stopping, I looked over the countryside to the south, and as I could see nothing in particular, I wondered where the line was going? The thing is, every time I follow an energy line to a circle or stone, it usually exits and goes on from there. At Machrie Moor I had followed one line that connected six circles. At a place like the Girdle Stains I see the line going on, but where? One of these days I will have to continue following a line like this to its next destination, and then to its next. I really wonder if in fact they just continue on and on? Maybe, like with streams and rivers, they flow on until they merge with a larger energy line?

There are quite a few scrubby trees and some brush growing along the outside of this circle, and it made for a very different and enjoyable atmosphere. It was a little like the vibe we experienced when Sharon and I were at Long Meg, with the big oaks inside the circle. It really is great when you get the interaction of the trees and plants with the rocks.

Standing there inside the circle I felt a very strong welcome from this unique collection of stones and I spent quite some time getting acquainted with them, moving slowly from stone to stone. I could sense a lot of energy here and when I came to a large toppled rock lying on the ground I lay down on it for a while, absorbing its energy. The air was getting even colder but here I found warmth and comfort. Opening to the stone I was blessed with a peace that I think one can only get from the stones.

Deciding to dowse the circle I began at the southwest stone on the edge of the river and immediately had a fun experience. As I walked around the stone I picked up energy lines coming off the rock in tight, elongated loops, much like thin petals on a flower. These petals were about two feet in length, an inch wide at the base, maybe three inches at the ends, and continued all the way around the stone. I took a stick and scratched the lines in the earth and indeed when I climbed up on the rock and looked down it was just like I was standing in the center of a flower. I have only had this experience once before, on Machrie Moor.

Though I did not check every stone in the circle, the six I did dowse had this same petal effect. Most notable was the large stone at the east. At this stone there were so many of these petals coming off the stone that I had a hard time separating them. They were also more like three feet in length. Quite an effect. When I ran a rod up alongside of this stone I found strong energies being emitted from near the top, pushing my rod away from the stone. This was all very exciting. My dowsing skills continue to improve and I become more sensitive to the subtleties of energy flows.

When it was time to go, I stood in the center of the circle and said thanks and farewell. Then following my rod back to the north, I was happy to find my path was consistent with the one I had walked in route to the Girdle Stanes Circle.

Returning to the Loupin Stanes Circle I once again settled in with the stones. I began walking the circle and singing the chant I had sung on the drive earlier. As I continued around the ring, moving in and out of the stones, my enthusiasm increased and soon I

was singing quite loudly and gesturing very dramatically with hands and arms. I could almost hear the stones joining in with me. It was great fun and I was glad to be there among friends. I noticed a van driving along a road on the other side of the valley and chuckled as I imagined the driver looking over to see the old "nutter" dancing around in the stone circle.

The temperature had been dropping and once again it was looking like it might rain. Standing there in the circle center, I opened to the stones. I began to visualize the stone complex from above and the higher I went the more I saw. Below were the three stone circles, complete with all stones in place. The platform on which the Loupin Stanes stood rose noticeably above the two smaller circles. From the Loupin Stanes there was a well-trodden path snaking south, going from stone to stone along the very route I had walked. There were more stones than now but they were still spaced quite a ways apart. This was clearly a procession-way between the two sites. As I looked further south I saw the largest of the circles, the Girdle Stanes in its glory, henge in place, no trees or brush near the stones, and the circle complete with the river a short distance away. It was really impressive. Thanking the stones for the visualization and a most wonderful day, I bid them all farewell and told them that even if I was never able to return I would always remember them. Along with an invigorating surge of energy came, "Return."

Today was to be my last chance for a stone visit on this trip. First, however, Sharon and I drove down across the English border to find Hadrian's Wall which I had long wanted to see. We spent four or five hours driving from place to place visiting portions of this incredible monument. Though much of the wall has disappeared over the years, the parts that still remain are a reminder of just how big and powerful Rome was 2000 years ago, as this wall was once the northwestern edge of the Roman Empire. It was a wonderful experience standing high on a section of the wall looking north, imagining the wild Picts gathering to challenge Rome's might, to drive back the intruders and tear down the wall. Did they have rallies and speeches condemning the Romans for building the wall? Was there a moment when Ronald the Pict yelled, "Mr Hadrian, tear down this wall!" (Please excuse the Reagan, Berlin Wall flashback.)

Near the end of the day I drove us just south of Penrith to find the Mayburgh Henge. The pictures I had seen, and the descriptions I had read, had not been all that enticing but something about this site always intrigued me to want to visit it, and this was to be the day.

Parking the car we took the walk around the base of the henge to the entrance. Mayburgh is a 15 feet high and 383 feet wide circle-mound made of rocks, with a wide entrance at the east. It is surfaced with a brilliant green grass inside and out, covering over the original river-rock surface. Growing sparsely along the top of the mound there are also the most wonderful old trees whose gnarly exposed roots reach out across the surface. Some of the trees have even worked their way down the inside wall to the henge floor.

Inside the circle is a flat grassy meadow in the center of which is a wonderful, stoic, nine foot tall standing stone. It is alone, but actually seems to prefer it that way. Standing outside looking in, the green earth ring topped with ancient trees, and the solitary stone in the center, provided a vision I doubt I will ever forget. And, along with this awesome visual was the feeling of being welcome and the inner voice clearly saying, "Please come in."

Dowsing rods in hand I found an energy line running straight through the entrance and on to the stone. Once there it circled around to the back side of the stone and then continued on across the grass, up the inside wall, and on out of the henge to the west.

Going back to the stone, which was all that remained of a destroyed stone circle, I checked to see if it had any energies being released from it and found there was a broad band at about two feet all the way up to six feet which pushed my rod away when passed over. As I stood there trying to get some personal hit from the rock I had the feeling the stone really didn't care one way or the other about our presence. In fact, I soon realized that the welcoming feeling I had experienced as I entered the henge was not from the stone but from the trees! The trees were happy to have us there, and I found myself wanting to just sit at the base of a tree and listen to stories. But, as you may know, trees can be as slow as a stone when it comes to talking.

As at Long Meg, and also at the Girdle Stanes, I really appreciated this interconnection of earth, tree, and stone here at Mayburgh, even if the stone did seem to be a bit of a curmudgeon.

Sharon had decided to walk up on top of the henge and had continued on along towards the entrance. At some point along the way she had seen a small rock on the ground which she picked up thinking to give it to me when we left. Continuing on she approached one of the old trees, whose roots were strung way out over the surface. She then heard a voice tell her, "Place the stone in the hole. Others have done so before you. You will then begin the process of becoming grounded with the earth." Wow! Under one of the roots creeping across the surface, she noticed a small cavern and dropped the rock inside.

By this time I had finished down below

and had climbed up to join Sharon. I could see her enthusiasm as she began telling me her story. I walked over to the hole to look for her stone, but it was quite dark inside. Using the flash I took a picture and sure enough, there sat her rock, nestled in among a collection of other small rocks. Life is rarely more precious than moments like this.

Turning to look down on the inside of the henge I tried to imagine it all as it once was. A large henge covered with river rocks with a ring of standing stones running around the interior of the henge. It must have been spectacular. The cool thing is, even in its deteriorated state, it still is.

Walking back to the car we were both quite happy and content with our visit to Mayburgh. It was everything I hoped for and more. This is a most special place and a wonderful way to end our journey. Though we did stop for a quick look at King Arthur's Round Table, another earth henge nearby, Mayburgh had filled my heart to overflowing, and I had little interest.

In just a few days we would be on a plane flying home. Over the last couple of weeks I had once again known the joy of being in the company of the stones and had been reminded once again of the "presence" of the marvelous old trees. Life was good.

I would also add that I have had a nagging thought as a result of dowsing on this trip. When I am following a line from one location to another I sometimes find myself making a loop or a figure eight along the way. What is that all about? Maybe there used to be standing stones in those places that have long since been removed, but the energies remain. Stones which had marked the procession way like between the Loupin Stanes and Girdle Stanes. Makes sense.

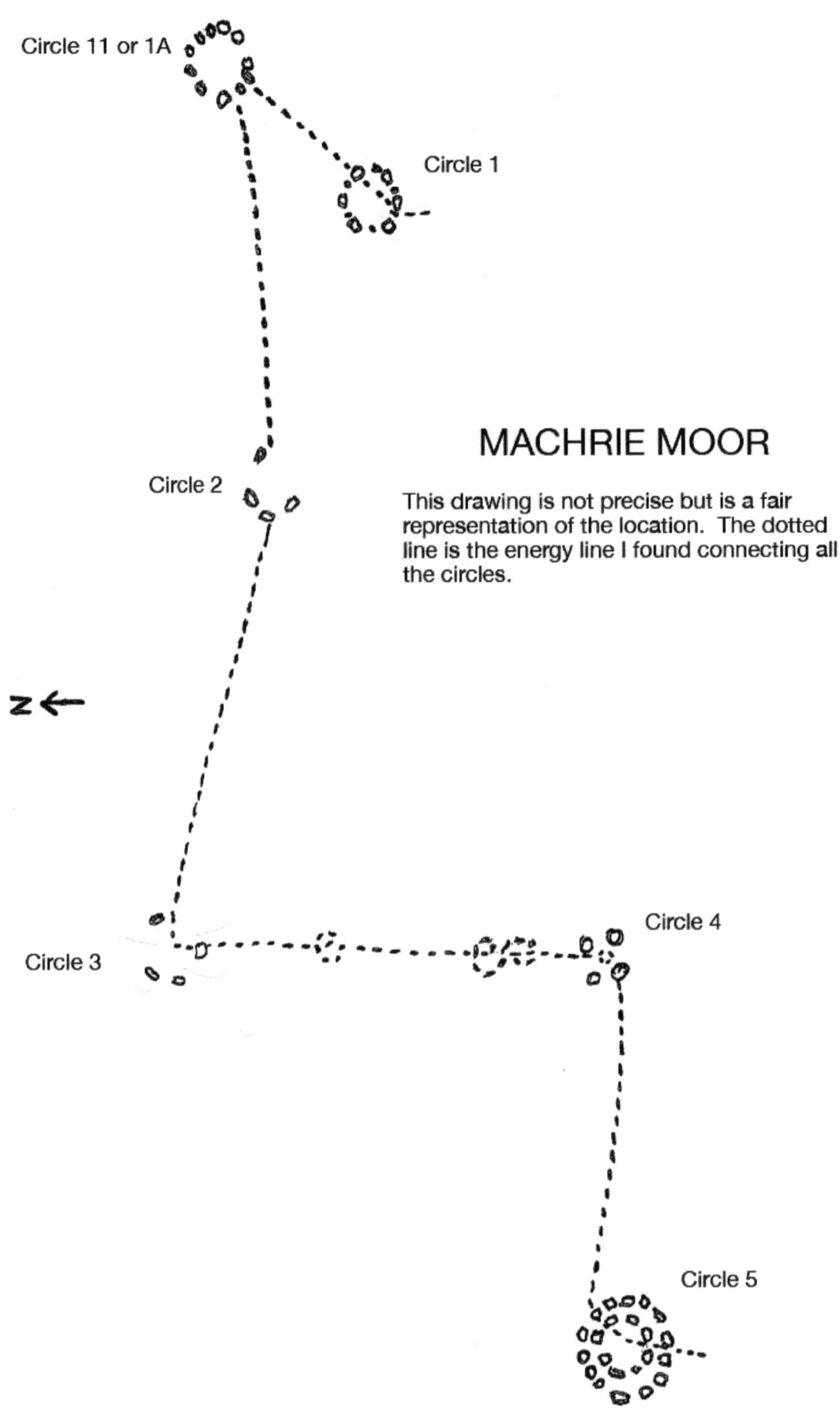

"It's no good just coming up to these places and demanding to know their secrets. They have to trust you first."
Paddy Slade

Stone Journey 5

SWEDEN

STONE JOURNEY 5 - November, 2012

I was on tour in Europe with my brother Robben's band. After a show in Malmoe, Sweden on the 1st, we were getting a day off. Having read about the standing stones in Sweden in Cope's *Megalithic European*, I knew just what I was going to do with my time. At the Malmoe gig I had approached the venue manager to see if he knew someone who would, for a fee, be willing to be my guide for a day. He made some calls and the next morning, I was waiting in the hotel lobby when Kristoffer walked through the door to pick me up. He had the look of a university student, a little rough around the edges but with a gentle spirit, and I knew we were going to get on just fine. In no time we were in his car driving south to find my first destination.

When I explained to Kristoffer what I was looking for, I was a little surprised that even though he had grown up in the region he had never been to any of these sites himself, especially as one of the sites is quite famous and known as Sweden's Stonehenge. Still, I have found during my travels that this is actually quite a common response.

Our first stop was Disa's Ting, on the outskirts of Svarte. It was easily found as it sits right alongside the road on a grassy bluff overlooking the Baltic Sea. However, as it was a foggy morning, I could not actually see the sea which was only about 50 yards away.

I should note that as I had not known I would have this opportunity, I did not bring along any tools for dowsing, measuring, etc. So, any such references are ones I figured out later from books or on the internet. I should also say, that after just three photos, my camera quite working. I did the remainder of this trip without being able to take photos.

Disa's Ting is a stone rectangle that is 118 feet long by 52 feet wide. Only 16 stones remain and they sit up on an earth berm. There are no stones on one of the short sides of the rectangle. The sea side of the rectangle consists of eight stones and includes the largest stone which is about seven feet tall and sits in the southeast corner. Though a few of the other stones are four to five feet tall, most are only a foot or two in height.

The morning was cold and foggy and the site location right alongside the road was somewhat noisy from traffic. As we got out to explore our find, I could sense Kristoffer watching me and wondering how long it would be before he might get out of the cold. I was not getting any kind of "feeling" from this site, and though it was cool to be in a rectangle rather than a circle, I had no desire to stay. So, saying goodbye to the stones we returned to the car and went in search of Ales Stenar.

After a short drive we parked the car in the provided parking lot and following the signs walked the path leading to the site, stopping along the way to read a well done information board about the Vikings and the stones.

This site is a Swedish National Monument and is often referred to as Sweden's Stonehenge. While this comparison might be a stretch, it is definitely a wondrous place, and I am happy that I got to see and experience this marvel.

As at Disa's Ting these stones were also set right on the bluff overlooking the Baltic Sea. Julian Cope, in *The Megalithic European*, describes the location as "extraordinary and spectacular, with such awe inspiring views along the southern Scandian coast that a monument half its size would still produce heart palpitations in its visitors." Sadly for me the fog was so thick as to reduce my views to a wall of shifting gray in all directions. I never saw the water.

Still, Ales Stenar itself was more than enough to make my heart skip a beat or two and to fill me with happiness. Whereas Disa's Ting had been a rectangle, these stones, and there are 59 of them, had been erected in the shape of a giant viking longship some 220 feet long. Now this is special! Standing there gazing at this ship of stones, I turned to Kristoffer and noticed he too was looking quite impressed. I was glad he was with me, and it made me feel good that I was the reason he had come to see these stones.

I was immediately drawn to the stone at the southeastern end of the ship. Was this the bow or the stern I wondered? Standing about nine feet tall, it was fairly square shaped at the bottom, maybe three feet or so across, and tapered towards the top. It was off-white in color with red swirls running throughout. It was obviously mostly quartz. Of interest was a small stone only about two feet tall which was placed several feet behind this tall stone, outside the ship, and in line with the center of the ship. I was to learn later that in fact this was the stern of the ship and the small stone was the rudder stone.

My first touch of the quartz stern stone was a comforting one as I immediately felt a sense of ease flow through me. Clearing my mind and centering on the stone, was that "Welcome" I heard? It was quite faint but it was there. This brought to mind a humorous question. Do stones from Sweden speak in Swedish? Since the interaction is more of a "spirit to spirit" thing, I guess it doesn't matter but fun to think about. Not wanting to make Kristoffer feel uncomfortable with this American musician who talked to rocks, I did not stay long with any stone, but kept moving around the site trying to get a feel for the place.

From the moment I first arrived at Ales Stenar I could feel its importance, and I mean just that. This place was important on several different levels. The visual of the stones and the location alone are enough. But once I opened up I could feel strength and comfort, joy and sorrow, knowledge and intuition. These stones were as proud as the people who had erected them. I think much could be learned here.

As I walked along the outside of the ship, I noticed that most of the 59 stones were maybe four to five feet tall and somewhat pointed at the top. Many were a composite of some kind, small chunks of rock held together by some natural bonding matrix. Quite interesting and, according to Kristoffer, quite common.

At the far, northwest end of the ship there was another even taller pillar of the quartz stone. This was the bow of the ship. This one was about 10 feet tall and was more pointed at the top. As I lay my hands on this megalith I initially felt only the cold stone. But as I stood there, I soon began to feel the energy seeping into my hands and arms, ever so subtle. I thought about quartz being a natural conduit for the earth's energies and here this definitely seemed to be the case.

Being aware of my guide patiently standing there in the misty cold, I knew I needed to move on. As with all other such places, time meant very little to these stones. If you want to fully experience them and learn from them, you must let go of any sense of urgency. As I could not do that in this situation, I said my thanks, gave the bow stone a hug and walked back to the car.

We were both quite damp as we climbed back into the little car and the heater was a welcome pleasure. I asked Kristoffer how he was doing so far, and he said he was really glad he had come along on this adventure. Though he knew of these stone sights, he had never been to them, and he too was enjoying the experience. "Where to next?" he said, and we were off.

Our next stop was at Kivik Kungagraven or "King's Grove." We had a bit of trouble finding our way but eventually arrived. Though it is located only three or four hundred yards in from the sea, the view in that direction was blocked by heavy fog. Parking in the provided lot we could see the most impressive looking cairn on the other side of the road. It kind of looks like the flying saucer from "The Day The Earth Stood Still" sitting there on the ground. Actually it is a 246 foot circular earth cairn completely covered over with what appear to be large river rocks.

Crossing the road we approached an entrance booth where you pay a fee. However, as it was winter, a sign was posted which said it was closed. That meant that one could still walk the site but not enter into the cairn, which is said to be very impressive.

We followed a path to this massive stone covered mound and then on to its entrance passage which led into the heart of the cairn. There we came to a large door barring our way inside. This was one of the coolest places I've been to, and I was bummed to be locked out. Walking back out we climbed up on the cairn and just sat admiring what had been built there. How great it would be to visit on a day when it was open. Really special.

Returning once again to the sea, we went in search of Havangsdosen, a dolmen burial site. It is interesting just how many stone sites there are here in the south of Sweden that are located close to, or right on, the sea. There was definitely a strong connection that these builders had with the earth, water, and air. When you stand at one of these sites you have the earth below and behind, the air above and around, and the water stretching as far as you can see on the horizon. There can be no doubt that these locations were chosen with these three elements in mind.

Once the parking area was found, we were soon following a nicely constructed wooden plank path through a lovely wooded area and we could hear the sound of the surf in the distance and smell the sea in the air. After a short walk the path exited the forest and headed downhill towards the sea where it suddenly ended among tall and seemingly endless sand dunes.

Though the fog was still heavy, it had lifted enough for us to see about 50 yards out to sea, and it was a calm day. The waves rolled in and out, rather than crashed, and provided a calming soundtrack to our adventure.

There were no signs guiding the way, so we began wandering among the sand dunes. We knew we were in the right area, and I had seen a picture in one of my books which showed the stones setting on the dunes up off the beach. The air was cold and damp and the dense fog provided a hint of magic brewing. As if to prove this point, in the distance three forms began to emerge from the fog, dark shapes seeming to move up and down as they slowly approached.

Then they began to take shape and soon Kristoffer and I saw what appeared to be wraiths on horses. It was quite eerie. In the fog one could easily imagine the dunes were barrow downs, and these were dark riders. But, as they bore down upon us we could see that they were, in fact, three young teenage girls out for their morning ride along the beach. Dressed quite properly in their light colored britches, knee high boots, long-sleeved turtle neck tops, zipped up vests, gloves, hats, and riding crops, they were a striking sight.

Kristoffer stopped them and asked if they could help us find our way to Havangsdosen. One of the girls cheerfully explained the route and off we went along the shoreline. After a short while the girls came riding up to give us a course adjustment and then decided to just slow to a walk and lead us to our destination. Once we were within sight of the stones, they smiled, gave a wave, and once again disappeared into the mist like apparitions who had been sent by Odin to show us the way.

Havangsdosen is one of the most precious dolmens I have seen. Not only is its location striking, sitting there on the sand overlooking the Baltic, but also its construction is most impressive. The dolmen itself is small and rather squatty, but the capstone is quite massive. Interestingly, the many uprights which form the chamber and support the cap stone are really short, standing only a foot or so above the ground. I did wonder if maybe the weight of the capstone had actually caused the support stones to sink into the earth to some degree? Also, sand could have been brought in by the wind and sea and deposited around the stones over the years. The dolmen may, in fact, have originally stood much higher above the ground.

The dolmen is surrounded by a stone rectangle made up of 16 standing stones of a variety of sizes and shapes. As at Ales Stenar several of these stones have pointed tops. On one of the short sides of the rectangle there are two larger pointed rocks which seem to form an entrance and look much like two canine teeth sticking up from the sand.

Kristoffer and I spent quite a while at this site. As we walked around he told me he remembered having come to this location on a school field trip when he was a kid. It was something he had forgotten all about. It made me feel better to think that at some point the children were being made aware of these wonderful stone treasures which are, in fact, spread throughout the country. Hopefully a few of those children hear the stones' call and cherish them.

Though I was getting no inner messages or energy connections, this place was very special. Standing there leaning against a stone, I gazed across the dolmen and the sand dunes to the sea below. The fog had once again become so thick as to block out all but an occasional visual of the sea. Still, I could hear the waves as they lapped up against the shore, and I felt at peace. This whole stone experience in Sweden had been so very different from those I've had in Brittany and the UK. Nowhere else has the water element been such an important part of the location and atmosphere of the stone sites. Saying good bye to this lone dolmen at the top of the sand dunes, I felt good all over. Turning away, I walked back into the mist. How appropriate.

Photograph of Ales Stenar
PhotoMartin - iStock

As my camera failed me on this occasion I felt I needed to get a photograph off the internet and insert it, so that the reader can see just how magnificent Ales Stenar really is. This photo is taken from the bow end of the ship. Beautiful photograph and a beautiful day. Nothing like the day I was there.

"In a crystal we have the clear evidence of the existence of a formative life principle, and though we cannot understand the life of a crystal, it is, nonetheless, a living being"
— Nicola Tesla

Stone Journey 6

SCOTLAND, NORTHERN ENGLAND

STONE JOURNEY 6 - July 22, 2013

Sharon and I have returned once again to Scotland. After a couple of relaxing days staying at The Carlton in Edinburgh, and our third visit to Rosslyn Chapel, we picked up a rental car and drove to the northeast. It was a pleasant enough day with just occasional light rains. Our final destination was to be Inverurie but I had planned several stone stops along the way.

First up was the Cullerlie Stone Circle. Although it seemed a simple enough task looking at our map, it did in fact take a while and required several stops for directions. I have found that such is often the way of these things when searching for stones. It is as if you are being tested to see how badly you really want to visit them.

When we did arrive at this site, it was sign posted. Looking over a low stone wall, you could see a circle of stones about a hundred yards away at the end of a wide grass alley which was lined on both sides with tall trees. It is a lovely visual. Parking the car, we hurried to see what we would find. The circle is about 33 feet in diameter and consists of eight good sized red granite stones. These stones were really intriguing composite type rocks, with big cube like crystallin chunks of reds and off-whites forming a rough exterior. I liked these guys, and they did feel like "guys" to me. Within the circle are eight solid kerbed rings, one in the center eleven feet in diameter, with seven smaller ones surrounding it. A kerbed ring is just a circle of stones called kerb stones (in this case six inches to eighteen inches high) which sit stone to stone establishing the exterior of the circle. The surface of the interior of the ring is then covered with smaller river stones. Though these rings are packed quite closely together there is still room to walk between them. This was my first time to visit a circle full of circles, and it was great.

Still, as I walked among the stones I was having trouble getting any kind of connection with them. Just a hundred yards away there was a busy farming operation going on, but actually that seemed to be having little impact on this wonderful place of stones. The circle felt calm and unconcerned with what was going on around it. Sadly, I think it was not too concerned with our being there either.

I dowsed the site and found two off center, but strong, energy lines. One ran northeast/southwest, the other northwest/southeast, and they crossed north of center.

Sharon and I did have one different but fun experience while at Cullerlie. Shortly after we arrived, this rather scraggly looking black and white dog came running over and into the circle. It walked around for a few minutes sort of checking us out. Then it walked out of the circle about ten feet, lay down on the wet grass and continued to watch us closely. When it came time for us to go, the dog, seeing we were leaving,

jumped up and trotted off down the alley towards our car. It would stop after about ten or fifteen yards, turn, and wait until we got close, then do the same thing over again. Once through the gate, the dog led us right to our car and then when it was satisfied we were actually leaving, ran back to the farmhouse. We both had quite a laugh. We felt as though this dog was the protector of the circle and wondered what it would have done if we had threatened to damage the stones in any way?

This stone journey had officially begun. I did not get any kind of special interaction with Cullerlie, but I did get the feeling the stones were quite content and well protected. I left feeling very happy and now we were headed for my first real recumbent stone circle. I was really looking forward to this.

A word about recumbent circles. Most seem to have been designed by the builders to be in line with the rising or setting of the moon in the southern sky and they were placed in locations with a clear view to the south. In many cases the recumbent stone and its flankers create a viewer, sort of like the original drive-in movie screen. Observers would stand or sit across the circle from the viewer and watch as the moon, or some other celestial body, would enter from the left, move across the recumbent, and exit to the right. These recumbent stone circles were built all over northeastern Scotland.

Midmar Kirk Stone Circle is located about three miles west of Echt on a little side road off of the B9119. Ever since I first saw photos of this ring, I wondered how I would like it? How would it feel? You see, this stone circle is located right out the back of a church, is surrounded by the graveyard, and is confined within the stone walled church grounds. Usually when churches were built on old pagan sites, places where there were standing stones, they would remove or destroy the stones. Here they actually embraced the stones, and the end result is, in fact, wonderful.

I was very happy with the way these stones had been treated. I was also happy to be at my first real recumbent stone circle, and the recumbent stone with its two flankers were very impressive indeed. The recumbent is very flat across the top, just under 15 feet long, and quite massive. The two flankers were eight feet three inches tall and shaped sort of like crescent moons embracing the recumbent. The combined effect really is something special. I wish I could have seen it before the church and trees. To have been in the circle on a ritual night and viewed the crossing of the moon or stars through this massive view finder would have been way cool. Even without the popcorn.

The remaining five circle stones were from maybe three to six feet in height and were of a variety of sizes and shapes. They seemed to be made of a pink granite, and were rather rough textured. Several also had intriguing mosses and lichen growing on them. One stone, which Sharon named the Goddess Stone, had a three inch wide band of a yellow/green moss growing across the inner surface (facing into the circle) at necklace level. In the center of the band there was a remarkable two inch long oblong "gem" of bright emerald green moss. It actually seemed to shimmer. Though we had wandered among the stones separately, Sharon and I had both discovered this stone with its necklace and were both impressed by the presence and the energy of this bejeweled megalith. Placing a hand on the rock, the energy flow was slow, steady, and comforting. There was a strong female presence here, a goddess presence, and as I stood there she bid me "welcome." I was, for lack of a better word, "charmed" by this stone, and I will never forget her.

Midmar was one of my favorite circles. Walking from stone to stone I found they were all alive with energy and three of them pulsed strong surges up from the ground, filling me with warmth. It had been quite a while since I had felt this earth flow and I relished it. With several of the stones, like with the Goddess Stone, I could also feel the flow coming directly from the rock through my hands. It was great, and I was soon feeling very happy. It dawned on me that this was because the stones themselves were happy. It was quite infectious.

Before leaving I did dowse the site and found a strong energy line running through the middle of the circle in a north/south direction. Though I was in no hurry to leave these stones we had one more stop to make this day, and so it was time to go. I walked the circle one last time thanking the stones. If only Christianity everywhere had embraced the stones instead of destroying them. So much was lost, both physically and spiritually.

Last stop of the day was the Sunhoney Stone Circle which appeared to be only a few miles away, just north of the B9119. Once again we had a little trouble finding this spot, but eventually we saw a small sign saying Sunhoney Farm and we turned in. These good people actually have a "stone circle" sign posted on a gate up behind the farmhouse. We could not get it to open, so over we went and followed a narrow path up to the top of a knoll where we found this recumbent stone circle half buried in grasses and weeds, nestled in among a small grove of trees. It was quite a magical setting.

Working our way through the grasses, which were knee to waist high in most places, and quite wet I might add, we arrived at the recumbent stone. It is close to 15 feet in length and though it once sat on its side it now lays flat on its back. The flankers are seven and a half feet, and six and a half feet tall and still stand guard over the recumbent. I am sure that when this stone was still upright, it, along with its flanker companions, made for an impressive viewing portal of

Stone Journals

the landscape and sky beyond. Now, with the recumbent fallen and with the trees grown up, it is hard to "get the picture."

Looking closely at the recumbent, we found many cup marks on one side of the stone. Who knows why?

According to Burl's *Guide* there are the remains of a ring cairn 64 feet across in the center of the circle, but it was overgrown, and we did not see it.

The nine standing stones of the circle were all of some pink stone, were for the most part quite thin, of different shapes, and about four feet in height. The recumbent was of a different, gray granite looking rock.

I decided to walk the circle, which was 83 feet in diameter, to see what I might find and by the time I had made it all the way around, all I had found was that my pant legs were soaked. No special hits or experiences here, though I did find a subtle east/west energy line running through the circle center. I would love to return when the weeds were cut down and the stones were revealed, especially if the sun was out. As I said, the location is magical and one can easily understand why it was chosen as a holy place.

Rising early, we tried to find several circles this day with mixed success. Just out of Inverurie, where we had spent the night, we went to visit the East Aquorthies Circle, but the road was closed due to storm damage. We then drove a few miles north to find the Balquhain Circle. We did find it, but it sat on the opposite slope of a wide valley that was planted with crops. I drove up and down the roads in the area trying to find a way to the circle without walking through some farmer's crop. I had seen a very enticing photo of this ring in *Circles Of Stone* by Milligan which showed a grand standing stone of quartz setting just outside of the small circle. I have looked at that photo many times and wanted to go there myself. Sadly, as I could not find a safe way to do so (by that I mean safe for the crops) and as it was raining, I had to give it up.

Looking at my map I saw that Loanhead of Daviot was the next closest circle, so off we went, and this time with success. We were soon parked and walking up a hill through a forested area. Much to my surprise we came across boy scouts camped in among the trees. It was still a little early, but they were up, building fires, laughing, and making breakfast. It brought back some really fond memories of my youth as a scout, and I must say I was very pleased to hear many of them say "good morning" to us as we walked on up the trail.

At the top there was a fenced off clearing surrounded by forest on three sides. To the front the hillside dropped off to expose a grand panorama of the countryside beyond. In the clearing sat a rather broody looking recumbent stone circle. It consisted of eight large stones along with the recumbent and its two flankers.

Entering the area through a gate, we crossed the grassy clearing to the circle. It was windy and rainy but we had dressed for it. Loanhead is approximately 68 feet in diameter. About four feet inside the circle of standing stones, the ground is covered with a kerbed ring of smaller rocks, except for the very center where there is an uncovered area 13 feet across, kind of like a bull's eye. Though it makes for an interesting visual, I am not sure what the idea was behind covering the ground with rocks like this. It definitely makes it more awkward to walk. Maybe it is a flattened cairn?

As we explored the area we also noticed that at least three of the standing stones had walkways of the smaller rocks stretching from the kerbed ring out to the stones. I wondered if there might have been others that were overgrown with grass?

One of these walkways led to a smaller, block shaped circle stone. The stone did seem to have been shaped (all the other stones were rather natural in appearance) and was placed in the southwest. Against its outside surface there were three flat rocks approximately 12 inches long and four inches wide, which were placed side by side on the ground right up against the stone, appearing to provide a platform on which to stand. Sharon first noticed it and stepped on to the two outer rocks. She stood there looking across the circle, quite calm and in no way bothered by the rain that was falling. She soon felt her body relaxing as a sense of peace came over her. After a while she called me over and without explaining to me what she had experienced told me I should try it out. I then took my turn with the same very gratifying result. We could not help but wonder about what had been the original intent with this spot? There was definitely something going on there.

The recumbent stone itself is squatty in appearance, about 12 feet long and maybe six feet high. The left flanker is not all that much taller than the recumbent but the one to the west is seven and a half feet in height. Together they do not really create all that impressive of a viewing portal. In fact the other standing stones are all about the same height as the recumbent and flankers, and it gives the whole circle sort of a symmetry as if not to overplay the importance of the recumbent and flankers over the other stones. I kind of like the idea of respecting each stone. I am remembering Sharon's experience at Stenness again. "You must acknowledge the smallest stone first."

An interesting thing about this recumbent is that though you don't notice it when looking at the stone head on, when you look down its length you see it has been split in two by ice over the years. Even the strongest stone cannot stop the effects of time and weather. Why do so many people have so much trouble accepting that fact, and spend so much time and money on a battle they cannot win?

Off to the east of the recumbent circle is a slightly smaller ring of rocks like those covering the ground in the larger circle. These have been placed side by side and rock to rock, creating a solid ring about two feet wide. Two entry ways were left in the ring and the interior surface remained uncovered, but for the grass. I read that the larger circle was a place for worship and this smaller one was a place for burial. Whatever the case may be, this just added to the wonderful atmosphere of this location.

Even with the rain and wind, I really liked this place. There was a good energy here with energy lines running north/south and east/west across the circle center. The east/west line also continued on out of the circle and through a small outlier stone further to the west. I had initially thought of this circle as broody but came to think of it as contemplative. This really was a peaceful place.

Standing in the circle getting ready to leave, I looked over into the forest and there among the trees I could see a few tents and see smoke rising up into the sky. I had forgotten all about the Scouts. How lucky these young boys were to be able to camp next to such a wonderful place. I can imagine them gathering among the stones at night, with the moon shining down through a heavy mist, and telling stories of ancient druids. You could feel the magic in this place. Could it get any better?

As we drove north on the A96 I took a slight detour on the B9002, and we stopped to see the Maiden Stone. This 10 foot tall Pict Symbol Stone stands alone alongside a country road. It is quite impressive. While it has Christian symbols carved on one side, the other side is covered with Pict symbols which include a mirror, a double sided comb, some kind of creature that appears to be a centaur, and a few other carvings. I was quite puzzled as to why this wonder sat out here in the middle of nowhere? But then, actually, ages ago it was probably in a place of some import that is now long forgotten.

I next hoped to find the Dunnideer Stone Circle. Taking a wrong road I found we were close to the Picardy Stone, another carved Pict stone, so we went to see it. Once again it was a lone stone in a field just off a small country road, and I doubt it gets much attention. It was much smaller and less dramatic than the Maiden Stone and was quite worn by the weather over the ages. However, I could see a couple of the same symbols carved on it, including the mirror. Why a mirror?

Just outside of Insch I knew we must be getting close to the Dunnideer Circle. We drove around the area for a bit, and though I had directions from several different sources, we were having no luck. So, I decided to go back to Dunnideer Hillfort, which we had passed earlier. This is the remains of an old fortification built on top of a cone shaped hill and my plan was to walk to the top in hopes of spying the circle from above.

Stone Journals

Pulling into the parking lot, Sharon and I put on our raincoats and headed off up the hill. It really looked like a tor to me and with the ruins on top it was quite reminiscent of Glastonbury. As we were working our way up, the weather turned very nasty, and soon it was windy and raining. I was thinking myself quite the fool for not having us switch to rain pants before starting out, and, in fact, by the time we made it to the top our pants were quite soaked. On a nice sunny day this would have been an exhilarating hike with a marvelous view, but for us it was wet and cold, and having hiked through the cloud line, once we reached the top we could see nothing below. This was beginning to remind me of the day on Sheepstor, and I decided to give it up. Back to the car, its heater, and a change of clothes. Another circle missed. On to Elgin.

One final thought about the hike up Dunnideer Hill. The closer to the top we got the more we came across what appeared to be rabbit burrows. Soon there were holes everywhere, and it looked like a scene out of *Watership Down*. At one time there must have been a huge community of rabbits living there. We did not, however, see any rabbits out for silflay, leaving us to wonder if they were still around? Or, had the site been abandoned for some reason, just as humans had abandoned it long ago?

We spent two lovely days in Elgin, and the Pines Guest House was a wonderful place to rest up. Along with the castles and cathedrals in the area, we also made a run to see the Suenos Stone in Forres. Of the three Pict stones we visited this was largest, being about 22 feet tall. In an effort to protect it from the weather, it had been put inside a giant plexiglass case, and though I understand the concerns, they should have made the case large enough so that you could go inside instead of looking at the stone through a plexiglass prison. It really was a bummer, and you could not see it that well through all the glare. Still, I did make an effort to examine what I could of the stone, and once again I saw several of the same images I had seen on the other two stones, including, of course, the mirror.

I have seen old photos of this stone before the plexiglass, and what a difference. I wish I could have visited it then.

On June 25 we made our way a little southwest to Balnuaran of Clava (or the Clava Cairns as many refer to them) located near Inverness. It is hard to prepare yourself for this sight. It really is something quite unique.

From the parking area you can barely see what awaits you, as it is hidden by the large beech trees growing all around the location. There are large stone covered mounds and standing stones all nestled into a lush, green, mossy, wooded area. But when you walk through the gate, it is like you have entered another dimension or gone through a time warp, far back in time. It really is kind of eerie, and yet very comforting at the same time. You can feel that this is a place where others have come for millenniums to celebrate both life and death.

Surveying the site, I could see three large cairns spaced quite aways apart from each other over an area about 120 yards long. The ground was covered with a carpet of green grass and moss. What really caught my attention was that each cairn was surrounded with a ring of large stones! Each ring and each cairn was a wonder in and of itself, but here you had them together. Spectacular! I had only seen this once before, and that was long ago prior to my first "stone journey." It was at Newgrange in Ireland and back then, sadly, I was not nearly as aware or receptive, and I did not spend near the time exploring the site that I would today. A missed opportunity I hope to one day put right.

We began by walking over to the most northern ring/cairn first. As with my first experience with the recumbents, I was more than a little impressed with the unique design and construction here. Though Kivik Kungagraven in Sweden was impressive, and in fact much larger, I had been unable to enter the cairn, and there was not this wonderful ring of stones around the outside.

Here was a huge mound covered with rounded river rocks and surrounded by a stone circle (or oval really) 114 feet by 104 feet. It had originally been a passage tomb and to the southwest there was a 20 foot long passageway which led into a central circular chamber, 55 feet across. Though this chamber and passage would originally have been covered over, the roof has now been completely removed. There are large kerb stones (and I do mean large) lining the entire base of the cairn, passageway, and center chamber.

Reading the information board for this cairn, I saw that this passage is aligned on the midwinter solstice, so that on the shortest day of the year the chamber would have been lit up by the setting sun shining down the passage. Now remember, this was some four thousand years ago! I am always so impressed by the awareness these people had of their environment. They were not an ignorant people.

The stone circle was built about 15 feet out from the cairn and consists of 11 stones of different sizes and shapes. The stone standing to the southwest of the entryway looks like a nine foot tall domino. It is the tallest stone at this site and commands ones attention. In fact, a little while later a tour group of some 20 people arrived and the fellow who was guiding them actually led them in some kind of ceremony in front of this stone. I was too far away to hear what was being said, but when I later returned to this ring/cairn, I found a large candle and some offerings placed at the base of this tall stone.

I moved on to the center ring/cairn. It was built much like the northern cairn, but this one did not have an entry passage to the circular same size as the northern chamber. The ring was about 103 feet in diameter and the cairn itself seemed a little smaller than the northern cairn. The stone circle here, as with the previous ring/cairn, was also made up of stones of various shapes though most were of similar height. Looking on to the southern cairn and then back to the northern cairn, I did notice that this middle cairn was flatter than the other two. I also noticed that this ring/cairn was not quite in line with those to the north and south.

Of interest here, similar to Loanhead of Daviot, we found three stone walkways connecting the cairn with ring stones, in this case to the east, to the southeast, and to the west/northwest. Once again we wondered what their purpose had been? We also noticed that none of the stones to which these walkways led had the platform on which to stand as we had experienced with the one stone at the Loanhead of Daviot Stone Circle.

Later on I noticed on the site information board a drawing showing four walkways. Evidently we missed one.

To the west of this middle cairn (some 50 feet) is a kerb-circle 12 feet across. It is just a solid ring of river rocks, each maybe two feet across and a foot or two tall, placed side by side. There was no cairn. It looks insignificant when compared to the ring/cairns alongside which it sits. Still, located there under these wondrous beech trees, this ring of moss covered stones had its own sense of place, and I was happy to spend some time there.

The southern ring/cairn was pretty much like the northern ring/cairn. This cairn too, was a passage tomb constructed with its passage in alignment with the midwinter sunset. Its roof, like the other two cairns, is missing and the exterior ring once again consisted of 11 stones. They seemed to be a mix of naturally shaped rocks along with a few that appear to have had some assistance.

I began to dowse the site by checking for energy lines at each of the ring/cairns. I soon found that each did have energy lines running through them, one northeast/southwest and one northwest/southeast. The northeast/southwest lines ran right down the passageways and through the center chamber of both the northern and southern cairns. Though there is no passage into the middle cairn, the energy line appeared to run right through the chamber's center there as well.

I next thought to start at the southern cairn and see if I could follow the northeast/southwest line all the way up through the complex. As mentioned, the line ran northward up the passage, across the chamber and out the northern side. It then

Stone Journals

bent to the left some and led me directly to the middle cairn. I did feel a little reluctant about crawling around on these cairns, but I was on a mission and so I followed the line across the middle cairn rocks, through the chamber, and back across the cairn to exit on the northern side.

I was a little surprised, as the line then continued on in this northwest direction and not back toward the northern cairn. But after a short ways it made a large loop and turned right again heading directly for the large domino stone referred to earlier. The line passed under this stone and turned right again. As I was following the line eastward, it took a sharp left as we passed in front of the north cairn passageway and headed right down the passage, through the chamber, and out the northeast side. This was too cool. These three chambers were connected together by one energy line. Where did it go next, I wondered? I followed it a little further going northeast until I came to a stone wall and I stopped there. One of these days I will not stop, but this was not that day.

Sharon and I spent a little more time just walking the location. The setting here really is as moving as the stones themselves. The trees, the moss, the earth, the stones, it is all connected, and you can feel something special here at Balnuaran Clavas.

Leaving these wonderful ring/cairns we drove south of Inverness alongside Loch Ness. We were in search of the Corrimony Ring/Cairn, located about 10 miles west of Drumnadrocht off the A831, and with very little difficulty we were able to find the spot.

Let me say at this point that Corrimony is without a doubt one of my very favorite cairn experiences to date. Once we parked the car and started walking towards the site, I could feel the "Magic." As we approached I could see through the trees, like at Balnuaran, a cairn surrounded by a ring of well- spaced stones. I began smiling and said to Sharon, "What a wonderful place."

Located right alongside a quiet country road, in beautiful pasture land, this small but impressive cairn with its ring of stone companions (for that is what they felt like here) emanated a real sense of strength and purpose. Crossing over a small creek on a little wooden bridge, we found ourselves standing at the entryway to the inner chamber of the cairn. Thinking it best to pay our respects to the stones, we walked the ring before exploring the cairn itself.

There was something very special about these standing circle stones. Each seemed to be uniquely shaped, many with sharp angles forming triangles, squares, pyramids, and arrow heads, and most were about four feet in height. There were a few ed and seemed like they were just used to fill the gaps, but who knows? There were also several of the stones with faces in them. We found two human faces and a horse head.

Another interesting thing about these stones is their number. In my notes I recorded that there were 12 stones in the circle. When I began putting this section of the book together, I looked up Corrimony in other books and on different web sites. I was surprised to see that most said there were only 11 stones. Pulling up my photos I saw that the information plaque at the site showed a drawing of the ring with only 11 stones. I then pulled up a video I had filmed standing on top of the cairn where I did a 360 degree view of the location. Three different times I counted the ring stones as they went by and there were in fact 12 standing stones. What's up with that?

Having visited each of the stones, I climbed up on the cairn to look inside the roofless inner chamber, which was well-crafted and about 12 feet across. I could have gone through the entry tunnel, which is still covered over, but it meant crawling, so I

Stone Journals

just walked up on top, being careful not to loosen stones. The passage or "crawlway" is about 10 feet long and still in excellent condition with the roof intact and the floor being one solid long slab. It and the chamber were built to last and, in fact, here they stand thousands of years later.

The cairn, an oval 50 feet by 45 feet, was built on the same alignment as the Balnuaran Cairns, with the chamber passage facing to the southwest for a midwinter sun alignment. The cairn is covered with well-rounded river rocks, and on top, near the roofless chamber, is a large slab with cup marks on it. Maybe it was part of the missing chamber dome?

Standing on top of the cairn really provided me a sense of place. You could imagine people long ago gathering to build this sacred space, and I had the feeling that if I were to have sat there on those stones for a while and opened myself, I might have had a much deeper experience. Hopefully, I will get that chance another day.

I kept being drawn to the stones of the circle, and so I went back down to enjoy their company. Though I had no conversation with any stones at Corrimony, two of the stones did give me strong tugs and I felt energies when I placed my hands on many of the rocks. But it was the communal feeling that radiated from this circle that impressed. The stones welcomed us and I could feel them smile at our presence. They were quite content. I would even say happy! And it was that contentment of the stones that you could feel. It is very interesting how often I encounter this same feeling when at stone sites that seem to have been so neglected. Maybe they are visited more often than I might think.

Sharon too picked up on a similar vibe here. She said she "had the impression that all those years ago a community of people built this site because they wanted to, not because they had to. They built this place to honor a person who was loved and respected." Once again I was surprised by her insight, and she said it as if she was reading a factual account from a book. Whatever the case, Sharon seemed to have tapped into something at Corrimony.

An interesting thing about Corrimony Ring/Cairn, and in fact there are many, is that even though this site is closely fenced in with a wire fence I never gave it a thought. That has always bothered me when visiting similarly fenced sites in the past. Here, however, it was not until days later when looking at my photos that I really took notice. The joy of these stones is so strong that any negatives seemed insignificant. I was reminded of our visit several years ago to the Long Meg Stone Circle with the road running through it. There too, Sharon and I had hardly noticed the road as the circle had such a strong and positive sense of place.

Dowsing the site I right away found an energy line entering the circle from the southwest, passing down the passage, across the inner chamber, on through the cairn, and off to the northeast to who knows where. But what really excited me was that as I continued my walk around the circle, I found an energy line running out from the center of the cairn to each of the 12 standing stones. I found I was giggling as I walked from stone to stone, checking to make sure of what I had found. I have read of such patterns in books by folks like Hamish Miller but I had never encountered it myself. Still, there they were, like spokes on a wagon wheel. What fun!

When we left Corrimony, I did so reluctantly. I was as happy as a lad could be, full of energy, and could only hope that I would one day return to this very special circle/cairn. There be "Magic" there.

Continuing back along Loch Ness we had to make a stop at Urquhart Castle. Who has not heard the stories of the Loch Ness monster and seen the pictures of the loch's famous castle? We thoroughly enjoyed exploring the castle and the views it provided out over the loch, even if we didn't get to see Nessie.

We spent a wonderful night at the Glenmoriston Arms (the meal was unbelievable) and in the morning set off for the Isle of Skye. We took our time, making several stops along the way, including a tour of Eilean Donnan castle which was informative and fun. We just don't have castles back home, and it's hard for me to pass one by. Once we arrived in Portree on the Isle of Skye, we settled in for the evening at the Duirinish Guest House. We stayed two nights at this pleasant place and were impressed by the owners' hospitality.

We started our day with a visit to Dunvegan Castle. Besides my inability to pass up a castle, we went there to see the Fairy Flag. Displayed in a glass case hung on a wall, the flag is said to have been a gift to the MacLeods from the fairies, and they treasure it. It is really just a wafer thin piece of disintegrating cloth but it is said to hold magic, and it remains under the protection of the chief of the MacLeod Clan. This flag and castle played an important roll in the first book of the *Adept* series by Katherine Kurtz and Deborah Turner Harris. I love the books and it was great to see both flag and castle in person.

Once we were back on the road we continued the fairy theme by heading for the Fairy Glen located on the northwest coast near Uig. In route I kept my eyes open for an alignment of two stones said to be located alongside the A87. Sure enough, just out of Eire, I saw the two lone stones standing on the edge of a bluff overlooking Loch Snizort. I left Sharon knitting in the car and crossed the road, jumped a fence, and walked across a wet field of knee high grass. It was overcast and had been raining off and on all morning. By the time I reached the stones, my pants were soaked from the knees down.

Arriving at these two lone sentinels, each about four feet tall, I was met with an immediate, "Welcome." Upon touching the southernmost stone, I received a strong energy boost for which I was quite thankful as I had very little sleep the night before and was feeling quite ragged. Moving on to the northern of the two, I sensed that this pair of stones were not so much content with their situation, as they were resigned to it. Standing with hand on stone, I centered. I was rewarded with a strong energy flow and a whispered, "Thank you for visiting us." Smiling I thought, "It is my greatest pleasure!" I then received the "impression" that there had originally been more stones in this alignment. That thousands of years ago they were part of a very sacred site overlooking the sea. I felt a bond with these two stones that I have not felt at many much more impressive looking stone sites. This is another place where time spent might yield good results, but I did not have the time and the weather was not conducive in any case, as it was once again raining. I left these stones thankful for having met them.

Returning to the car I told Sharon about my experience, and she was sorry she had not gone with me. Until that is, she noticed my pants were soaked through.

Off we went, and it was not long before we were parking the car in an area referred to as the Fairy Glen. I will not go into all the details of our visit there, but I must say that if you ever get a chance to go, you should not miss it. We began by walking through what appeared to be a scene out of middle earth. First were the little pointed peaks looking like conical pyramids here and there. We then entered into a forest of gnarly miniature trees. The ground, the rocks, the trees, all were covered with a lush green moss. Little streams trickled down narrow little valleys and there was a tall pillar-like rock outcropping called "The Castle" nestled right in the middle of this marvelous landscape. I, of course, had to climb up to the top. The view was breathtaking and in a cliff face nearby I could see a small cave opening. Surely this is where the fairies live. Everywhere you go, you "almost" see a fairy. You know they are there, but you just miss them out of the corner of your eye. I would love to visit the Glen with my grandchildren.

After this magical experience in the Fairy Glen, we drove back towards Portree. Along the way we stopped near Borve to check out another stone alignment. This one was three smaller stones, maybe three feet tall, and set right alongside a narrow country farm lane. It was cold, windy, and rainy, and the stones were overgrown with grasses. I took a few photos, wished the stones well, and got back in the car. It is kind of a sad location. The stones are right across the road from a farmhouse, on a narrow shoulder of land, with the road on one side and a wire fence on the other. You get no

sense that anyone cares about them, and that they don't care much either.

Leaving Skye the next stop on our tour of Scotland took us south to the Kilmartin Valley. This is another one of those places like Machrie Moor where a large number of stone sites are located within close proximity of each other. There are standing stones, stone alignments, stone circles, cairns, rocks with carvings, hill forts, and more. In fact I read that at this location there are more archaeological monuments within a six mile radius than anywhere else in Scotland. This has been on my list of must visit places for many years now. Today it would happen.

Just south of the town of Kilmartin, right on the A816, we arrived at, and checked in to, the Dunchraigaig B&B. As we were settling into our second story room, I looked out the window and there, just across the road, standing in an open field, were the Ballymeanoch standing stones. Absolutely spectacular! Life could not get much better.

As the weather was quite nice we immediately headed out. All of the sites in the Kilmartin Valley are easily accessible from established parking areas, along maintained walking paths. This arrangement keeps the traffic controlled and keeps people out of farmers' fields. It is laid out quite well.

Driving back north of our B&B, just a short way up the road was one of these designated parking areas. Getting out of the car we crossed the road, and there just on the other side of a low stone wall, sat the Dunchraigaig Cairn. Passing through a wooden gate, we approached the cairn. It is surrounded by large old trees, and, in fact, the location itself just "feels" old. That might sound odd but places do have really different vibes to them. Most are, of course, quite old, but that is not how they all feel. Some don't "feel" at all.

The mound is similar in size to Corrimony and covered with rocks like others we have seen on this trip. It seems a bit squatty and though the entrance is still there, and in good condition, you would have to get down on your belly to crawl in, and even then you can only go a yard or so as the passage is blocked. There is also a small cist in the top of the cairn.

As I walked around the cairn, dowsing for energy lines, I found strong lines running both north/south and east/west. I followed the southern line, which in fact was more to the southwest than true south, until it came to a stone wall which fenced off a grassy field. Looking out across the field I could see the Ballymeanoch Stones off in the distance. There was an assigned pathway running alongside the wall, so we followed it and after passing through several gates we entered the field in which sat the stones themselves. The very stones we could see out the window of our room.

Looking over the site, we saw the remains of a small cairn to the east, an alignment of four tall stones in the middle, and an alignment of two more tall stones further west. We decided we would go to the cairn first.

The cairn is really in a sad state. There are a number of the larger kerb stones, which would have formed the exterior base, still standing in place. Other than that there isn't much there. I also noticed a couple of good sized stones outside the cairn which lay flat on the ground and were being slowly absorbed back into the earth. The one on the south side had a large hole in it that was smoothed and definitely looked manmade. It was maybe as big as a cantaloupe in size, and I puzzled over its purpose. While Sharon was looking at the information board for this site, she read that this holed stone originally stood by itself to the west of the two tall stones alignment, and that the hole went all the way through the rock. Evidently it had fallen over long ago and had been moved to its present location.

Why didn't they just stand it up again? Now it lies there sinking into the earth. Very sad really.

I did dowse this cairn and found energy lines running both north/south and east/west.

Next Sharon and I separated and spent time just wandering among the stones of the two alignments. They had been placed parallel with each other running northeast by southwest and were about 50 yards apart.

Walking from stone to stone in the four stone alignment, I received good responses from three of them, especially the end stones. Placing my hands on the one to the south, I felt it pulsing a strong, satisfying, warm energy. This stone definitely had a strong male energy and I quickly felt charged. The stone at the north end was almost its opposite, but with just as wonderful a result. This is one of those rocks that makes you feel relaxed, as its energy flow is slow and steady. This is a "crawl up in Grandma's lap" kind of stone, good when you are feeling stressed. This stone definitely had a female energy going, and I had to wonder if this effect, of having a male stone at one end of the alignment and a female stone at the other, had been planned by the builders? There may of course have been many more stones in this row once upon a time. These two alignments may be all that remains of some long avenue which once connected different sites. Who knows?

Now, the second stone from the south in that alignment was something else. When I first walked up and placed my hands on it I felt a strong energy flow, but it would come and go like an ocean wave, back and forth. As I stood there I started getting kind of dizzy and pulled away. This was sort of like a roller coaster ride, or like standing up on a branch near the top of a tall tree on a windy day. When Sharon and I got together a little later, the first thing she asked me was if I had any strange hits from that same particular rock? She said it made her feel unstable like she was standing on a moving surface and being pulled towards, and then being pushed away from, the stone. It had actually made her a little nauseous.

When I tell others about my experiences at a certain stone site, I never expect for them to necessarily get the same results from those stones that I got. I have noticed that energy flows can change from rock to rock, and that they can change over time. Also, individuals are receptive on different levels and some, it seems, are not receptive at all. There have been occasions when I have gone back to visit a site again, and I have picked up different results than I did the time before. Here at Ballymeanoch however, Sharon and I both had the same weird experience with this same megalith. It was great.

Rather than going on to the two stone alignment, I decided to dowse the site overall. I went back to the little cairn and picked up on the line leaving it going west. As it headed towards the four stone alignment, about one third of the way there it made a small loop and then carried on. It passed between the two middle stones, then went straight across the field and passed right between the two stones in the shorter alignment. I was having fun now, and said to Sharon, "Let's see where it goes from here."

The line turned southward and zig zagged around a bit before going straight east. Suddenly the line bent back south and after a short distance began going around in a four foot diameter circle. After a few laps, it continued on. Shortly I arrived at a low henge which, from a distance, had been completely concealed by weeds and grasses, but was quite obvious when you found it. Crossing over the henge mound and across the shallow ditch, I found a low earth platform in the middle of which was a cist. From there the line continued on and exited the henge to the west. I followed this line until I came to another fence. Once again I was wondering, "Where does it go from here?" I was one happy boy! I had followed a line through four different stone placements, and it was still going. To me this is magic! Earth Magic.

Full of joy we returned to the two stones in the western alignment. The southern stone we called the "Martian" as it looked just like a martian head. This stone had a strong "male" energy that immediately made me feel more energized. I could almost hear this stone talking to me, but not quite. Maybe another time. The other stone seemed asleep, but present, and I felt a very subtle energy.

While I had been interacting with these stones, Sharon had gone back to have another look at the information board which was placed near the ruined cairn. There was an aerial photo of the site, and she saw that on it they had marked the original location of the holed stone we had noticed earlier. It had been located to the northwest of the two stone alignment, and she wondered if we might be able to find where it had been standing? We looked around the area where she thought it should have been but found no signs. I decided to try my luck dowsing the spot. I went well away from the area that the photo indicated and using one rod I began working. My mantra was "Where was the holed stone standing?" I repeated this over and over as I walked. At first nothing, but then

slowly the rod began moving, and I followed it's direction.

After a bit of wandering the pull became steady and soon I arrived at a place where the rod bent back on itself, and as I turned, it stayed that way. I told Sharon I thought I might have found the spot, so she went back to look at the photograph on the info board. Looking back past the stones and across the field toward where I was standing, she yelled, "You're right on it!" What a fun day.

There was one more line to check. I went back to the ruined cairn, found the line going out to the north, and began following it. As I suspected, it went pretty much in a straight line until it came to the walled-in field to our east. Looking across the field in the direction I had been going, I could see it was in a straight line with the spot where earlier, I had been stopped by the stone wall when going south from the Dunchraigaig cairn. It was all connected by one energy line! I wondered if from the Dunchraigaig cairn it continued on north to connect with other stone sites throughout the valley. Maybe another time I will see if I can get permission to follow this line. Feeling happy and content, Sharon and I decided to go back to the B&B for a rest before dinner.

As it didn't get dark until about 11 PM, when Sharon and I finished dinner we felt rejuvenated and decided that since the weather pattern (cold but no rain) was holding, we would do a bit more exploration. We began at the Nether Largie Stones. Sitting in an open field this is another very unique grouping of megaliths. At the south end are two tall, thin stones standing side by side with a gap in between. To their north is a ring of small stones which were probably originally part of a cairn. A bit further north is a single standing stone and then still further north are two larger megaliths similar to the first two in this alignment. Though the ring is a little off line, the lone stone standing in the middle is right in line with the gaps between the two pairs of stones on either end. Looked at from above, this grouping forms an X and is, in fact, referred to as The Great X.

It was getting colder, so we decided to move on to the Temple Wood Stone Circle a few hundred yards off to the west. Comfortably nestled under some trees, this unique circle of small stones gives off an interesting vibe. As I walked up, I immediately got the impression that serious things used to happen here. This was a place where many gathered for celebrations of life, not of death. The large cairns placed throughout the valley were places to honor the dead, but this circle had performed a much different function.

First you come to the edge of a circle of small river rocks which completely blanket the ground like a flattened cairn, about 40 feet by 44 feet in diameter. Located well in from the edge of this flattened cairn, is a ring of 13 low, thin, standing stones, of various heights, none more than three feet tall, and placed about two feet apart. In the very center is a small rectangular cist which is surrounded by a ring of small kerb stones about 10 feet in diameter. The surface being completely covered with river rocks makes walking in the stone circle kind of awkward. However, one really needs to walk inside to get the full impact of these stones. It was, in fact, while walking among the circle stones that I received my "impression" of the purpose of this circle.

Now I must say, when I discovered the cist in the middle of this circle, it kind of threw me, for, as I said, I really did not get the feeling that this was a place for celebrating death. However, I later read that the cist was added long after the circle had been built and used.

I would also point out that originally this circle sat out in the open and that the trees that now surround it were planted in more recent times (the 1800's I think) by the land owner who thought it would provide good affect. I must say, I agree with him. This place feels of magic. The trees really do add to the overall atmosphere, creating a comforting, "why not stay awhile," feel to the site.

I dowsed the location and found strong energy lines running north/south and east/west across the middle of the circle.

Just a little to the north, also under the trees, there lies another of these rings of surface stones. It is smaller than Temple Wood being about 34 feet in diameter. It only has one short standing stone along the exterior, but I imagine there were once many more. In the center is a single, low stone, sitting on its side like a mini recumbent. The result overall is a simple but powerful circle of stone. Cool place. When dowsed, this ring, too, had energy lines running both north/south and east/west.

As it was getting darker and colder, we decided to call it a night and drove back to the B&B. What a great day! What a great place!

Could there be anything more exhilarating than waking up in the morning, looking out our window, and seeing those impressive Ballymeanoch Stones beckoning from the field beyond the fence? I could not wait to pay them another visit.

We decided, however, to begin the day by going back to where we left off last night. Walking through the Nether Largie stones, we followed the path on over to Temple Wood where we then joined a farm lane which ran alongside it and on north up the valley. As we followed this lane, we encountered three large cairns in a row, constructed quite a distance apart. They are surrounded by pasture land, and each is fenced for protection. There is a fenced-in walkway leading from the lane to each site. These are large, rock covered cairns much like we had seen in the north, but these do not have stone rings around them. However, I did read some information later on at the museum that said one of these cairns had a stone circle inside of it when it was excavated. Now there is a puzzle. Was the decision made to just make an existing stone circle site into a cairn and not to even bother to take down or move the standing stones? Or, were they may be part of the original plan? More questions without answers.

The first cairn we came to (Nether Largie South Cairn) has a large rectangular burial chamber in its center built with large slabs for entrance, walls, and ceiling. The roof is still intact, and the chamber can be entered from either end, but you must squat down inside. Pretty cool.

I also found a good sized cist on the south side of the mound that was in good condition. The lid, which was a huge rock slab, had been pulled off the opening, so you could see into the empty cist. It was well constructed with single, solid slabs for the walls. The remains of whomever had been buried there were, of course, long gone.

This was a really interesting place to experience, but I had no special connections there.

Moving on up the valley, we next came to the Mid Cairn. Though less impressive than the South Cairn, this cairn has an earth ring built up around it which gives it an aura of strength. As with the South Cairn, there is also an empty cist on the south side of the cairn that has its stone lid held open by some metal bars. Strange to think there once was a body buried there. I found myself wondering, "Is this really how we should treat the dead? What right do we have to remove the bones of some person who was honored with such a burial?" I understand the search for knowledge about the past, but what do we gain by such an act as this? And, what do we lose? While I recognize that some of this activity was done by grave robbers looking for personal gain, often times it is done for research.

The next cairn in this alignment was Nether Largie North. As we approached this site, it looked quite impressive with the village of Kilmartin and its church as the backdrop. It was a good sized mound with an indention in the top, and it kind of reminded me of a small volcano. Climbing up on top I found a large metal door which obviously covered an entrance. I was able to slide the door open and climb down inside to a good sized square chamber. This was beautifully built with stacked stone blocks that seemed to have been shaped for a tight fit. In the middle of the floor is a large burial cist with walls constructed of solid stone slabs. The lid is missing. The floor of the chamber was covered with small crushed rock making a comfortable

walking surface. I read that this had been the burial place of just one person. This was a large cairn for one person, so he, or she, must have been very important to the people who built this site. Notice, I said important, not powerful.

I dowsed all three cairns and found north/south and east/west energy lines crossing through the center of each. The lines going south ran through the cists on the mid and southern cairns. Though I did not cross over the pasture land between the cairns, it appeared as though there was, in fact, just one energy line running north/south connecting all three cairns. Standing on top of the northern cairn looking south across the other cairns I could see the standing stones in the distance. Were they too on this line?

There was actually one more cairn much further to the north, but Sharon and I decided we would check it out later from the northern end.

In route to the car, we walked the lane to Temple Wood and then took the path back towards The Great X.

Along the way I noticed a lone stone standing in the field between the south cairn and the Nether Largie stones. Pulling out my dowsing rods, I picked up an energy line which appeared to run from the south side of the cairn, through the standing stone, and on to where I was. I followed the line as it continued on south, but it soon took a turn to the northeast going away from the Nether Largie stones. After a short ways the line made a four foot diameter circle, continued on and then made a much larger circle, and then turned south again. From there it was straight on to The Great X standing stones. The line passed under the westernmost stone of the northern pair of standing stones of this complex, and then continued on to the center standing stone where it curled right around its base, about a foot away. Then it was a straight line south to the southern pair of stones where it passed right through the gap between them and on to the south.

As I stood there looking to the south I felt sure that if I could follow this line it would continue on to the Duncraigaig Cairn and would, in fact, be the same line I had found there that passed on south to the Ballymeanoch Stones. I am in awe of the energy lines I have found here in the Kilmartin Valley. This is such a special place and really needs more time spent.

It was time to return to the B&B. When making plans for this trip one of the reasons I chose the Dunchraigaig B&B was because they offered a cupcake decorating class to anyone interested. I knew Sharon would enjoy it, so I had booked her a session. As the class was to take up most of the afternoon, I returned her to the B&B and then set off to explore the Valley by myself. I first went in search of a tall standing stone on the north end but failed to find it. So, working my way south I drove to Dunadd Fort, a massive outcropping of rock which protrudes from the valley floor and formed a natural castle like fortification. It is quite an impressive site and was once the place where Scottish Kings were said to have been crowned.

Parking the car I followed a barely marked trail as it wound its way over boulders and through slight ravines until eventually it came to the top. What a cool place. Near the top you pass through a long natural entryway through rock that opens into a bowl like enclosure in which people once lived and where there was a natural spring/well.

Once at the top I had a wonderful view of the valley below and the hills beyond. There I also found a large rock slab in which set a perfect human footprint. It is said this is where the Kings would place their foot when being crowned. Standing there with my foot in the print (it was a good fit I must say) I did get a really good feeling from this place. I had forgotten to bring along a rod, so I did no dowsing, but I did

sense some good strong energies on top. The weather was turning bad, so I decided to head back to the car. Dunadd became just one more site on my lengthening list of places I would like to visit again.

I returned to the B&B and checked in on Sharon who was having a great time. I thought maybe I would just relax for a while, but looking out our bedroom window I saw the weather break again and so I was up and out the door. I knew I wanted to spend more time with the Ballymeanoch Stones, so that is where I went.

I walked past the Dunchraigaig Cairn and followed the pathway to the field in which the stones sat. Looking across the rich green grass at those tall proud stones, my feet began to tingle and I felt a flush. This is one of those places where the earth energies are strong.

Since I really had not spent enough time with the two stone alignment on our last visit, that was where I went first. I squatted down, back against the west side of the northern stone, and opened myself to the stone. It was a slow, subtle sort of experience, where I kind of lost track of time as I seemed to merge with the earth and stone and was welcomed. I had an idea to try to interact with the stone in a different way, and having brought along my rods, I took one in hand. Centering, I asked, "Is the stone happy I am here?" As I repeat the question, the rod began to slowly "pulse" four or five times to the right and then stopped. A solid "Yes." I began to laugh and turning to the stone said, "Thank you. I am happy to be here." I sat, back against stone and enjoyed its company. A relaxed but steady pulse of energy came from the rock, and I just sat there absorbing what was being offered.

After quite a while I got up and moved to the southern stone of the pair. What an experience. I stood there looking directly into the face of "my favorite martian," and though his mouth did not move, he welcomed me back just as loudly as if he had spoke with an audible voice. "Hearing" this welcome, I reached out and touched the stone. I felt a warm infusion of energy coming from both stone and earth and was soon fully connected. Whereas the first stone had filled me with a soothing, healing energy, this was a joyful, "Let's go do something" kind of experience.

Deciding to try my luck dowsing the stone, I pulled out a rod. This time I stood in front of the stone and asked the same question. "Is the stone happy I am here?" With no hesitation, the rod jerked all the way to the right. Hugging my new friend I said, "Thank you."

I stood there for quite a while sharing in the company and energy of the stone. When I look back on this experience, I am sorry I did not take full advantage of the moment to ask more questions of the stone. When I visit the stones and get a strong welcome, I am just so happy to be with them I rarely think beyond the joy of the moment. It was an opportunity missed. Still, it was one of my strongest interactions with a stone and I know I must go back.

I then returned to the B&B to see Sharon's beautifully decorated cupcakes. It had given her a lot of satisfaction to spend those hours working with Lynn in her most charming kitchen, and she was quite proud of her efforts. It was great fun for me to see her excitement as she showed me her colorful, flowered creations.

Sharon and I took the late afternoon to visit the Kilmartin Museum. It was small but pleasant, and we enjoyed the interactive exhibition. One thing that caught my eye was a pile of small, smoothed quartz stones on display in a case. There were 33 of them. They were said to have been discovered at the base of a tall standing stone somewhere in the valley. The stone had been placed in such a way as to face sunrise on Midsummer solstice. Why the pile of quartz stones was there no one really knows, though there were several possibilities suggested.

Next door in the church graveyard, there was a collection of ancient carved tombstones that were really impressive and worth the visit.

After a most enjoyable stay in Kilmartin, the next morning we were on our way to Dumfries. It was not until we were about an hour south that I realized we had forgotten to go to the cairn on the north end of the Kilmartin Valley. And, we had not visited any of the cup/ring marked stones for which this region is famous. It was too late to turn around, but it gave me two more reasons to want to return.

The main purpose for returning to Dumfries this time was because Sharon had finally tracked down a cousin who lived there. This was to be the culmination of five years of search into her family's Scottish heritage and she was very excited. Her cousin, John Kirkpatrick, and his family were wonderful and welcoming people, and we enjoyed two days of their company.

However, this brings me back to a reoccurring situation concerning old stone sites that always surprises me. When talking with John I asked if he had ever visited the Twelve Apostles Stone Circle which was located just a few miles south of where he lived and right alongside the road he drove to work. He had not, and, in fact, he had never heard of it. When I explained it was the fifth or sixth largest stone circle in the UK, he was amazed that he knew nothing of it.

So, the next day I took him to see the stones. As it was raining we did not stay long, but standing there looking at the circle, John said he could not believe he had lived in the area for 50 years and did not even know of the circle's existence. I was happy that I got to introduce him. Now that he knew they were there, I told him he needed to take his nine year old grandson to meet the stones. Young Jamie just might feel their magic.

Leaving Dumfries we had a long day of travel ahead of us, and so as we entered the Lake District of northern England I reluctantly drove past the sign pointing to the Castlerigg Stone Circle. As much as I wanted to go there again, I knew we needed to keep moving.

Our first stop was not at a stone site but at Hilltop Farm. Located right in the heart of the Lake District this was the home of Beatrice Potter, the writer of those wonderful children's stories. Having read them to our grandchildren over and over and viewed the animated film versions of the stories many, many times, Sharon and I were excited to visit the place where Ms. Potter had imagined, and written about, Peter Rabbit, Jemima Puddle-Duck, Farmer McGregor, and all the other wonderful characters. As we walked the grounds where cotton tailed rabbits jumped across the lawn, and passed through the very gate which she had drawn in her stories, and then toured through the old stone house that had been her home, we could feel just how special this place was. We were really happy we had made the stop.

That said, the drive to Hilltop Farm once we had left A591, and the drive from Hilltop on south to Broughton Furness, was absolutely "hellacious." I was on edge the whole time. Now I have been driving in the UK for a long time, and I am for the most part quite comfortable doing so, but in this case, I met my limit. The winding roads were very narrow, and lined with unforgiving stone walls. Add to that the large number of cars, busses, and tractors and the speeds at which they were traveling, and it was absolutely awful. When we finally got through it all, I told Sharon it was one of the most beautiful and one of the most nerve shattering drives I had ever made. Luckily for me our next stop was to be just the restorative I needed.

We were in search of the Swinside (or Sunkenkirk) Stone Circle which was located near Broadgate, north off the A595. With the help of a couple of locals, we soon found the private road which climbed steeply uphill to the Swinside Farm. As is often the case throughout the UK, the landowner has kindly allowed the public access to this megalithic site. Parking alongside the public road in a slight lay-by, we began our walk up the hill. After a mile or so we were beginning to wonder if we had made a mistake? We could see for quite a ways and saw no sign of a circle. And then, as often happens when looking for stone sites, there it was. Looking over the stone wall that ran alongside the road we saw a massive stone circle positioned proudly out in open pasture.

This is one of the most impressive and complete stone rings I have encountered. It is about 94 feet in diameter and made up of 55 rather large naturally shaped rocks all placed tightly together. Some stones actually touch each other. Climbing over the gate we approached the circle and were struck not just by the stones but by the setting overall. This ring sits high on a mountainside with the mountain's top for a backdrop and a beautiful panoramic view of the landscape below. Though the setting is spectacular one has to wonder why the builders would choose this location for their temple, so far from the sea where their villages would probably have been situated? That said, the location of this circle provides one of the most peaceful, nourishing environments I have experienced.

Walking among the stones I could sense the wonderful energy just below the surface, but I did not feel it flowing up into my body. This was different, and a bit puzzling.

Deciding to begin dowsing I quickly picked up strong energy lines running both north/south and east/west which crossed near the circle center. I also came across a third, and most interesting, energy line. To the southeast there is an established entrance that is about five feet wide. It is clearly marked by the presence of two exterior portal stones which frame the entrance passage. As I had walked by the passage I picked up this third line which I then followed through the passage and into the circle. Near the center my rod bent back on itself, and I was soon going around and around in a circle about four feet across. I kept going around asking for an exit, but I could not find one. This was a first for me. I have read that energy lines sometimes "go to ground" and that seems to be the case here at Sunkenkirk.

I next thought to see if I could find energy lines coming from any of the individual stones. I did not check them all, but I did get strong responses from five of the stones. The north stone, which sets right on top of the north/south line, was where I started and where I got an immediate response. This stone, by the way, is the tallest stone in the circle, being seven and a half feet tall. It is also narrow and pointed like a marker pointing the way. As I was saying, I did get a strong energy response here, and it was in the form of flower petals. I always find this to be so very intriguing. The loops were three or four inches wide at the rock, about a foot wide at the end, and protruded about two and a half feet out from the stone. There were seven petals total. I found the same effect coming from the rocks to each side of the north stone. I also found this

flower petal pattern emanating from the two circle entrance stones but not from the portal stones.

Feeling a bit tired I decided to lie down on one of the fallen circle stones and soon felt a mild and comforting flow of revitalizing energy. After the stress of the Lake District drive, this was much needed and much appreciated. I had wondered if I was going to be able to connect here and was quite happy now that it had happened.

Rising up I looked around the circle, and noticing that quite a few of the stones had fallen over, I decided to count them. There were 23 stones that had fallen over the years. What I found interesting was that all had fallen into the circle. None had fallen out. As I thought about the reason for that it occurred to me that maybe the strong energy line coming into the circle through the entrance and then "going to ground" in the center created a kind of energy pull on the stones. Sort of an energy whirlpool. It kind of makes sense.

Walking the ring again, when I got to the entrance I stood between the two entrance stones, placed a hand on each and settled. Soon that same calming energy came flowing through the rocks and into my body. I was hooked up now, and all was well with the world.

Sharon and I then walked up on the rise above the circle, looked down on it and out across the landscape beyond. We stood there smiling and felt blessed to have experienced this most special place. We were also thankful to the folks who own Swinside Farm for allowing people like us to continue to visit this amazing site. I imagine that back in the States the road would have been gated with no trespassing signs posted every-where.

The day was getting on and I was hoping to make one more stop before going on to tonight's B&B. We were in search of a small ring of stones called the Druids Circle, or Birkrigg Stone Circle, located to the east. Using information I had found on one of the internet sites, we were able to locate the stones a short ways off the A5087 to the south of Ulverston.

The circle is situated on a grass and bracken-fern covered hillside overlooking the village of Bardsea with its imposing cathedral, and Morecambe Bay beyond. The view from this circle of small stones is spectacular. Though the Druids Circle is not nearly as impressive as the Sunkenkirk Circle, this does seem a much more practical location for a place of worship. But then maybe in the case of Sunkenkirk, that was the point. It was not meant to be convenient. Maybe the effort of getting there was an essential part of the experience.

Having parked the car we walked up the hill towards the stones. Whoever maintains this location has done a good job of clearing wide walking paths through the bracken-ferns and grasses up to and around the circle. They have also kept clear the inside of this ring of stones. Sadly, there is an outer ring of low fallen stones that they have left overgrown, and most cannot be seen at all. Why they chose to leave this outer circle covered over, I cannot understand.

There are 12 stones in the inner circle, with two just visible. They are small in size with the largest being only a few feet tall. They have a bright white affect to them and really stand out against the green backdrop of the grass and bracken-fern. Walking among the stones, I got the feeling that this was a serious and sacred place. As much time as I have spent in the company of stones I find it interesting that some sites leave me completely unmoved with no connection at all. As insignificant as this circle might appear when compared to some others, (it is only about 30 feet across) these stones felt of strength and importance.

We found several intriguing things about this circle. The largest of the stones had some strange growth on it that looked like blood running down its sides. It really did look like a bleeding stone. I have never seen this before. In *A Guide To The Stone Circles Of Cumbria* by Robert Farrah, there is a photo of this bleeding stone.

There was also one stone around which had gathered a large number of small snails with the most beautiful multicolored shells. Why just at the base of this stone? I found myself thinking of those wonderful books in the *Duncton Wood* series in which the moles would gather to worship at the base of the stones. I also remembered the snail that was on pilgrimage to the top of The Blind Fiddler and wondered if it ever made it?

And then there was the "Serpent" rock. It really did look like the head of a serpent coming up out of the ground to me, and I kept being drawn back to it as if it had something to tell me but I was not hearing the message. There was indeed something going on.

In *The Stone Circles Of Cumbria,* by John Waterhouse he too refers to this rock and describes it as "a sperm whale, mouth ajar, rising out of the sea."

I decided to do a little dowsing and soon found north/south and east/west energy lines running through the circle. Then I decided to dowse to see if I could find the outer circle and following my rod I was led to a grass covered stone. Continuing to follow the direction of the rod, I worked my way through the thick growth and soon had found 14 stones making up a circle over 80 feet across. Was that all of the exterior circle stones? I don't know but it was great fun! As I went from stone to stone I would pull the plants back to reveal the stone buried underneath. If they would just remove the growth out past the outer ring I think people would really enjoy the result. Double circles are not very common.

It was getting late, but still I did not want to hurry as this was to be our last stone visit of this trip. I stood in the circle looking down on Bardsea below, and I could imagine a small group of druids leading a procession from the village up the hill to this circle of stones. This was not any inner vision, just my mind having fun. I think modern religions have done us a great disservice by taking nature out of the mix. Those who worshipped at the Druids Circle did so with the land as their cathedral floor, the stones as their walls, and the sky as the ceiling over it all. I believe that we have lost our ability to talk with our God (or Goddess) as we have closed him, or her, out and closed ourselves in.

As Sharon and I started the walk back to our car, I felt a strong tug and I turned to look back. It was a strange experience. My eyes were drawn directly to the Serpent Rock which seemed to be smiling at me, and I was filled with happiness. Saying a quiet "Thank you," I started back down the hill. I took Sharon's hand and I, too, smiled. This ended another wonderful journey to the stones.

As I sit and write this, I am missing the stones and wishing I could just walk out my door and go sit with my back resting against The Blind Fiddler, or wander in and out of the stones of Sunkenkirk. There is so much to learn.

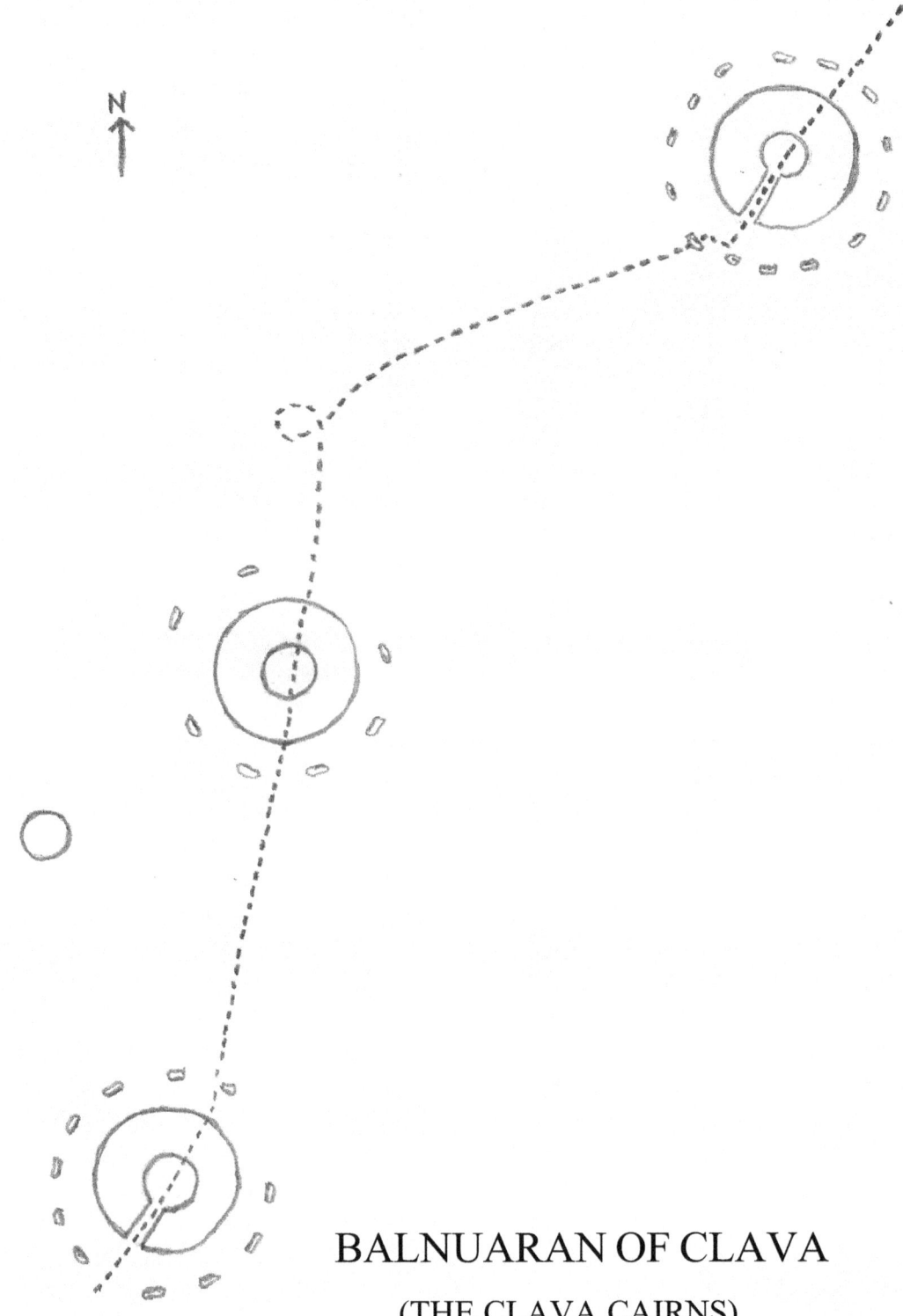

BALNUARAN OF CLAVA
(THE CLAVA CAIRNS)

This is drawn freehand and not meant to be precise. I do feel it fairly accurately represents the site. The dotted line is the energy line I dowsed flowing through the location.

"All that we can say, ultimately, is that these sites possess a curious power which still draws us to this day. To stand within any of the stone circles, or to touch one of the great standing stones, is to feel a special kind of energy which one may, perhaps, call the heartbeat of the earth."
John Matthews
Landscapes Of Legend

Stone Journey 7

ENGLAND, SCOTLAND

STONE JOURNEY 7 - June 15, 2015

Well, it took 29 hours to get from SFO to York, England but when Sharon and I finally arrived, at about 8:00 PM, we were tired but happy to be back, and we had just enough time to get to Betty's for a bite to eat before they closed. So began another "journey to the stones."

After a surprising good night's sleep we decided to start our vacation with a visit to the Brimham Rocks, referred to as "Nature's natural sculpture park." This unique site is located just off the A6165 out of Ripley and there are some six acres of natural rock formations that are as impressive, in their own way, as the best known of the man-made stone sites. As you walk the paths through this partially wooded wonderland you come across one massive monument after another. Many appear to be just wondrous piles of rocks stacked in the most haphazard and precarious ways, but others seem to have been sculpted to specific forms. Among the latter we came across stone formations appearing to be a dog, a dancing bear, a flower pot, a druids table, and even a humongous Mickey Mouse head, though they surely called it by a different name in ages gone by.

There are also balancing rocks of various sizes and shapes which seem as though they would fall over should you give one a light push. Most fantastical of all is the Idol Rock, which is a huge stone some 12 feet tall and maybe 10 feet wide, that is balancing a couple of feet in the air on the smallest imaginable pillar of sandstone. It just does not seem possible that it is still standing. By all rights the stone should long ago have either crushed the insignificant pillar or fallen off it.

When we had finished the walk Sharon commented that it seemed as though at Brimham, "Mother Nature had just been having fun." It really is the most wonderful place. And, they allow you to climb on the rocks (within reason) which provides not only amazing views of the countryside below but also allows you to get close and personal with these amazing stone formations.

At one point along the way Sharon had taken a photo of me standing at the Druid's Table. As I stood there with one hand on the table I did feel a strong energy surge flow from the rock. I was not expecting this kind of response and though surprised, I accepted the gift of the stone joyfully. Though there are no records of Druids actually using this site it is hard to believe they wouldn't have. It is just too magical for them not to have appreciated, and been in awe of, what Mother Earth had created.

Once we were satisfied with our time spent wandering among these unique rock formations we headed towards Ripon to make a stop at Fountains Abbey. The abbey ruins are quite impressive and the gardens are fantastic and well worth the visit.

Later that day we made a stop to see the Devil's Arrows just out of Boroughbridge, near the A1. These three tall, massive, pillar stones are as much as eighteen and twenty two feet in length, with the smallest being a rectangle about six feet by four feet wide and the tallest being about four by four feet wide. They were placed in pretty much a north/south alignment. Sadly, the timing of this visit was not good as the field in which two of the stones sit was covered with a crop, leaving me no access to the stones. This was too bad as I was getting a strong pull from one or both of those stones.

The third, and I think tallest stone, sits alone across a road and outside the field in which the other stones stand. It is surrounded on three sides by a grove of trees and is locked in by a gated fence fronting the road. It feels imprisoned. Whereas the other two stones stood closer together out in an open field in the full sun, this lone sentinel felt separated from them and was almost hidden among the trees where it was cold and dark. Standing there with my hand on the stone I could get no response at all. Well, actually, when I first touched it I thought I felt something but it stopped as quickly as it started, and then there was nothing. I did dowse an energy line running right under the stone headed north towards the stones out in the field.

Stone Journals

I left this sad, lonely stone and went back out into the sun to climb the fence and gaze upon its two distant companions. They looked magnificent out in the field and I could feel them calling to me. I would not tramp on the farmer's crop to get out to them, and so had to leave without making the acquaintance of those two charming megaliths. I can only hope I will one day return when the crops have been harvested.

Worth noting, all three stones have long, deep grooves worn, or cut, into them that run down from the top like wax running down a candle. Whether they were carved, or caused by weathering, is up for debate. No matter what the case, it is a most interesting effect. One I have seen several times before, like on the majestic megalith in Circle 3 on Machrie Moor.

After a travel day and a visit with some friends in Outwood, Sharon and I headed for the Cotswolds. We decided to try to find Wayland's Smithy Long Barrow just down the ridge from the Uffington White Horse. After two unsuccessful attempts (we had been on the wrong ridge) we returned to our car and drove a little further north on the B4000 where we found a parking area and sign which declared that we were, in fact, at the infamous "Ridgeway." The Ridgeway is an 87 mile long section of an ancient roadway that went from Norfolk on the East Coast, across England, and down to the Dorset coast in the south. It is thought to be the oldest existing roadway in England and was used at least 5000 years ago by both traders and travelers. All along its route you find megalithic sites like the Uffington White Horse and the Rollright Stone Circle. Knowing we were in the right place, we hiked about a mile up the ridge to find the long barrow beautifully nestled among a grove of trees, just a short way off the path.

As you approach the site the stone entrance to the barrow really is very impressive. There are four large stones, 10 feet tall, placed across the front, and in the center is the entrance to the actual burial chamber which is blocked off. The earth mound that is the long barrow stands about five feet high and is some 55 feet across at the front. It then stretches some 200 feet long, narrowing somewhat as it goes, to a rise of just one foot at the far end. Due to the slope and chamber construction when you look along the top it is pretty much flat.

As I walked around it dowsing, I found a strong energy line running right down the middle. It ran from the far end, down the full length of the barrow, out through the entryway, and onward in a southern direction. There was a real "comfort" to this place and I enjoyed being there.

Today Sharon and I were joined by our daughter Galadriel, her husband, and their two children ages 8 and 11, who were vacationing in the Cotswolds. When visiting stone sites I am used to traveling by myself, or with Sharon, so I did not know how this was going to go. But, it seemed to me that as they were in the UK they should meet some stones, so off we went to Avebury.

As it was the day of Summer Solstice there were still hundreds of revelers remaining from last night's, and this morning's, activities. There were also many people who, like us, had just chosen this day to visit Avebury. People were everywhere and I must say it did kind of kill the Avebury groove. Many were walking among the stones, some were just lying here and there in the grass, and others sat leaning against one megalith or another. Then, of course, there was the occasional couple making out, seemingly oblivious of the people around them. There was also a motley bunch sitting up on the henge top playing reggae music through a boom box. I was not digging it at all. They had no respect for anyone else, and I don't think they cared much about the stones either. It was all about the party.

Speaking of caring about the stones, we had an interesting experience out walking the Avenue. My grandchildren wanted to know if it was ok for them to climb up on the stones. When they are at our house I am more than happy to have them connecting with the stones of our stone circle by climbing on them. The rocks are quite solid and I see no harm, and it just may be the thing that enables them to get in touch with the stones' energies. I also think the stones enjoy their youthful enthusiasm and imagination. So, I told them to go ahead.

In any case, as the kids had climbed up on one of the avenue giants a woman came up to reprimand us for not being more respectful of the stones. That they were thousands of years old and we should not treat them in this manner. While I respected her views I think she was way off base. If these stones were made of a soft material and in danger of being injured in some way, I too, would have told my grandchildren it was not a good idea. But not only have they stood there thousands of years, they are "solid as a rock" as the old saying goes. I knew the stones were quite happy to have these young children, with big smiles on their faces, climbing up and sitting on them. It reminded me of watching the young girl climbing on the stones at Castlerigg years ago. No harm, no foul.

Our visit to Avebury was not what I had hoped. I did get away by myself at one point while the family was eating at the Red Lion. I went to spend some time with the two remaining Cove Stones, but there was a woman there who was being filmed for some program and she was talking about the stones and energy lines. I was happy when she finished and they walked on, leaving me alone with these two wonderful old megaliths. As I opened myself to them, wondering how they were holding up with all this chaotic activity going on around them, I received a quick, and surprising, response of contentment coming from both stones. I was welcomed with a warm pulse of energy through my hands, which I had placed on the shorter of the two, and I felt a sense of thanks for my concern. Though I am sure the stones appreciate those who come to celebrate with their hearts in the right place, I could not help but wonder just how trying all the nonsense of the last twenty four hours might had been on them.

I went back to join up with my family, thankful for those few moments with the Cove Stones. I felt blessed that in all this chaos, I had made this connection.

Next, it was on to Stonehenge. As I knew they had been expecting as many as 20,000 people for the Solstice I had decided to stay away during the activities. We arrived a little after 3:00 PM and were told the site was closed but would reopen at 3:30. The crews were still finishing cleaning up the mess left over from the Solstice crowd.

When we were allowed entrance, Sharon and I were overjoyed with the new Stonehenge experience. You now pull into a parking area about a mile and a half away from the stones where they have constructed a really nice information center, cafe, and shop. I was not expecting any of this.

We jumped on a shuttle (you no longer drive to the stones) and were soon being dropped off near the site. What a change! No shops, no kiosks, no parking area with cars and buses, and no road! It was all gone and replaced with earth and grasses. I was blown away. As we made the walk to the stones the setting was impressive to say the least. The landscape could have been what you would have seen thousands of years ago.

Another bonus to the new set up is that it seems as though they have moved the path closer to the stones at one point, improving on the overall experience. And, a plus for us was that we were in the first group to enter after the reopening so there were only about twenty people walking around the site. To think there had been up to 20,000 people here in the past twenty- four hours seemed unreal. This was more like it. Aside from the time Sharon and I actually walked among the stones with our small group, this was my favorite visit to Stonehenge.

It was a beautiful sunny day with white clouds and blue sky and though I had no personal experience with the stones this day there was an overall sense of contentment to the place that I have never felt there before. It was as if the stones felt appreciated and were beginning to awaken. I left Stonehenge quite happy, with hopes that I might one day return to see if I can finally make a real connect with these stones.

What a fantastic day! The sky was clear, no winds, and no need of a coat. Sharon and I were on our own today and the first point of interest that we were in search of was the Minchinhampton Long Stone which was, appropriately, located near Minchinhampton. Finding it was a bit tricky. The directions I had from one of the websites proved to be inaccurate. When I asked a local for directions she was not sure but said she thought we were on the wrong side of the village and pointed in the direction she thought I should go. As I drove through the town I stopped to ask another fellow and he pointed me in yet another direction. He did say however, that he was not sure and suggested I stop at the postoffice/store in the middle of town, as the lady who worked there grew up in the area and would surely know. This proved to be good advice.

When I walked into the store and was greeted by a kind woman behind the counter, I asked her if she knew where I might find the Minchinhampton Stone? She smiled at me and proclaimed, "Certainly, that was my grannies place!" She gave me accurate directions and soon we were parked in a small lay by along a country road.

The stone sits in an enclosed area just off the road. It really is a grand old stone, close to eight feet tall, maybe six foot wide, and about a foot and a half thick. I could sense something magical about it as we approached, almost as though it was pulling me into its spell. It looked like a larger version of one of the Rollright Stones with the same coloration and rough texture. It also had a similar gnarly shape with holes worn all the way through it, the largest being maybe the size of a football.

As we walked around the stone, examining it closely, I could see that Sharon, too, was being "charmed" by this most interesting stone. "Hello Old One" I said. I do not know why I referred to this stone in that way, but "Old One" is just what came to mind when I was trying to connect with it, and I said it with sincere respect. "Greetings" was the reply.

About this time a woman came walking into the enclosure and passed around to the other side of the stone. I could not help but notice that she stooped to place a small bouquet of flowers in one of the holes in the rock and then stood back as if in prayer. After a several minutes she walked back to the stone and stuck her hand through one of the larger holes holding it there for just a few moments.

Once she had done what she came for she said hello and we had a nice conversation with her. She had grown up in the area, moved away for a while, returned, and was now living just down the road from the Minchinhampton Stone. She walked past the stone going to and from town and often stopped for its blessing. She said it was a healing stone and that passing an injured part of your body through one of its holes could help with the healing process. I did not doubt her. She had a nice spirit and we enjoyed our visit with her.

After she walked away, I stood with a hand on the rock's surface and felt a subtle surge of energy. I felt the stone's presence but knew it would take more visits before it would open to me as it obviously had done to the woman who had just left.

In search of our next stop we traveled north of Cheltenham on the B4632. Just before Winchcombe we turned off on a narrow country lane and drove about a mile and a half to a designated parking area for the Belas Knap Long Barrow. From the parking area the long barrow is another mile and a half hike up a fairly steep hillside, part in a dense wood and part in open fields.

Belas Knap is quite different from other long barrows I have visited, both in construction and in location. Rather than sitting out on a ridge top where it could be seen from long distances, Belas Knap sits in a more concealed location. Though it is still up high on a ridge you do not see it until you have arrived, and then you cannot help but be awed by its presence and unique construction. Unlike at West Kennet, where you enter the large burial chamber area from the front and through an obvious courtyard and doorway, here, though you have a rather wonderfully constructed courtyard, what appears to be the front entrance seems to have been a decoy. The appearance is all correct, with two upright pillar stones on the sides of the entry, a lintel over the top, and a solid slab covering the doorway. However, when excavated, there was no chamber to speak of. Instead, here at Belas Knap, you find a number of smaller chambers dug into the sides of the mound. They originally would have been covered over with dirt and easy to miss by grave diggers. There is one small chamber on the west side and there are two on the east side. These side chambers are wonderfully constructed and I spent time in each. Nothing out of the ordinary happened while I was visiting these chambers, though I did feel a real sadness that the people who had been so respectfully buried here had had their remains disturbed or destroyed. But that said, there was an overall good vibe to this site that was quite comforting.

There is also, what may have been, another chamber at the south end where quite a notch has been dug into the mound.

The long barrow is about 190 feet long and is oriented in a north/south direction. The front of the mound is at the north end, and is about 60 feet wide, 13 feet high, and shaped sort of like a crescent moon (a Goddess representation perhaps), or like a bull's horns (could represent the God). Looking at a photograph taken from above one can easily see how actually, this long barrow really does have the appearance of the female anatomy with the front entryway being the entrance into the womb.

Belas Knap is a unique and really wonderful place on many levels and along with the amazing views it is well worth the hike.

Speaking of the hike, I was very surprised to encounter 12 or 13 people in ones and twos making the same trek. Lucky for us only one arrived at the long barrow while we were there.

After a fun visit to Sudley Castle we went on to the Rollright Stone Circle. I had not been to this site since my first stone journey back in 2009 and I was excited to be returning. When we arrived there were two adults with their two small children enjoying the circle. One boy kept climbing all over the stones and while I was happy to see him having fun with these gnarly old rocks, the owner of this site has posted a sign asking that there be no climbing on the stones. These rocks are made of a soft oolitic limestone and do appear to be fragile, so I could understand the concern. But more than that, the land owners have been allowing visits to these stones for years and we should respect their wishes.

Sharon and I wandered the stones separately. This is a compact circle, 104 feet in diameter, and about as perfect dimensionally as a circle can get. Its stones were often placed quite close together, almost like a stone wall. They are very rough and oddly shaped, and most are not much more than three feet tall.

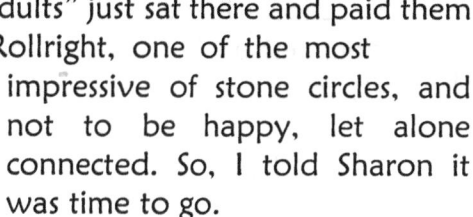

I must say I was a little surprised that I did not get the strong connect I had experienced last time I was here. I did feel welcomed but the energy level was barely noticeable, with no strong pulls from any of the stones. Actually, the stones felt tired. Could it be a result of the Solstice celebrations a few nights before? I saw lots of ribbons and dry flowers lying on the rocks here and there and the Rollright Stones do attract large crowds for the Solstices. There was kids climbing on these fragile "old timers" while the "adults" just sat there and paid them no mind. Whatever the case, it was sad to be at Rollright, one of the most impressive of stone circles, and not to be happy, let alone connected. So, I told Sharon it was time to go.

Sharon and I then walked down to the Whispering Knights which could be seen off to the east about a half of a mile. There you find five large stones kind of piled together, the remains of a dolman I think. As on my previous visit, I was bummed by the metal fence enclosure which surrounds them. We did spend some time there just relaxing on a bench nearby and enjoying the evening. At one point I got up and walked over to the stones. One of the stones seemed to be calling me and as I moved closer to it I was surprised to see that this stone did, in fact, look like a knight! I had never noticed this before. This knight seemed to be looking across the distance towards the Rollright Circle. I could feel a strength in this stone and realized it was not only aware, it was actively doing all it could to serve as a protector of these stones. I know, you might ask, how can a stone

Stone Journals

do anything at all, let alone actively protect something? By whispering. By speaking softly to the hearts of those who come to the stones. By encouraging them to be respectful and letting them think it is their own idea. Is he not, after all, a Whispering Knight?

Feeling much better about everything, and knowing the stones were protected, we crossed the road and stopped at the eight foot tall King Stone which is, like the Whispering Knights, caged by the same metal fencing. I could not make any kind of connection with this stone and decided to call it a day.

Now, this was another great stones day. We started out with a visit to Stanton Drew. I had been disappointed with myself the last time I visited this site as I had let the weather get to me and had left before visiting all the stones. Today was a lovely day and we would be in no big hurry. Arriving at the small parking area I was surprised to find it full, so we went on to park by the Cove, which I had missed last time around.

The Cove consists of three large stones. Two are standing and facing each other, one being about 10 feet tall and the other closer to 12. The third, of similar size, lies fallen between them, but when standing they would have created a U shape. The Cove is located behind the Druids Arms Pub in a garden area with picnic tables and a rabbit hutch. There is a large tree that has grown quite close to the stones, and while I normally enjoy the interaction of tree and stone, in this case I wished the tree was not quite so close. The stones felt a bit crowded, but all the same, they seemed content and I was happy to finally meet them.

Standing there, opening to the rocks, the smaller of the standing stones seemed quiet, rather than unresponsive. The larger of the standing stones however soon made me feel welcome. This stone was shaped sort of like a flattened horse head. Facing it "head on" I placed my hands on each of side the head, caressing it, and put my forehead against it. I was intrigued by the presence of this stone. The energy was there but it was deep and I doubted I had the time needed to make a connection. We had much yet to see and we needed to be in Bath in the afternoon to meet up with family. So, saying my thanks to this interesting rock trio, we went to the Druids Arms for morning tea before going on to the circle stones.

What a wonderful feeling to be back at Stanton Drew on such a beautiful day. Nothing like my last visit, with those extreme, cold winds. Along with the Cove, this site has three stone circles which were constructed in a southwest/northeast alignment, the largest in the center. There are also the remains of several stone avenues. It really is one of the best of the stone sites.

Though there were a lot more people visiting the circles this time around, they were well spaced and did not impact us all that much.

I led Sharon around the Great Circle (which is 370 feet in diameter) to give her an idea of its size and to introduce her to the stones. So many of the stones have fallen over the years and are being absorbed back into the earth. When you stand looking at the circle from a distance, you really only notice a few standing stones here and there, but as you walk the perimeter you realize just how many stones are still present. There are, in fact, still 26 visible stones, though some just barely. I think only four remain standing. I continue to be puzzled by the lack of interest in standing these fallen megaliths back up in place. How impressive it would be.

We then followed the remains of an old avenue over to the Northeast Circle. It is much smaller in size, about 100 feet in diameter, but its stones are quite large, all eight are still in place, and half are still standing. This is a "Look at me" kind of circle.

After spending some time in the Northeast Circle we walked the avenue of stones going off to the east, and I talked with Sharon about my experience there during my last visit. It had quite an impact on me. This time around I was getting nothing special. Quite a few people were beginning to gather around these stones and I think maybe I was

Stone Journals

getting distracted. It was not affecting my ability to enjoy being back at Stanton Drew however and for that I was thankful.

Next we walked to the Southwest Circle which you cannot see from the Great, or Northeast, circles. It is located in another field, up on a rise, and is separated from the other two circles by a couple of hedges and fences. Having missed the Southwest Circle on my last trip I was looking forward to this. As we entered the field in which the circle sits, at first we almost didn't see it, as the thistles, grasses, and other weeds had overgrown the site. Over the years, the stones have all fallen, and are being absorbed back into the earth. Thankfully, someone had cleared around some of the stones making them easily accessible.

The thing is these stones, though fallen and neglected, were a pleasant surprise. This circle is actually larger than the Northeast Circle, being about 140 feet in diameter. Its stones however, appear to be much smaller than those of the other two circles. I found 12 stones in the circle though several had obviously been moved over the years. As I walked from stone to stone, most were giving me a strong welcome, and when touched, a mild surge of energy. When I reached the west stone I sat on the rock and immediately felt a warm embrace as my feet began sinking into the earth. Yes! I had been hoping for this to happen and I gladly sat there absorbing the energies the earth gave so freely. Once fully charged I thanked the stone and continued my walk.

Moving south, the next stone I came to was quite overgrown with thistles and yet I could feel its welcome. Looking closer I noticed it had that same ultra-polished effect that I had seen on the stones at the Twelve Apostles Stone Circle near Dumfries a number of years back. This is only the second time I have come across this and I don't know what causes it. I guess it could have been sheep but I have my doubts.

The last couple of stones I encountered made me welcome with fairly strong surges of that, "relax and stay for a while" kind of energy. This was great fun for me and most unexpected. Sharon had been sitting on the north stone watching me as I made my way around the circle. As I walked up to her she smiled and commented on what a peaceful place it was. In the hour or so we were there no one else bothered to visit this neglected, small circle of stones. Though Stanton Drew had drawn a good crowd, the people were all visiting the Great Circle and the Northeast Circle, and missing the joy to be found just to the southwest. This was to be my last visit to a stone site before going on to Scotland. I was so glad I had made the effort to return to Stanton Drew and to meet the stones of the Cove and the Southwest Circle.

On June 30th Galadriel had joined Sharon and I for a week in Scotland while the rest of her clan headed home. We started with a few days in Edinburgh and decide to take Galadriel out to Rosslyn Chapel. It really is a must see and upon arriving we were so happy we had made the decision to do so, as they were actually done with the face lift. Finally we could see Rosslyn in its full glory. No scaffolding!

We then went to Dumfries to spend some time with Sharon's cousins, the Kirkpatrick's. While there we took Galadriel to see several of our favorite sites in the area. These included the Gem Rock Museum, Cairnholy I & II, and of course the Glenquicken Stone Circle.

Upon arrival at Glenquicken I was saddened by how overgrown the circle was this time around. Some of the circle stones were almost completely covered with grasses and thistles. Nonetheless, I could sense the welcome of the 29 small, rounded circle stones, as well as that of the impressive tall center stone, and I was happy to be there. This was not a time for me to attempt to get close to the stones. With everyone else there, it was enough to just share in the stones' company. Still, though the others did not realize it, they too were being affected by this marvelous old circle of rocks. We had a wonderful time walking among the stones and had many a laugh, especially when Sharon tried, unsuccessfully, to show us the face she saw in the large center stone. The magic of Glenquiken is alive and well, and if I am ever able to return to this part of Scotland again, I will also return to visit this grand old circle. The energy of the stones pulsed just under the surface and I could feel them smiling as the four of us trekked back through the tall grasses, still bubbling with the joy of having been in the company of stones.

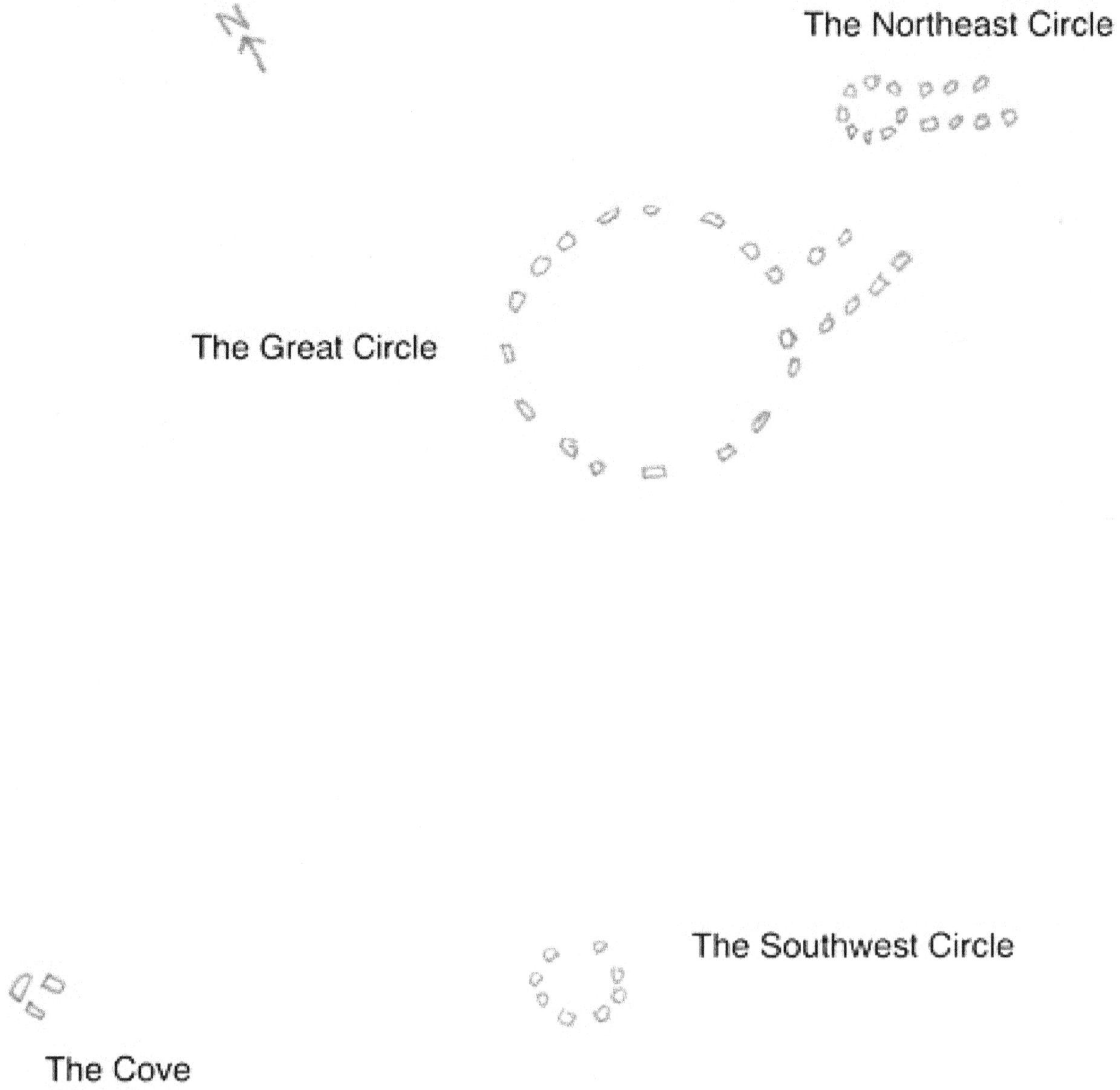

N

The Northeast Circle

The Great Circle

The Southwest Circle

The Cove

Stanton Drew Stone Circles

Though this is not drawn exactly to scale it does fairly accurately represent the site.

"It is not possible to comprehend the purpose or meaning of the megalithic monuments without understanding something of the sacred nature of the landscape."
Jack Roberts
The Sun Circles Of Ireland

Stone Journey 8

IRELAND, NORTHERN IRELAND

STONE JOURNEY 8 - June 3, 2016

After the usual exhausting journey, (three hour ride to the San Francisco airport, three hours check-in and wait, 11 hour flight to Dublin, customs followed by a one hour queue for our rental car, and then a 40 minute drive) Sharon and I arrived at the Maudlins Hotel in Naas, Ireland. It was around 2:30 in the afternoon, we were tired, and I had been feeling kind of funky since just before the plane had landed. Regardless, after getting settled in we decided to head out and see if we could find a couple of standing longstones located near the Punchestown horserace track. It did not appear to be far from where we were staying.

Though the directions I had seemed pretty easy we were having no luck, so I stopped into the raceway to get directions. The track was closed but I managed to find a couple gals who were working in the office, and when I told them I was looking for the two standing stones in the area they were happy to help. This was the first of what was to become a very common event, me stopping for directions and being rewarded with good information from the kindest of people.

As we were exiting the main entrance gate we were surprised to see a large megalith standing in a field directly across the road. When I had been driving along the road towards the racetrack I guess the stone had been blocked from view by a hedge, but from this angle, there it stood in a planted field, just upslope from the road. In *The Megalithic European* by Cope, he refers to this stone as the Racecourse Longstsone. Knowing now how easy this impressive megalith was to access, I decided to go find the other stone first.

Just a short way back up the road was another entrance gate used by the workers, horses, etc. The gate was locked but I could just see, over a wall and off in another field, the top of a tall stone. If you stand looking towards the gate, it is in the field to your left and very near the R411. It too had been blocked from view by the hedge that runs along this side of the road. I had to climb a stone wall, jump a thistle lined ditch, and climb a railed fence, but soon I was in the field and approaching the stone. I could tell from photos I had seen in *The Megalithic European* that this was the Punchestown Longstone.

The stone is narrow and pointed, kind of like an elongated finger pointing at the sky. It stands straight, is 23 feet tall, and is the tallest standing stone in Ireland. It is quite impressive. There is a low rail fence around it to protect it from animals and tractors, but this barrier is easy to climb and really did not bother me much. What immediately got my attention was the male energy flow emitted by the stone, strong and steady. Standing there with one hand on the rock I could feel the fatigue from the travel dissipating into the earth, and along with it, the stomach sickness I had been feeling for several hours. Soon I felt quite invigorated, and caressing the stone I said, "Thank you." What a way to start this journey to the stones of Ireland. I was a happy fellow.

Looking closely at this elongated megalith I saw large deposits of quartz throughout and assume that its presence had something to do with the strength of the strong energy flow, as quartz is, as I have said, an excellent conductor of energies. I also noticed that though the stone starts off being a rectangle at ground level it becomes a triangle near its top. Kind of cool.

Dowsing the site I found an energy line running right under the stone but as I had forgot my compass I was not sure of the direction. I also picked up a line running off in the direction of the Racecourse Stone, and so, with a nod and a smile to this magnificent menhir I decided to follow the line. It led me right back to where I had left Sharon with the car and continued on in the direction of the other stone. We drove back to the main entrance where I parked. I walked back up the road and crossed to the other side where I picked up what I was sure was the energy line coming from the Punchestown Stone. I followed it over a fence, into a field, and up the slope towards the Racecourse Stone. Luckily there was a tractor track running through the crop that went up towards the stone so I didn't have to worry too much about damaging plants. With just a little line-of-sight checking, I was able to once again pick up the energy line coming from the Punchestown Stone. It ran right to, and then passed under, this lone sentinel before continuing on.

Leaning at an angle, and not quite as tall as the Punchestown Stone, this also was a dramatic, finger shaped rock. The Racecourse Stone too, flowed with a warm energy, though it was subdued compared to its neighbor. I enjoyed its company for a short time and then returned to the car quite content. As I got back into the car Sharon commented on how much better I looked. Thank you Longstones!

We decided to finish our rather long day with a visit to St Brigid's Well. This shrine to the saint, who was originally a Celtic Goddess, and for whom I have a strong affinity, is located just off the R415, south of Kildare. It is a beautiful and peaceful place located out in the countryside. The site is rectangle shaped with fence and trees lining its sides, and it is carpeted with green grass. From the wellhead the water runs underground for maybe 20 yards before surfacing again to form a creek, and it is there you find a lovely statue of Brigid holding her flame. It really is a very comforting place and was a great way to end our first day in Ireland.

6/4

What a day this turned out to be! We went off in search of three stone circles, all located on, or just off, the N81, south of Naas. First up was the Broadleas Stone Circle. At one point we had to stop at a post/grocer for directions, but as usual, a kind lady walked me out to the street and pointed the way. Her directions, of course, included a couple of pubs, a church, a junction, and a left at a fork. No road names or numbers. Still, we were soon parked and climbing over a gate into the field in which we could see the stones. The circle sat up on a low knoll and appeared to have some trees growing around its edges. There was another couple already there when we arrived and as they seemed to be interacting with the stones we stayed on the fringe of the circle until they finished up. Then, with a quick hello they went on their way.

After having spent a little time walking among the stones I decided to dowse the circle, which is actually more of an oval 105 feet by 92 feet, and I soon found an energy line running north/south across the ring and under the two corresponding stones. As I walked around the circle I was being charmed by these stones, which were, in fact, more what I would call large granite boulders. There was a real sense of contentment here. I also noticed that many of the stones had large amounts of quartz in them, even more than I had found in the Longstones.

The stones of the circle, and there are 27 of them still standing, along with several others that have fallen over, had in most cases been placed right up next to each other, not unlike kerb stones, creating kind of a wall effect. In several places the trees had grown up among the stones and seemed to infold and even caress them in the most comforting way. In the case of the south stone however, a tree had grown right up through the rock, cracking it in two. Also of interest I noticed that the stone circle had been built around, and right up against, a raised earth platform. The ground level inside the circle of stones was definitely higher than outside. I do not know that I have seen this before but it is a really fun effect.

As I walked the circle I was reminded of Sharon's experience at the Stones of Stenness, noticing that the north and the south stones were about the smallest stones in the circle and yet it is through them that the energy line runs.

The only real experience I had at Broadleas was a calming flow I received when I placed my hand on the stone just east of the south stone. It was full of quartz and emitted a steady and soothing energy.

Sharon, on the other hand, had one of her rare "wake up call" type experiences. As she walked the circle she heard, "If you are always looking where you're stepping you will never see where you are going." This just frustrated her and she called out, "Tell me something I don't know!" The reply was, "Where are you?"

Now this may seem a little odd to you but it is right-on for Sharon. She has a problem experiencing the moment, and a fear of tripping, so she is often looking at the ground, and misses much of what is going on around her. This simple little message had a profound effect on her for the entire remainder of our trip. She really took it to heart and every now and then I would hear her say to herself, "Where are you?"

There was something very different about Broadleas. The placement of the boulder type stones with the raised interior, and the intriguing trees growing up among the stones, provided a most wonderful and comforting experience. To sit on a rock was to feel the peace of the stones. This circle was up there with my favorites.

Next up was to be the Athgreany Stone Circle, or The Pipers Stones as the locals call it. Though I was pretty sure we were going the right way I stopped at a small garden supply center to ask directions. The fellow laughed and said, "Have ye not seen the giant sign yet?" He then told me the circle was not far down the road on the left but to keep our eyes open as the sign was quite small.

We were soon parked and walking through another field. This circle sits up on high ground and you do not see it until you crest the knoll on which it sits. Athgreany is now missing some stones, has a thorn tree growing up along the edge, and is in a bit of disrepair. It remains impressive nonetheless, and I am sure that in its hay-day The Pipers Stones would have had quite an impact on those who approached it at a time of ritual. Great location with great views.

I was very pleased to see that this circle too, was made up of large granite boulder stones rather than the angular, squared off, somewhat sculpted stones that are common in many of the places I have visited elsewhere. There are 14 of these rocks placed in a near perfect circle about 75 feet across, and they are from around three to six feet in height. Some of the stones stand upright while others are lying on the ground. Of those on the ground some kind of look like they were intentionally placed that way.

I was getting a real different vibe here in Ireland. It was extremely earthy and rooted and I must say, I was liking it. I was also liking this wonderful sunny weather. Two days in a row!

There was a large outlier stone off to the north so Sharon and I went there first. Right away we noticed that the stone, which is about six feet across, had two grooves carved across its top which were just like the cross pattern you would see carved in the top of a loaf of Irish soda bread. Interesting if nothing else. I also noticed that one of the cuts followed a vein of quartz. Was it easier to chisel along that line or did they want the quartz for a purpose? Piles of small quartz chunks, and of small quartz river rocks, have been found in ceremonial and burial areas all over the UK and Ireland. No idea why, unless of course, they were aware of quartz being an energy rock and were using them to energize the site or ritual.

Dowsing the outlier I found an energy line heading south towards the circle and as we followed it the line passed between two large stones, entrance stones maybe, and on into, and across this lovely ring of stones. Surprisingly, the couple we had seen at Broadleas was there, so I stopped to introduce us and to assure them that we were not following them. They were from Koln, Germany and this was their last day of a two week trip before going home again. They too, had been traveling Ireland in search of megalithic sites and had in fact visited quite a few. They were a nice couple who had a real love for, and concern for, the stones. They not only reveled in the energies of these sites, they gave their own energies back in an effort to heal those places which had been damaged or were struggling. I was very impressed with their concern and their enthusiasm.

On his iPad, Alex showed me aerial photos he'd had taken of many Irish circles using a drone he carried along with him. Great photos, and it was good fun to be able to see those circles from above. I have often wished I could soar above these sites to see them from that perspective. I did have one experience at The Loupin Stanes in

Scotland where I had a visualization of soaring above the site, and it was quite powerful and fun, but I don't know if that counts. This technology allows him to do it. It also allows him to use the drone to find sites that he is having trouble finding on the ground. Way cool.

After they left, Sharon and I went back to exploring the circle. We soon found four more stones that had obvious markings carved into them. On one rounded boulder, shaped like a large head, was carved a groove in the shape of a huge smile, above which was carved a large cup mark. I told Sharon it looked like a smiling cyclops. Alex had told me that if you placed a staff in the cup at the right time of year it worked as a sundial to mark an event, or events, like solstices. I do not remember which events.

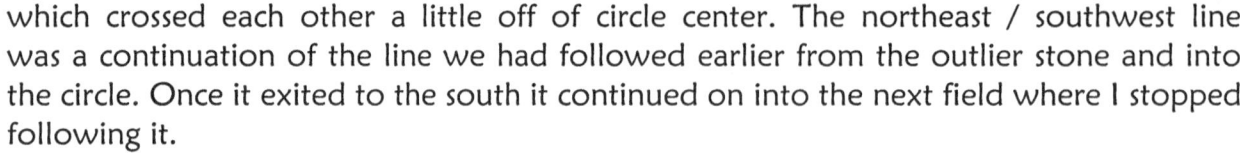

Carved in a line across the top of one of the entrance stones we found four narrow rectangular slots, maybe 2 inches deep, 3 inches long, and 8 inches apart. What was that about?

Dowsing the site I found energy lines running northeast/southwest and northwest/southeast which crossed each other a little off of circle center. The northeast / southwest line was a continuation of the line we had followed earlier from the outlier stone and into the circle. Once it exited to the south it continued on into the next field where I stopped following it.

It was a beautiful sunny day and I was quite content. Ireland was being very good to us. Deciding it was time to go, we took off to find the third circle of the day, Castleruddery Stone Circle. For some reason this circle gets lots of praise for what it once was, but I found it to be a very sad place that was home to lots of sheep. It is 100 feet in diameter but has been poorly treated over the years. Though about 40 stones remain, many stones are missing, fallen, or have been moved. There is a four foot high earth berm around the outside which makes more of a circle than do the stones. Really, the only neat things about this place were the two large quartz entry stones on the northeast side. One stone is 10 feet long, by four feet wide, by four feet high. Its partner is nine feet long, by six feet wide, by four feet high. Even in this place of chaos they sat proud and strong. I noticed that in one of these massive quartz blocks there was a pocket of gold maybe three inches long and an inch wide. I am sure it was probably something like pyrite but it looked just like shinny gold.

There are a number of stones lying on the ground outside the entrance that Burl says in his *Guide To The Stone Circles Of Britain, Ireland, and Brittany*, were originally part of an avenue. I did not pick up on any of that. I did find an energy line passing into the circle between the quartz entry stones which continued across the circle. I also found one

other energy line but I forgot to note the directions of either line. They crossed in the center at a point marked by a small stone that was disappearing into the earth. Was it original to the circle? I do not know.

Needless to say we were quite surprised when we were joined at the circle by the German couple. Alex immediately got out his drone and put it in the air. I must say it was very annoying, like a giant mosquito flying around above us. Though he did not have it in the air for long I did not dig it, and Sharon was getting upset. Time for us to go. We left them to do what healing they could to this sad place.

6/5
Today we left for Waterford stopping in route to see the Brown's Hill Dolmen located just outside Carlow on the R726. One word. Impressive!

Parking, we looked over a stone wall and off in the distance, sitting alone in a vast field of grain, you could see the massive capstone of the dolmen. You follow a lovely treelined walkway around the outside of the field until you draw even with it. At that point the pathway crosses through the crop to the

stone giant. I have visited a number of dolmens, but none more impressive. And, while the dolmen overall is in good shape it is the capstone that demands your attention. It is said to be the largest in Europe and weighs a guesstimated 100 tons. Surrounded by a brilliant field of green, the location of this megalithic structure could not be more comforting. Though originally it would surely have sat out in open uncultivated terrain, I found this grain field to be a most calming, peaceful, and respectful place.

I did find a north/south energy line running under the dolmen disappearing into the fields on each side. I do not always find energies at burial sites which puzzles me.

6/8

After having settled in at the pleasant Hotel Isaacs in Cork, today we were on our way to Skibbereen to meet up with Finola and Robert, who have a blog called Roaringwater Journal. I just happened across their site while surfing the internet, planning our Ireland trip. They do a wonderful job of presenting Ireland, especially the southwest, in the most charming way. If you read their blog and look at their photos, you cannot help but want to visit there.

In route to Skibbereen, we stopped at the Bohonagh Stone Circle, just off the N71, east of Rosscarbery. Finola had given me perfect directions and with no trouble at all we had parked, had crossed a couple electrical fences, and walked across a field to find the stones up on a rise. Approaching the circle we first came across a rather large boulder setting off to the west. In fact, it is a "boulder burial site," or boulder dolmen, where you have a large stone (often boulder shaped) sitting up off the ground on several much smaller stones. These sites are found all over this part of Ireland. Whether they are actually burial sites is, I think, still up for debate.

The circle, which was maybe 30 feet across, was quite overgrown with weeds but the stones stood out clearly. In short order I had found in the east a large recumbent stone and to the west two nice sized (about seven feet tall) lateral standing, entry, or portal stones. This is one of the cool things about these Irish circles. The portal stones often are placed laterally, or even diagonally, in the ring to better mark the entrance so there is no mistaking it. I have not seen this arrangement elsewhere. Also of note is the placement of the recumbent stone in relationship to its flankers. Whereas in Scotland the flankers are usually taller and placed right up alongside the recumbent, here the flankers can be of any size and there is usually a good gap between them and the recumbent. The important thing here seems to be in the relationship between the recumbent and the portal stones on the opposite side of the circle. At Bohonagh, the alignment is such that on certain dates the sun would either rise over the recumbent and shine across and through the portals to the west, or the sun would set to the west between the portals when viewed across the recumbent.

The location of this circle is quite wonderful. You have grand views in all directions, looking out over the southern coast of Ireland and to the sea beyond. Dowsing the site I first found an energy line in the west which entered the circle through the portals, then went into the center where it circled once before going to ground. I had experienced this once before at Swinside Circle in England. From the east side of the circle I picked up another line crossing under the recumbent and then going straight across the circle and out to the west passing right over where the other line had gone to ground. I was a little confused by this and still do not understand it.

Next, I found small quartz blocks buried in the weeds several feet outside of both the north and the south stones and I found an energy line running under, and connecting, all four of these stones. Did the quartz blocks amplify the energy of this north/south line maybe?

Also of interest, one of the tall circle stones over on the south side of the ring has large inclusions of quartz in it and there is a big block of quartz stuck under it on one side to prop it up. Lots of quartz in this circle. Maybe lots of power?

At one point, while standing between the portal stones with a hand on each, I was looking across the sea to the west when I had a momentary vision of someone long ago standing in that same place, also looking across the sea, and watching the sun set. I suddenly felt the power there, flowing up through me, out my arms, and around the circle to the recumbent stone where it returned to the earth. Then, there was a shift in the energy flow, and some of the energy did not go to ground but instead continued circling all the way around the circle, back through me, and round and round. It was an exhilarating moment. One I shall never forget.

When we walked back to the car I could "feel" the earth under my feet. The energy was strong here and I was liking it.

Continuing west on the N71 we soon saw the Burgatia Stone standing out in a field on the sea side of the road. We parked and walked a short distance just inside the fence line before crossing into the field and to the stone. This is a really fun rock. It stands six and a half feet tall, is maybe five feet wide, and I did find an east/west energy line running under the stone. It has a human face in its southwest side which appears to be gazing across the sea towards sunset. It also has some basic rock art on the northwest side that has, sadly, been affected by weathering over the years and much of what is there is now very hard to see.

We met up with Finola and Robert in Skibbereen as planned and found them to be a most pleasant pair. They said they would like to show us a few of the local sites so off we went. They began by taking us to Castletownsend, a charming little village, with castle, located right on the sea. Up on the hill sits the Church of St. Barrahane. We went inside to see some stained glass windows done by Harry Clarke, a true master. I have seen a lot of stained glass in my travels, and in some of the most famous religious structures, but I have never seen work more wondrous than these windows in this little known church on the Cork Coast. We were so thankful to have had the chance to have this experience.

Next up was Knockdrum Stone Fort. Located higher up on the hills this is a Bronze Age circular stone fort and I really don't know much more about it. I did read that it is 95 feet in diameter and that the stone walls were almost 10 feet thick and about six and a half feet high. A few of the stones had some basic rock art carved in them including one with a cross. Overall this is a really great spot, but the prize here goes to the views over the Cork Coastline. With a cup of hot tea in hand, one could sit there for hours.

Last of all, we went to the next ridge over to see The Fingers (or Gurranes) Stone Row, an alignment of three standing stones which do, in fact, look like long fingers protruding from the earth. The longest of the fingers is about 15 feet tall. There is also a fourth finger, and maybe a fifth, lying on the ground, fallen or broken off in time gone by. They are located right on the edge of a very high and flattened ridge, with wonderful views far off into the distance. How mysterious, and maybe even intimidating it would have looked with all its fingers in place. Especially with a mist all around.

I did check and the alignment was in a northeast/southwest direction. Because I was with friends, and new ones at that, I did not bring my rods nor did I spend any time trying to get acquainted what the stones. I was sorry about that, but I was also quite happy and thankful that we had been brought to this wonderful place. I hope I can return to this spot again to see just what I might experience there. Finola and Robert had been wonderful hosts and we will always be in their debt.

Starting back for Cork, we decided to stop at the Drombeg Stone Circle. This is probably the most famous stone site in the south of Ireland and arriving at the circle it soon became apparent why. It is in perfect condition, the location is spectacular, and the overall site is a wonder. Though I had no special interaction with these stones, they reminded me of Avebury. Not in physical size or shape of course, but in the sense that something was going on there, and I just needed enough time to tap into it.

When we first arrived we were lucky enough to have the site to ourselves and we took full advantage of the time. The near perfect circle is only 31 feet in diameter but seems larger. There are 17 stones in this circle including recumbent and portal stones, and the tallest is around seven feet in height. I was also struck by the shapes of the stones. Unlike the circles we had visited further north and east, this circle, and Bohonagh as well, was made up of rougher, squarer, taller stones, more like what I am used to. A cool thing here is that several of the stones, including the recumbent, were cut smoothly off at the top as if done by some modern cutting tool.

I quickly set about dowsing the circle and once again found some really interesting energy lines. I had thought that Bohonagh was fun but this circle really brought a smile. When I followed a line into the circle from between the east portal stones, it wound part way around the inside of the circle stones to the left and then went into the center where it looped around and went to ground at a small stone marker in the circle center. Coming at it from the west, I followed a line from outside the circle which passed under the recumbent stone and then repeated a similar pattern to the line from the east. The difference was only that this line stayed closer to the center as it circled left, but it too went to ground at the stone marker. About this time people began arriving in small groups of two, to four, and that continued for the rest of our stay. I did, however, finish dowsing the circle and found a strong line running right across the circle under the north and south stones. I also followed the east line away from the circle for quite a ways before deciding to give it up and call it a day.

There was another really unique thing about Drombeg. The builders of the circle also seem to have planned to provide for the people who would be involved in, or attending, the rituals that must have been held at this site. A little to the west there are the remains of shelters for housing people and there is also something else quite special. A rocked in area had been built around the spot where a spring surfaced, creating a cooking area. In the center they had built a large, rock lined pit which could be filled with water. Next to it was a fire pit which was used to heat stones which were then thrown into the water filled pit. Tests were done which showed that by filling the water pit with hot rocks it would have taken only 18 minutes to bring the water to a boil to then cook meat, vegetables, whatever. Pretty amazing! So, the question is, was this set up to take care of travelers coming for ritual, or was it maybe for the druids (I am using this term quite loosely) who ran the place?

One more point of interest. The location of this circle is a shelf, which had been carved into the slope to create this flat platform on which to build. The implication is that this was the spot on which the circle needed to sit. It was not chance or haphazard in any way. It was thought out, planned, and executed. In fact, Drombeg is one of the finest examples there is of stone placement for ritual purposes. When the sun rises on Winter Solstice, if you stand on the far side of the circle you see it come up out of the ocean between two stones and right in line with a small stone on the opposite side of the circle. Then, when it comes time for sunset, the sun drops down behind the hills in line with the recumbent stone, and right in line with the entrance between the portal

stones, thus creating a long shadow from the recumbent right to the base of the entrance stones. This was well planned and required a smooth earth surface, perfectly placed stones, and an angled flat surface on the recumbent stone which would create just the right shadow effect. It really is quite amazing.

Continuing to Cork I had one last stop in mind. Just off the N71, and on the edge of a small village called Shannonvalle, is the Templebryan Stone Circle. It seemed like it should not be too hard to find so we took a chance, and I am so glad we did. The circle sits in a field just behind a plant and tree covered, long, narrow, earth mound, which serves as a wall separating the field from the road. If you are not looking close it is easy to miss the stones.

Once we did find it, and had parked our car up the road a ways, I was having trouble finding an entry through the overgrown wall and into the field. A nice lady pulled up in her car and asked us if we were looking for the stone circle? I had a chuckle and then said that yes we were, in fact, trying to get into the field to visit the stones. She said to follow her and she started off slowly down the road. After just a short way she stopped and pointed to a break in the barrier. Then, with a joyful smile, she said to have fun and off she went. I love these Irish.

I had been told Templebryan was in a state of disrepair but when Sharon and I arrived we found it to be a wonderful circle, 31 feet in diameter, with four good sized stones standing in place and one fallen over. The tallest stone was about six and a half feet tall. I felt drawn to this circle the minute I saw it and as we approached, I sensed an earthy rumble under my feet, a welcome. It was overgrown with grasses and wildflowers but nothing like at Bohonagh. All the stones were flat topped, like some of those at Drombeg, but most dramatic were the two bulky stones in the southwest.

The one that was the shorter and wider of the two was the circle's recumbent. I found both stones quite jovial and they made me want to laugh.

At Drombeg I had found a marker in the center where maybe a stone once stood, but this circle actually had a small quartz center stone. I walked over and sat on it and immediately felt the stresses of a long day flowing out my feet and into the earth. Where I had begun the day with an infusion of energy at Bohonagh, now I was being relaxed. This was one of those "Let's just curl up with the stones and go to sleep" moments. But of course, that wasn't going to happen.

Making myself get up off the stone, I got a dowsing rod and went to work. As always seems to be the case here in Ireland, the results were surprising and fun and I found myself smiling as I followed where the rod led me. The line I followed into the circle from the south passed between the two big flattops, circled half way around the west side and into the center where it then did a tight loop before it exited out to the north. The line that entered from the east, arched around the south side and exited to the west. The line from the west, arched around the north side and exited to the east. Though I cannot explain what this means, or why this happens, I just enjoy knowing the earth is alive with energies and that I am aware of their presence.

I really did love these stones and I thanked them for sharing with us. Since arriving in Ireland I continue to be surprised at just how strongly I feel the connection with the earth. Something special is happening and I hope it continues.

6/9
We were off to Blarney Castle today. What a joyful place this turned out to be. The castle is good fun (though we did not kiss the Blarney Stone) but it is the gardens surrounding it that really impressed us. Whoever planed the gardens did a great job of incorporating a more wild and natural garden, with a taste of history and fantasy, mixed with old Irish traditions and stories. It really brings out the spirit of the child, and by that I mean the willingness to believe in possibilities.

I was originally told about this garden by the author, Herbie Brennan. Though I did not know him, I had read in *Astral Doorways*, about an experience he had at a longstone near Naas, and wondered if it was a stone I had seen written about in another book. I emailed him my question and he kindly responded with a confirmation that it was the same stone. He then suggested, as I was interested in stone circles, I should check out the stone circle at Blarney Castle. He said, "The stones are not prehistoric, but whoever erected them knew what he was doing, because the energy in the area is quite palpable." I am most grateful for this tip as it led Sharon and I on a most wonderful journey through the gardens of Blarney.

Upon entering the castle grounds we began walking through the garden and soon found ourselves approaching the Seven Sisters Stone Circle, and it was indeed quite special. The stones are some of the most beautiful I have seen in both shape and composition. They were tall and dramatic and seemed to shine with a light. While we were at the circle we saw many other people walk up to the stones and all were smiling. It was interesting because I have watched people at many stone sites over the

years and most just take a look and move on. Here at the Seven Sisters, everyone seemed to be uplifted and would take the time to stand with, and touch, the stones. The energies Herbie referred to were at work and the visitors to this circle left happier than when they arrived. On a scale of 1 to 10, definitely a 10.

From the circle we wandered throughout the garden visiting a witches' kitchen, a dolmen, a druids cave, a fairy glade, the witches' stone, the druids stones, the wishing steps, and several waterfalls. And then there was the castle! I would love to take my grandchildren to Blarney. What a wonderful and magical place.

Stone Journals

6/10

After breakfast at the Tara Tea Room (just a few doors down from Hotel Isaacs in Cork), which I highly recommend, we began our journey to Kenmare. In route I planned to attempt finding at least two stone circles. Our luck so far had been quite amazing. There had only been one site that we had failed to find, making us twelve for thirteen. And then there was the weather which had been stunning! I am just not used to this many nice days in a row in this part of the world.

Just west of Macroom we had taken the R582 to the north. Before entering Carriganima we turned up a small road to the right and after a little drive we saw a sign posting, "Archaeological Site." We had arrived at the Knockraheen Stone Circle location.

Passing through a gate into a field I could see in the distance a large block of white quartz standing in the grass. As I approached it I saw another rather flat slab of bright white quartz standing alongside the big block, and both, though very different in shape, stood about three and a half feet tall. Looking past the two white stones, further to the north I could see the stone circle and realized that the circle and the stones were in an alignment which ran southwest/northeast.

Placing a hand on this large wonder, the stone felt really smooth and pulsed with a subtle, but strong, energy. I began feeling warmth flowing from the stone as I sensed I was welcome. I could feel a real pride coming from these stones and I got the impression that they were once part of a larger complex of stone monuments, and that this area had been a very holy place. I was encouraged to explore further.

A little to the south there was a lone stone that was obviously not part of the alignment. It was small and rounded with a cup mark on top. Though I could not see how it was connected to the others, it felt as though it was.

Sharon joined me and we walked on to the stone circle which we found was overgrown by grasses. It was small in size (12 to 13 feet across) but full of energy, and it seemed so happy to see us. Once again I was laughing as I passed through the entrance and crossed over to the recumbent. I felt the energy bubbling up from the ground, massaging my feet with each step. There was much more to this circle than met the eye. Closing my eyes, I was suddenly alone in the circle, dressed in a white robe, and the air seemed to vibrate with a sound, soothing yet joyful. I realized it was the stones welcoming me and I thanked them. When I opened my eyes the sound stopped, but my body continued to vibrate. I was feeling the power and joy of Knockraheen!

There are five rather rough and natural looking stones in the circle and none of them are very big. The recumbent is long and low being only about two feet high. The largest are the two portal stones and I don't think they are much over three feet tall. They are, however, set up at angles to accentuate the entry to the circle. I was

really enjoying this Irish approach to the portal stones that I was finding at many of the circles.

Going back to stand in the entrance and looking south, I could see right over the top of the recumbent to the two bright white row stones, all in a perfect alignment. This was, once again, well thought out and I wish I knew what the purpose was.

Dowsing the site I did find an energy line flowing south through the portals, across the circle, and on past the recumbent towards the quartz row. Turning, I then followed the line north out of the circle. It immediately swung towards the west before then arching back to the east. I continued on across the field until the line turned back north where it came to a rock wall. Looking across the wall I could see the remains of a cairn in the distance. I decided to return to the circle and from there, looking northeast, I could see the top of the cairn maybe 150 yards away. This must have been part of the complex.

I then walked down to the quartz row. Standing on the south side of the row I looked towards the circle and could see, there beyond it, the top of the cairn. It too, was a part of this northeast/southwest alignment. This site just kept getting cooler.

It was time to dowse the quartz row stones, so starting about 10 feet south of the big block I picked up an energy line which led me towards the pair. As I approached, the line stayed about three feet to the left of the stone and started snaking back and forth in long, narrow, tight loops about two feet long until I was half way between the two quartz stones. It then crossed between the two and about three feet out it turned north and repeated the snake like pattern. A foot or so past the second stone the line straightened and headed towards the circle. I continue to be surprised by the energy lines I am discovering.

Leaving Knockraheen was not easy for me, even though it was sprinkling at the time. I had made a strong connection with these stones and I was really sorry to go. I doubt I will ever get to come back to these stones and that is a sad thing. As Sharon and I walked back to the car, I "heard" a strong call from the stones. Looking back at the quartz row and the circle beyond, I could feel, rather than see, that they were happy we had made the effort to find and visit them and that they too, were sad we were leaving.

Driving north of Carriganimmy (same town as earlier but I found three different spellings of this town) on the R582, we followed signs towards the Knocknakilla Stone Circle. The signing was pretty good. Along the way we came across the Glantane (or Glounthane) Stone Circle off to the left. Looking across the field we saw quite a few large cows and Sharon decided to wait in the car. The plus to the cows is that they had kept the grasses down to the point that all the stones were visible, not just the 12 foot tall megalith standing just outside the south side of the circle. Once at the site I found another of the tall megaliths fallen on the opposite side of the circle. Whether it

had been a part of the circle itself or another outlier I could not tell. But in any case, there most certainly would have been a north/south alignment of the two tall stones and the circle.

There are six circle stones still standing along with several that have fallen. All are small in size, none more than two feet high, and they are all very thin. The circle itself is also quite small being only 16 feet in diameter.

Dowsing the site I picked up a line south of the stones which I followed around the tall outlier, across the south circle stone (maybe a recumbent), and through the circle where it exited to the northeast. I really had no special experiences here but I must say I enjoyed this spot. I would love to have seen it before the stones fell over. I do not recall ever seeing or reading about a circle with two tall outliers on opposite sides of the circle like this. Was it just the "style" of the designer or was there a real purpose to the alignment?.

Another mile and a half up the hill we came to Knocknakilla Stone Circle, which is actually more complex than just a circle. This site is under state protection and is fenced in to protect the stones from animals.

These stones were erected on a small shelf on the rough, rocky, hillside of Musherabeg. There is a noticeable slope but I wondered if maybe the creators of this complex had not leveled it some. At the top of the site, to the southwest, is a unique shaped 12 and a half feet tall standing stone. It has three flat surfaces at the base which then rise to a point, reminding me of the Punchestown Stone. It has a large gouge out of one side which might be man-made. There is also a most interesting bowl carved out of one of the edges. Twelve feet to the northeast is another fallen menhir as big as its standing partner, but it lies horizontal to it on the surface and I am not sure where it originally stood.

Continuing northeast is the charming small stone circle, about nine feet across. Three of the five stones are still standing including the two portal stones which are four and a half feet tall. The recumbent has fallen over but looking through the portals and across the recumbent, the tall menhir stands right in alignment. Was this set up to mark a solstice or equinox? I don't know.

Stone Journals

Some 20 feet to the east of the circle is the remains of a small radial-cairn. Sharon spent some time sitting on a stone alongside this cairn, which just looked like a circle full of small stones, and she said it really was a very peaceful feeling place.

Deciding to try my luck dowsing I started at the top. I picked up an energy line going northeast around the tall outlier stone, continuing across the fallen stone and over the recumbent stone, through the circle, and out between the portals. It then took a turn further to the north and went down the hill about 100 yards before it passed between to rather large block boulders that I had noticed on the hike up. They had caught my attention not just because of their size and shape but because they did not look at all like the other rocks in the area. The line continued on but I had gone far enough. Standing there looking at these two large rocks I sensed that they were indeed important to the site. That maybe they had been the original entry point to this sacred place. I have seen no mention of them in other books or web sites so it is another mystery.

Returning to the fallen recumbent I lay down on it with my feet towards the opening between the portals and my head towards the tall outlier stone. Immediately upon laying flat I felt surges of relaxing energy flowing into my head and out my feet. It was like laying down in a shallow stream with your head into the current and feeling the water as it moves around you, only in this case it was moving through me. Just another wonderful experience with the stones of Ireland, and when we left Knocknakilla we did so thankful for having found it.

Arriving in Kenmare we checked into the Rockcrest House. We had a most wonderful room (Room 4) with a spectacular panoramic view of the hills in the distance. We were told that you used to be able to see the Kenmare Stone Circle out the window but the trees that have grown up over the years have blocked the view. As this is one of the circles I had on my "must see" list, a little later we took the walk to the circle, which is just a five minute walk from the center of the town.

The owners of this site have treated it like a park, with manicured grass, a wall of pine trees forming an enclosure around the circle, and a variety of garden plants at the entry. Now, some folks have been very negative about this treatment, preferring a more natural setting, and I get that. I too, would have loved to have seen it when the views of the surrounding country side and of the river, would have been part of the esthetic. But I found this near perfect circle to be happy and healthy and well treated. I was reminded of New Grange. It also looks nothing like it originally did, but if you let that go, it is a wonder.

When we arrived it was late evening and no one else was there. There is a small unoccupied kiosk at the entrance where they ask you to pay an admission fee, which we happily did. This is the largest ring in the Cork/Kerry group of stone circles. There are 15 good sized stones making up a circle that is 56 feet by 49 feet in diameter. In the center sits an impressive large round boulder burial capstone. Burl claims it weighs about seven tons and moving it into its position here would have been no easy task. This is a very fun and yet serious place and we enjoyed a short visit knowing we would return in the next couple of days to get better acquainted with these stones.

6/11

It had been beautiful weather so far but it was beginning to cloud over and threatening to rain. This is really the weather we had been expecting from the beginning, so it was all good. Our journey today took us out onto the Beara Peninsula, driving along the R571. Our first destination was the Uragh Stone Circle which we discovered was well signed and easy to find.

Uragh is a perfect example of a five stone circle, complete with a large outlier stone. It sits on a bench in the hillside, at the end of a valley. Rocky walls rise on three sides with Lough Gleninchaquin below, and a long, narrow waterfall runs down the rock face at the valley's end. This is a most magical location and I can understand why it was chosen for the setting of this circle. Upon arriving at the parking area, Sharon had decided to put on her rain gear while I had impatiently gone on ahead, the walk being only five minutes or so. As I stood there looking around me, I could sense the power of this place, and knew I was welcome. I could feel the energy all around me in a much more inclusive way than I had ever experienced before. The earth, the water, the sky, the plants, the rocks, all seemed to pulse with a strong and yet subtle and soothing energy. Standing in this enclosed valley made me think of what it must feel like for a child snuggled in their crib. Completely at peace with the world. Safe.

The outlier stone is a massive rock about 10 feet tall which sits just a foot or so outside the small, eight foot in diameter, circle. The stone, which is a flat, rectangular, domino kind of shape, was placed with a narrow side towards the circle. The five stones of the ring itself are no more than three feet tall but have real presence, and the axial, or recumbent stone, has some good bulk to it. This arrangement of smaller circles with large outlier stones, which I had also found at Glantane and Knocknakilla, seems to be unique to this part of Ireland and is to me most intriguing.

I did take a moment for some dowsing and I soon found an energy line running northeast / southwest under the alignment stone, through the circle, and exiting between the portal stones.

As I examined the scene before me I could think of no better location for a sacred site. This was as beautiful and perfect a spot as one could want. The closed in canyon provided the seclusion, the lake below provided a calm and peaceful atmosphere, the rocky hillsides surrounding the circle provided the structure, the waterfall proclaimed the power of nature, the earth underfoot gave the grounding, and the sky above gave access to the eternal. Perfect!

Uragh had won my heart. I loved these stones and I loved this place. It had begun to rain and as we began our walk back to the car I thought that I must return here again one day, settle in with the stones, and just wait.

Back on the R571 we continued southwest in search of Shronebirrane Stone Circle. Once again we had little trouble and were soon driving down a long, very narrow, high stone walled canyon. At the end of the canyon the road came to a stop in front of a house, in the rear of which we could see the stone circle. I knocked on the front door and a nice lady told me we were welcome to go out to the circle. She then asked if I would mind paying two euros each which was fine with me. Though they have done very little to maintain this site, it is still their property and I appreciate that they let us visit the stones.

I must say, I found this to be a sad place. The sheep have made quite a mess of the site, it is missing some stones, and the house built right alongside the circle kind of impacts the feel. Nonetheless, there were nine rather interesting stones here with six still standing. I especially liked the vibe I got from the south stone which had a fun face in it. I also enjoyed what I thought was an outlier stone (as it was so much taller than the remaining stones at eight and a half feet), but the closer I looked, it really did appear to be a part of the circle, maybe a portal stone? And, across from it is what appears to be a recumbent, which sits flat on the surface, is only two plus feet in height, and about seven feet long. The circle was about 25 feet in diameter.

I found energy lines running both north/south and east/west, crossing just off circle center. The east/west line flowed under the tall stone, across the circle, and out under the apparent recumbent stone in the west. This circle seems to have been mucked about over the years and it is kind of hard to tell what originally went on. But if you close out all the negatives and imagine Shronebirrane as it might have been, this would have been a really cool place.

As with Uragh, I was struck with the location of this site. There really is only one way to get to these stones and traveling down the canyon, as you approach its end, you can sense the walls of the canyon closing in on you, setting the perfect backdrop for the circle. The visual for those approaching the stone circle in ages gone by would have been most impressive.

Returning to the R571 we backtracked a little way to have lunch at Petals And Boots Cafe, and we were quite happy with our meal.

Continuing southwest we were looking for Ardgroom Stone Circle, which everyone says is signed right on the main road just before the village of Ardgroom. However, after several passes along the stretch where we knew the sign should be, we finally just took a road and drove until we saw someone. Asking if he knew of a circle in the area he said we were on the wrong road and gave us directions. He too, said it would be signed but evidently someone had removed it. His directions were spot on however and we took the road he described. Just a short distance up the road there was a sign for the circle, and in fact, it was well signed from there on.

After parking the car we took an old path of partially sunken paving stones which crossed through several fields and over several fences. There was a heavy mist in the air and as we approached the dramatically shaped stones standing up on a rise, we could just see through the mist the pyramidal form of Skellig peak, brooding in the distance. It had the appearance of a volcanic cinder cone and the visual really was impressive, if not oppressive, as were the occasional views of the bay below. This place has a strong vibe about it and though the moisture in the air was becoming a

steady sprinkle, and there were occasional strong gusts of cold wind, I knew we would be in no hurry to leave here.

This is a powerful circle and though it is only 23 feet in diameter, I could feel the energy before we entered it. There are 10 stones remaining with nine still standing and they range from four feet to almost seven feet in height. Many of them are pointed on top with one severely so.

About 20 feet to the east of the circle is an outlier that is close to nine feet tall, maybe six feet wide, and on the west side is what really appears to be a lions head carved into the stone, watching over the circle.

Everything about this stone proclaimed it to be the circle's protector, and I did not doubt it.

Dowsing the circle I found an energy line coming from the east that wound around the outlier, continued into and across the circle and exited to the west. It seemed to be off center. While Sharon nestled up against a stone to get out of the wind, I walked over to stand on the energy line where it entered the circle from the east. I was facing into the circle with my hand placed on the stone to my right. I immediately felt energy pulses coming from behind, flowing up through my body and on around the ring to my right. Strong gusts of wind suddenly began pushing at my back and this seemed to intensify the earth energies. I was really enjoying myself, and what had now become a mild rain was not bothering me at all.

After a while the winds began to relax and so did I. Sharon decided to head back to the car while I took more time to walk among the stones. I did not connect on any deeper level with Ardgroom but what a great place this is. I thanked each rock, hugged the outlier, and began the walk back through the rain. At one point I turned to look back and there stood the stones, alone, tall and defiant. The peak was no longer visible through the rain but I could sense its brooding presence.

6/12

After a fun day visiting manors, a waterfall, and a couple Irish woolen outlets, we returned to Kenmare. Later that evening we decided to go back to the Kenmare Stone Circle. Quite a change from the circles we had visited yesterday. You have none of the mystical, gnarly, rough terrain of Ardgroom, or the wonderful views and atmosphere of Uragh, nor do you have the magnificent tall stones of either, but here you have symmetry and clean lines, smooth and rounded surfaces, a neat park like setting, and a sense of calm that cannot be denied. This is a grand circle.

As you approach the ring, which consists of 15 stones and is actually an ellipse 56 feet by 49 feet, your attention is immediately drawn to the boulder burial in the center. This boulder is quite massive, being over six feet long and wide, and about two and a half feet high. You cannot help but be drawn to it, and placing my hand on the stone I found the surface to be very smooth, and I was rewarded with a soothing energy flow and an ever so quiet, "Welcome."

When I dowsed the ring I found several different energy lines. I picked up one outside the circle's north stone which ran south across the circle, passing around the burial boulder on its east side, and then on and out under the south stone. From the west I followed a line over the axial (recumbent) stone to just inside the circle where it then swung in an arc left to the north stone and then on to the center boulder where it turned to the east, and going straight, it exited the circle at the east stone. Very peculiar!

Then, coming from the east, I picked up a different line that repeated the same pattern in the opposite direction. Entering from the east the line went straight to the bolder where it turned south to the circles edge and then made an arc back to the west stone where it exited.

Last of all I walked the circle just inside the stones and found a line running from each stone to the center boulder like spokes on a wagon wheel. I have found this same effect at Corrimony Stone Circle in Scotland and at my circle back home. The more time you spend at the Kenmare Circle the more you realize just how important the center boulder is to this site. It seems to be the source of the circle's energy, flowing out to all the stones, strong, calm, and soothing.

After some time, Sharon and I met up and sat on the north stone, leaning shoulder to shoulder. Relaxing, my feet soon settled into the earth and all was well with the world once again. I thanked the stones.

6/14

We were spending a couple of nights in Limerick but today our goal was to the find the Grange Stone Circle located to the south about 11 miles, and near Lough Gur. With the directions provided by a taxi driver we had no trouble finding the circle right alongside the R512. This ring is on private property but is open to the public. They do ask for donations and we were happy to drop some Euros in the box.

Grange is said to be the largest stone circle in Ireland, being 157 feet across, and impressive it is. I have never seen another like it. You first walk up on to an earth mound that rises three or four feet above the ground level, is around 20 feet wide, and forms the exterior of the circle. There are 113 stones of all sizes and shapes that are placed rock to rock, right up against this earth mound, forming a stone wall around the interior. The floor of the circle then sits a foot or so below the level of the mound. To the east is a stone lined entryway cut through the mound, with large entrance stones on each side as you enter the circle. The stone to the north is six and a half feet tall while its partner to the south is over seven feet. Standing on the mound to the west, looking across the circle towards the entry, it was easy to imagine hundreds of people walking through the passage and spreading out over the interior surface, waiting for the ritual to begin. Adding to the atmosphere there are a number of large old trees growing up among the stones and it brought to mind that the other name of this circle is The Lios, or "Fort of the Fairies." It is definitely all that.

Dowsing the site I followed an energy line down the entry from the east and across the circle where it exited just south of west. I also found a line running across the circle north/south and the two lines crossed near the middle.

Standing on the mound and looking around I saw what appeared to be an outlier in the next field maybe 100 yards away. I followed the line from the south as it led me across a fence, into the next field, and right to the large, rather rough looking boulder

type stone, which was overgrown with tall grasses. The line swung around the stone and continued on to the southwest. It was definitely an outlier to the circle. Pleased with the discovery I headed back. I later found out that this stone is called the Stone Of The Tree.

I knew there was another circle said to be in the field to the north so I decided to go in search. Once again following my dowsing rod it led me across a stone wall, over an electrical fence and northeast across the next field. I was soon standing at a much smaller, though seemingly complete, stone circle of the more typical kind. There are 15 stones forming a ring 55 feet across. The stones are rather squatty, quite dark in color, and have large white splotches of some kind of growth all over their surface, like the stones at Knockraheen.

The energy line had led me to the west stone where it entered the circle and crossed over to the east side. There, brambles and grasses had overgrown several of the stones and blocked me from following the line. I did pick it up again outside the circle where it continued on to the east. There was also an energy line running pretty much north/south across the circle. The whole area was overgrown with tall grasses

and my pant legs were getting wet, so I soon returned to join Sharon at the main event.

Walking down the entry passage I saw Sharon standing opposite me on the west side. Stopping at the portal stones I placed a hand on each, and centering, opened myself to this amazing ring of rocks. I soon could feel the energy coming up from the ground, through me, and flowing out and around the circle in both directions. I visualized yellow energy going out to my left and red rushing out to my right, creating a whirl of color and energy flowing around and through me. Wow!

After maybe five minutes I crossed over to join Sharon. She told me to check out the two large stones where she was standing. They were composed of small square chunks of some type of red/brown rock bonded together by a matrix. I realized that they were of the same material as one of the entrance stones across the circle. Checking the compass I found that these stones were in a true east/west alignment with the entrance, and in the entire circle there were only a few of this kind of stone, all placed at specific points of the compass.

Sharon also pointed out that one of these west stones had a bench on which you could sit. When you did, you were then looking straight across the circle and down the entrance passage towards where the sun would rise in the east at Solstice. That would be dramatic.

Further to the north of the entrance is a massive eight foot tall stone with squared off edges, looking like a big block. It is not only the largest in the circle, it is said to weigh over 50 tons. Just to the north of it is a flat slab of a rock standing on edge that has three slots carved into its top like the stone we saw at Athgreany Stone Circle. What was the purpose?

The interaction of trees and stone at Grange really is special and the trees seem a real player in what goes on there. I had no communication with them but I could sense their pleasure at our presence. When at The Lios, you cannot help but imagine fairies congregating there and holding playful dances in the ring at night.

Sharon and I had both felt a real welcome at Grange and I had made some serious connections with these stones. I was sorry to leave, and once again, I knew I would need to return to this place. As we were leaving Sharon put it well when she said, "This circle needs time."

Walking back to the car we saw a fellow sitting in his tractor in the parking space. As we approached he greeted us and asked if we had enjoyed our visit? He was, in fact, the owner of the site and he got real pleasure in seeing people visiting the stones. It was obvious he took pride in his circle and he spent some time telling us about not only Grange but also about other circles and standing stones in the area. He also told us that when the weather allowed, on the morning of summer solstice there would be a large group of people there to watch as the sun rose and shone down the entrance into the circle. I thought about the bench on the west stone and how fun it would be to be sitting there for the event. He was a great fellow and we really appreciated him taking the time to talk with us. I must also say he has done a wonderful job maintaining the site. The fence is not obtrusive and it does, for the most part, keep the cows out, and the grass clear for walking.

Along with these circles there are actually a number of megalithic sites in the Loug Gur area and before returning to Limerick we decided to visit a few. We climbed to the top of Carriage Aille Ring Fort, an earth fort that was built up on a high point overlooking the surrounding area. The view was quite impressive and it was easy to see why this spot was chosen. We also stopped to check out the Giants Grave, a burial chamber located right off the road. It was still in really good condition and a cool place to just walk about.

6/16

While staying in Galway we took a trip out to visit Brigit's Garden located east of Rosscahill, off the N59. This is a truly amazing garden designed in four sections so that as you walk through it you take a journey through the seasonal cycle of the year. Each section also celebrates one of the Celtic fire festivals; Samhain, Imbolc, Bealtaine, and Lughnasa, which mark the beginning of each season.

While you will find stone circles and stone passageways, it is the garden as a whole that pulls you in, releases the child within, and makes you want to play. It is a beautiful and marvelous place and I would highly recommend it to anyone who is in the area.

6/17

Continuing our swing up the west side of Ireland, in route to Sligo, we took a side trip to Cong to visit the Glebe (or Cong) Stone Circles, which are located on the R345 about a mile east of the village. Cong is a beautiful village in and of itself, but its claim to fame seems to be that it is where *The Quiet Man*, starring John Wayne and Maureen O'Hara, was filmed. There is even a life size statue of the two of them in the center of town. We had lunch and a nice walk around the village, and then we went in search of the stones.

The main circle is signed and easy to find. Sitting up on a knoll surrounded by a grove of beech trees, you can just see some of the stones from the road. You have to park a ways back up from the entry and walk back to the fence crossover. The road is narrow so you need to hurry along and keep a look out for the traffic.

Once in the field, it is a mild walk up the slope to the stones which you find hidden by the trees and surrounded by a metal rail fence placed so as to protect them from the animals. This fence also provides you a clean surface on which to walk while enjoying the circle. The fence is not too substantial and is placed far enough from the stones so that it really did not bother us.

While Grange may have been the "Fort of the Fairies," this marvelous place was definitely a "fairy ring." This spot just oozed magic of a calm and soothing kind and if I was a local, and in any type of trouble, this is where I would come to ask for help. We spent quite a while walking among the stones getting acquainted, and several made me welcome with a subtle but steady energy flow. The circle is 45 feet in diameter, consists of around 18 stones (some nearly buried), and as a whole, just feels good.

Deciding to dowse the site I had soon found a strong energy line running pretty much north/south. In the south was a really different looking domino shaped stone, the surface of which was covered with large, rounded, bowl like indentions creating a very dramatic affect. The line ran under the stone, across the circle, and out to the north under what appeared to be a recumbent stone, with its flankers on both sides. I was really enjoying this circle and took a moment to sit on the recumbent, allowing my feet to settle into the earth. The energy flow increased and I felt great!

Continuing around the outside of the circle I picked up another line in the east which crossed the circle, exited out the west side, and continued on. Now, when I had first arrived at Glebe, and had climbed over the fence into the field, I'd seen a fellow and his dog walking across the field towards me. I'd asked him

Stone Journals

if he knew of any other stone circles in the area, as I had read somewhere that there were supposed to be several. He pointed towards the west and said he remembered one circle in the field in that direction but he had no idea what kind of condition it was in as he had not been there in years. He also said there was another circle behind the house back up the road where we had parked. So, since the first circle he had mentioned seemed be in the direction the line I'd found was headed, I decided to follow it.

I followed my rod to a high stone wall, climbed over, and there in the next field, maybe 100 yards out, I could see what looked like the remains of a circle. As I approached it I saw that this was, in fact, a much larger ring than the last, about 100 feet across, and although many stones seemed to be missing, those remaining, both fallen and standing, still declared their presence. The line I had followed entered the circle between two standing stones, one having the same bowl cup marks as the south stone in the last circle. I wondered how these two stones had been created? Maybe through some natural process like gas bubbles. In any case, they were quite unique and seemingly of some import. The energy line continued on through the circle and out across the field to who knows where.

The stones were placed on, or alongside, the remains of an earth bank, and most seemed to favor the squarer, thin shape. There were also a couple of trees grown up on the circle edge.

The ring is neglected and battered but these stones have not given up. I could feel a very subtle energy here, but it was buried deep. This is definitely a place I would like to return to and stay for a time, as I think these stones would respond to someone of good intent. In fact, as I walked away I felt a strong tug from the circle along with, "Come back." "I will try" I said. I hope one day I can.

Returning to the main circle I decided to spend more time with the trees, as they are obviously an important element of this place. I am sure there were no trees here originally but that does not mean they cannot have a positive impact on the site. So, I dowsed several trees inside the circle to check their auras. Yes, I said aura. I'm going all New Age on you now. Call it what you like, a tree's aura is a good gauge as to its health. The healthier the tree the wider its aura. Using a dowsing rod you can approach a tree looking for its aura and the rod will show you how far out it extends around the tree. I have dowsed many trees at our place back home over the years, and as we have been in an ongoing drought for many years now, the auras around our trees have shrunk a little each year as they struggle to survive.

Here at Glebe, I approached one of the trees, looking for its aura, and found it circling the tree about 20 feet out. I walked up to the tree, introduced myself, told the tree how much I appreciate it, and how wonderful it was. I then went back out to check its aura again and found it to have expanded to 30 feet! I find this is often the case with trees. They really do like it when you show them some positive attention. The trees of this grove seemed to me to be quite happy, healthy, and content with their situation in the company of the Glebe Stones.

As we prepared to leave I noticed something, that may be nothing. It struck me that here in this ring there are several groupings of three stones together, and it is an interesting effect. It is quite common to find a recumbent and flankers grouped together, but usually only one grouping in a circle. Here there are three such groupings and there may have been more. A puzzle.

Saying our farewells and giving thanks to both the stones, and the trees, we went to find the circle behind the house that the fellow had told me about. Sure enough we found a near perfect stone circle sitting in a corner where two stone walls met. There was metal fence put up around the exposed portion, but unlike at the main circle, here the fence was quite depressing. I climbed over it and walked among the stones but found the circle had no vibe to it at all. It was strange because here we found a

near complete circle of good sized, interesting looking stones that should have filled me with joy, and all I felt was sorry for them.

Looking out across the stone wall to the east I could see the remains of the large neglected circle I had visited earlier, still holding on to its pride. What a contrast! Time to go.

6/18
Having arrived in Sligo yesterday, today we decided to drive out to the Carrowmore Megalithic Cemetery just a few miles to the southwest. It is located right in the geographical center of the Cuil Irra Peninsula, a very sacred and holy place to the ancient Celts and to those before them. Further to the west, and overlooking the entire peninsula, is the imposing presence of Knocknarea mountain. It is wide and flat topped, stands 984 feet above the surrounding terrain, and on its top is the massive cairn known of as Maeves Tomb. Maeve was the warrior queen of western Ireland. Knocknarea can be seen from anywhere on the peninsula and for me conjured up memories of a movie I saw when I was a child called *The Lost Continent*, on which were discovered dinosaurs and cavemen living on a secluded, flat topped, mountain in the jungle of South America. No dinosaurs here however.

The cemetery covers an area about 2/3 mile by 1/3 mile and consists of 30 different burial sites, or passage tombs, of several different types and in varying conditions. Most commonly, they appear as a ring of good sized stones, often placed close together like kerb stones, in the center of which are the remains of a burial chamber. There are several chambers that remain in good condition with their capstone in place, looking like dolmens found elsewhere around Ireland and the UK. A few of these dolmens seem to stand alone without a circle, but I do not know if that was originally the case. There were also a few of the stone circles that had no apparent burial chamber and I wondered if maybe they were just stone circles?

As you walk around you will see in the center of this vast complex, a big stone cairn, site 51, also called Listoghil, and it is indeed the largest burial site in the cemetery. It is also the only complete cairn and is 111 feet in diameter. A little south of east there is a long entry passage leading to a large inner chamber in the middle of which sits a complete burial tomb. The tomb consists of six good sized stones forming the walls and a six ton slab for the roof. Also of note, resting on the ground at the entrance to the passageway is a large flat stone on which is carved a human footprint. Natural or manmade I do not know, nor do I know its purpose. It does remind me of the footprint on top of Fort Dunadd in Scotland however. In any case, the whole thing is very impressive. When it was reconstructed they used gabion baskets to support the inner walls for obvious safety reasons and though the wire does look a bit odd, it makes complete sense.

Also of note as you walk the location, to the west stands Knocknarea, and no matter where you are in the cemetery you can see the mountain and feel its presence. You can also see and feel the presence of the nipple on top which is Maeves Tomb. She must have been of great importance to have been honored in such a way. The proximity of the mountain and tomb to the cemetery is not happenstance.

Having dowsed many of the Carrowmore sites I came up with a variety of very fun results. At site 49, a small boulder burial, I found a simple straight energy line running east/west across the site. Site 57 had one of those unique Irish patterns where the line entered the circle, which was a ring of 33 boulders about 66 feet in diameter, from the west, then curved to the north and around the interior just a few feet in from the circle stones. When it got to the east it curled in on itself once and then went to ground. The pattern was repeated with a line coming in from the east side, which curled around the circle to the south, and arriving at the west it looped in on itself once before going to ground. Great fun!

I found a line leaving the north side of the circle at site 2 that I followed to the east side of site 1. This site has an outer circle about 40 feet in diameter and also the remains of an inner circle. Entering from the east, the line looped around the ring, in-between the two circles, until it reached the north where it crossed the outer circle and exited. The line then made a jog to the west before it turned back to the east until it returned to where I had just exited the ring. It then continued off in a northern direction to who knows where.

At site 7, a wonderful circle of 32 boulders, about 40 feet in diameter, and with an impressive dolmen in the middle, I picked up a line outside the circle to the southeast. It curled around the outside of the circle up to the north. There it entered the circle and curled back to the south before turning due west, crossing through the burial chamber, and exiting out to the west. The line continued on under an outlier stone and on towards Knocknarea off in the distance. Going back to the east side of site 7 and looking west, I could see that the burial chamber in the circle and the standing stone to the west were in direct alignment with Maeves Tomb on Knocknarea.

Site 4 consists of an earth ring with a dolmen in its center and a standing stone to the west that is all that remains of a ... rom the northeast and followed it as it wound around the outside of the ring. Going around to the east it was at the southwest point that the line entered the ring and swung back to reverse the pattern on the inside. Getting back to near the north, the line curled back on itself again and went east until it got in line with the dolmen entrance. There it turned westerly to enter the dolmen and upon coming out the other side it turned to the north and exited. I love these Irish energies!

Last was the connection of sites 58 and 59 by a straight line which ran from the southwest right through 58, and then on to 59, where it traveled down its center and exited to the northeast through what appeared to be a recumbent stone.

While I received no special interaction with the stones at Carrowmore, I have rarely been so happy to be someplace. The weather was near perfect and the energies of this location were alive and well. It would be way fun to spend several days here delving deeper into what the energies had to tell. For example, what had I missed? Were all the sites connected by one energy line, and did that line go all the way to Knocknarea? And then, of course, there were the stones themselves! The wonderful stones!

Leaving Carrowmore we decided to climb Knocknarea, and to visit Maeve's Tomb. Maeve was not only a warrior queen but also a Celtic goddess. This mountain is a very sacred place and as its presence had loomed over us for a couple of days now. It seemed only right that we should pay our respects. Also, we could not have asked for a nicer day to make the hike.

We were told to allow two hours round trip but even though it is quite steep in places, and the path can be rough, Sharon and I had arrived at the top in about 40 minutes. The views in all directions are spectacular but it was Maeve's Cairn, standing proud and majestic at the top, that drew our attention. We did not climb to the top of the cairn because it was obvious that damage is being done to the cairn by people doing so. Still, just to stand there and think about how very important Maeve must have been to the people of her time, for them to have made this effort to honor her, was quite moving. From the moment I stepped up onto the top of Knocknarea I could feel the energy pulsing through the ground as Maeve made her presence known, and I was happy. This is indeed a very powerful place.

There are several other smaller burial sites on top of the mountain but we did not spend long checking them out. Preparing to leave, I thanked Maeve for her blessings and promised to keep her in my thoughts. We both felt energized as we began the walk down the mountain and it seemed no time at all before we were back at the bottom and approaching our car. I should add that there was a lady with a crepe truck set up at the parking lot who made the most wonderful apple crepe. The perfect way to end a lovely day.

6/19

The weather was iffy today as we headed north out of Sligo on the N15. The rain came and went off and on all day. Not too far north we saw a sign for Creevykeel

Court Tomb just off to the right of the road, so we stopped to check it out. A court tomb is a burial chamber that has a court area in front. While the burial chambers would originally have been roofed over, the court area would have been left open to the sky.

In the case of Creevykeel the overall site is 164 feet long, 65 feet wide in the front, and narrowing towards the back. You enter through a narrow passage which then opens into a large courtyard that is oval in shape. Beyond that you find several burial chambers. The interior walls of the passageway and chambers are all lined with large stones. It is a cool place. Also of interest is a speaking platform, not unlike the pulpit in churches, where a person, or priest, would have been able to stand above a crowd gathered in the court to address them.

Walking around the outside of this structure we found several more burial chambers along the sides towards the back, reminding me of Belas Knap.

Driving east on the A47 we crossed onto Boa Island, on the north end of Lower Lough Erne, and soon had arrived at Caldragh Cemetery. It was raining, but I was anxious to be out of the car and down the path in search of a pair of stones called the Janus Stones. This is a small overgrown graveyard surrounded by forest, and with the rain falling from dark, broody skies, there was quite a mysterious atmosphere to this place. Entering through the metal gate I immediately saw the stones standing in the middle of the site. Though they sit there like just two more tombstones in the graveyard, they were, in fact, brought there from some other location and do not mark anyones grave. They are also much older than the graveyard itself. How old is up for debate.

Carved into the stones are what appear to be male figures, from about the waste up. The taller of the two stones has a face carved on both sides (thus the name Janus) and is both unique and very cool. The faces are long and pointed at the chin, and they have long fingered hands crossed at the waste. The bottom of one of the stones, on which the hands are carved, seems to have been broken off at some point in time and the piece sits leaning against the stone. In the top of the head of the stone with the two faces there is a notch carved out, as if to hold something. Maybe antlers were placed there during rituals thus designating the figure as the god Cernunnos?

The other stone is smaller with carving on just one side. Still, it has a real presence about it and together with the larger stone they make an impressive pair. I have not seen their like anywhere else. Caldragh Cemetery had the feel of fairy about it and the potential for magic.

After an unsuccessful attempt to find the Drumskinny Stone Circle we were once again headed east. Entering Northern Ireland we were on the A505, looking for the Beaghmore Stone Circles, and I do mean circles. This is another of those unique Irish sites where they have uncovered in the peat, seven stone circles, 12 cairns, and ten alignments, all grouped together in the most marvelous complex. The stone circles are made up of smaller stones (accept in one circle where there are two larger stones), and most interesting, with the exception of the circle furthest to the northwest, the circles are built in pairs right next to each other.

When we arrived at Beaghmore there was a light rain, but we were dressed for it so out we went. Because of the low height of the stones they do blend into the environment, but right away we saw two circles made up of stones no more than a foot and a half feet tall and sitting quite close together. There were four long rows of stones coming from the northeast leading into the gap between the circles. The outside rows were made up of the same small stones, but the inner rows contained a few larger stones maybe three feet in height.

Further to the west we found another group of two circles which actually bumped up against each other for a short distance leaving no gap between them. There was a single short row of the small stones leading up to the circles intersection point also coming from the northeast.

Stone Journals

Northwest of this group we found a larger circle the interior of which was covered over with small rocks. Some of the ring stones were a bit larger here. There was an alignment of small stones coming in from the northeast which led right to the east side of the circle. Looking back I noticed that this alignment was pretty much parallel with the alignments leading to the previous circle groups.

Placed a distance to the southwest from these circles, was another grouping consisting of two stone circles, and an earth ring with a cairn in its center. The most northern of the two circles contained two stones maybe four feet tall which were the largest of all the circle stones.

By this time it was really raining and Sharon decided to head back to the car. For me however, the setting could not have been more magical. The surrounding hills were shrouded in mist. The terrain was fairly flat and covered with lush green grass mixed with low growing, bright yellow and white flowers. And the stones themselves seemed full of joy as "Honor the mother, honor the earth" rolled through my head like a mantra, and I began chanting it as I walked.

Pulling out a dowsing rod, I immediately found energy lines and began to laugh. Ignoring the rain, I walked among the stones, happily embracing the moment. The air was alive with an audible energy creating a subtle sound like a gong in the distance. The earth too, pulsed under my feet. It was an incredible moment. I loved this place and its small but dynamic stones.

The first energy line I followed was at the southwest grouping. It entered the earth ring from the south, crossed through the cairn and exited the ring to the north. The line then ran straight north to enter the stone circle, cross to the middle, and then turned to exit to the west. Deciding to follow the line, it headed north until it came to the one separate stone circle I had previously visited. It circled around it to the north and then back to the east where it met up with the row alignment and entered the circle and went to ground. This was really good fun.

Sadly, as it was now raining pretty hard I was no longer taking notes and could not later accurately remember the details of the remainder of the dowsing I did at Beaghmore. I did continue to walk the whole site finding energy lines connecting several of the circles. I also remember that there was a line running right up the long avenue that leads to the first circle pair.

Returning to the car I was quite wet, but I was also quite happy. Several times as I had walked among the stones I had felt and heard their encouragement and had laughed out loud as I thanked them. I also heard, "You need more time, we need more time." But I did not have more time. I am going to have to return. This is a most unique and magical gathering of stones.

6/20

After a wonderful night at the Kensington Lodge in Dungannon (and a great and very entertaining dinner at Viscounts) we headed south. We were looking for the exit off the N1 to visit the Proleek Dolmen, but for whatever the reason we missed it and were soon reentering Ireland. Changing plans we set out to find the Boyne Valley and its famous burial mounds. As Sharon and I had visited New Grange on a previous trip, this time we decided to go to the other two tombs of import.

Whereas New Grange and Knowth have both been completely restored, draw large crowds, and are in fact quite magnificent, Dowth sits alone and ignored by all but the few who search it out. No parking lots with shuttle busses, no restaurants,

kiosks, shops, or restrooms here. Driving down a country lane (L1607) we saw a sign on our left and parked in a pullover. Just a hundred yards or so across a field we could see this tall earth mound, some 50 feet high and 280 feet in diameter, covered with grass and brush, and looking quite neglected.

Approaching from the north we began walking around the base to the west and soon came across the entrances to the two tombs in Dowth. Both are closed off to the public. The entrance to the south tomb, which is

Stone Journals

aligned to the sunset at winter solstice, still has its large entrance stone in place though it is about two thirds covered with earth. You can just see a bit of the rock art that is carved into it. Sad really that no effort is being made to reveal what is there.

Looking up on the mound it really does have the appearance of a volcano with a crater in its top, one side having been blown out. Originally, Dowth had been the tallest of the three main cairns in the Boyne Valley but years ago there was excavation work (or more likely grave robbing) done here and the result was the caving in and washing out of part of the mound. To my knowledge this did not affect the chambers underneath.

Continuing on south around the mound we began to find that lots of its kerbstones had been uncovered over the years and that 15 of those had rock art in them, which was quite weathered, but there nonetheless. Here we also found a large tree growing out of the side of the mound. It seemed out of place at first, but the more I looked at it, I began sensing it had a purpose. The tree was doing its part to assist in holding the mound together and in return the mound was providing all the tree needed to grow strong and healthy.

On the east side there is a grouping of kerbstones visible with some really fine artwork. One stone, called The Stone of the Seven Suns, is most impressive.

Sharon returned to the car while I climbed to the top of the mound. I had been enjoying a nice grounding feeling since we had arrived at Dowth and up on top the feeling grew even stronger. I heard voices and so walked over to the edge of the crater. Looking down in I saw a group of maybe seven people sitting on blankets in a circle. The center was completely covered with flower petals. Not wanting to bother them I went on around to sit on the outside edge of the mound. As I crouched down I felt as if my whole body was being drawn down into Dowth, down into the earth, down to the chambers. It was dark and cold but exciting. Suddenly my eyes opened and I was back on the mound. Closing me eyes I tried to go back but with no success. Whoa!

Eventually I went down to sit on one of the kerbstones on the south side. Centering, I could feel the energy of the mound, soft and subtle, yet strong and present, if that makes any sense? Unencumbered by crowds and chaos Dowth made me welcome. Something I doubt I would ever experience at New Grange. I was quite the happy man when I began the walk back to the car, but I was also longing to return down under, down into the chambers.

Next we went to the visitor center to book a tour of Knowth. While it limits you to an hour on site, the tour was well presented and a good value. The Knowth site is actually a large complex of 22 burial cairns, with Knowth sitting in the center and being the largest of them all. It has been beautifully restored, and most astounding of all are the kerbstones around the base of Knowth. As a part of the restoration they were left uncovered so that you can see, and appreciate, the incredible rock art that appears on the stones. There are 123 of these kerbstones and 90 of them have rock art carved into them. As you walk around the mound you move in awe from stone to stone, with each having its own unique carvings in it. The artwork really is amazing, and though there are some good ideas as to what the carvings mean, it is all conjecture at this point. It was pointed out on our tour that in fact about 40% of all the existing rock art in Europe is found on the Knowth kerbstones and in its inner chambers. Sadly, you are no longer allowed to go into the inner chambers which are said to be most impressive.

Stone Journals

6/21 - Summer Solstice

This whole day was to be a celebration of the Summer Solstice and we began with a trip to the Loughcrew Cairns. Finding the parking lot we began the steep climb up Carnbane East to the summit where the views were spectacular and where you find a complex of seven cairns, in various conditions, with the massive Cairn T in the center. This cairn is 115 feet in diameter and is completely covered with rocks. Walking the exterior you find on the north side a huge slab of stone that appears as though it is a giant stone chair or throne and it is called the Hag's Chair. There are a number of legends about the stone, which include that it was a witch's chair, or Queen Maeve's throne.

The entrance is located on the east side and on this day there were two docents at the site to provide information. They were quite helpful and provided us with flashlights before we entered the chamber. You have to crouch down as you enter the 16.5 feet long passage. The central chamber itself is sort of circular with three smaller chambers off of it. On the Spring and Fall Equinoxes the rising sun shines down the passage to illuminate the stone at the back end of the chamber. This stone is beautifully carved and on this occasion had a bright green lichen growing on it.

Standing in the main chamber, I felt, once again, that connection with the land that I have felt so often in Ireland. Moving my light across the interior stones I realized just how many of them had been carved and how each was distinct from the others. Passage stones, too, had been carved and I could sense the artists' presence here. Many hands had spent many hours preparing these stones before they were placed in specific locations. Why were these particular carvings made in the stone on which the sun shown during the Equinoxes? What was their meaning?

Exiting the tomb we walked around to the north and sat up on the Hag's Chair. It is a really fun place to just sit, to absorb the energies flowing through the mound, and to enjoy the spectacular views to the north. Did Queen Maeve herself once sit here?

Walking around the top of Carnbane East you begin to appreciate the real complexity of the location. To the east is Patrickstown Hill on which are located six more burial tombs. To the west you see a small hill which has several more sites on it and even further west is Carnbane West with another nine or so tombs. All in all Loughcrew consists of about 30 cairns. Sadly, much of it is closed off to the public. Happily, what we did see was spectacular!

Starting back down the hill I decided to go exploring. I crossed over a fence onto private property to the west and soon came across the remains of a cairn. Just five or six stones remained, but there was one standing stone to which I felt drawn. As I stood next to it, hands on stone, I felt a good energy coming from this impressive old rock. Looking past it I saw Cairn T high on the hill directly to the east. I had read that Cairn T does indeed seem to be the center of the whole complex and that many of the tombs on the other hills were aligned to it. Whatever the case, there can be no doubt that Cairn T held a place of import. As I walked back to the path and continued on down the hill, I could feel Loughcrew tugging on my backside. Turning and looking back up the hill, I knew I must return to this place. There is more here for me. With a smile and nod I continued back to the car.

We were feeling quite hungry so Sharon and I went to the Loughcrew Gardens Cafe where we had a wonderful meal. As we had gone up to see the cairns, we were given free entry to the gardens. Walking through the gardens we had a fun time. It is a little rough around the edges but well worth it. Plus, it is a grand place for children.

We finished our day at the Hill Of Tara which is, aptly, located near the town of Tara. When we arrived in the late afternoon there was already quite a crowd gathered for the Solstice, including a gathering of Travelers. Most of the people were mingling around the small shops and parking area, so we decided to go straight up to the monument.

Tara is said to be the place from which the ancient Kings of Ireland reigned, and is the location of The Lia Fail, or Stone Of Destiny. Though the hill is only 500 feet in height it commands a grand view of the surrounding landscape. At Tara there are actually quite a few different sites but we only managed to visit the main ones. Starting to the north, there is what appears to be a long entry way, referred to as the Banqueting Hall, which is created by two parallel rows of earth mounds. If you approach from the side it just looks like some earth mounds and you do not get the hall effect. At its end you come to a set of earth ring enclosures, one inside the other, which are called the Ring of the Synods. One side has been overrun by the grounds of St Patrick's church, originally built in the 1200's. I would assume this was done in an attempt to replace the old gods with the new god as Tara was central to the ritual practices of the Celts. Continuing south you arrive at the Rath of the Kings, a 16 acre earth enclosure (ditch and bank), inside which you find the Mound of the Hostages, the King's Seat, and Cormac's House. The Mound of the Hostages is a good sized ancient ritual and burial mound, but the entrance had been gated so that we could not get in.

The King's Seat is the center of the complex. It is a flat surface with two outer banks and ditches around it. On it sits the five foot tall Stone of Destiny, not to be confused with the one in Scotland. Though it was originally located nearer the Mound of the Hostages this location does seem to be the proper place for such a wondrous stone. Its round, smooth, phallic appearance just seems right jutting from the heart of Tara. Standing with my hand on the stone, the grounding energy I had been feeling all over Ireland flowed comfortably up from the earth. Even with people continually coming and going, (and the crowd was beginning to build up) this place felt alive, and willing to give. Great place for the solstice.

Butted up against the east side of the King's Seat is Cormac's House, or King Cormac's Seat, another large earth ring enclosure. After a visit there we went on down to the church grounds in search of Block and Bluid, two standing stones said to be located in the graveyard. Easily found, they too, are reported to have been moved to their present location among the grave stones from somewhere else on Tara. Was this to christianize the stones rather than destroy them? No one really knows.

As we approached the two stones I was immediately charmed by them. I could feel their presence and I could feel their welcome. They stand about eight feet apart and are quite different. The one stone is only a couple feet tall and rounded. The other, also known as St Adamnan's Pillar, stands maybe five feet tall and is shaped like a domino. Also, if you look closely at this stone you will find there is a figure, maybe 18 inches long, carved into its east side. Weathering is making the figure difficult to make out but if you look closely from the right angle, it is there. In a pamphlet about the Hill Of Tara site that I picked up in the book store, I read that the carving is of the Celtic god, Cernunnos, which was good fun as I had been wearing a Cernunnos pendant on this entire trip.

The church has now been converted into an interpretive center and they were having a solstice celebration concert at 8:00. So, Sharon and I went to check out the shops and to get a bite to eat before attending. The setting for the concert was perfect. The small stone church provided a rich sound and the colorful stained glass window behind the performers provided a rich atmosphere. We saw several fine artists but the highlight of the evening had to be Coscan, a truly wonderful band performing all types of Irish music. Listening to the music we could feel ourselves being drawn deeper and deeper into the soul of this amazing land. It was a perfect way to celebrate the Summer Solstice, and though clouds blocked the view of the sun as it set, we left Tara with our hearts full of joy.

So ended our trip to Ireland. We had made a complete circle of the island and had been blessed beyond our expectations. We had been welcomed by the people, the land, and the stones, but 23 days was not nearly enough and we knew we would have to return.

The entrance to Grange Stone Circle looking east

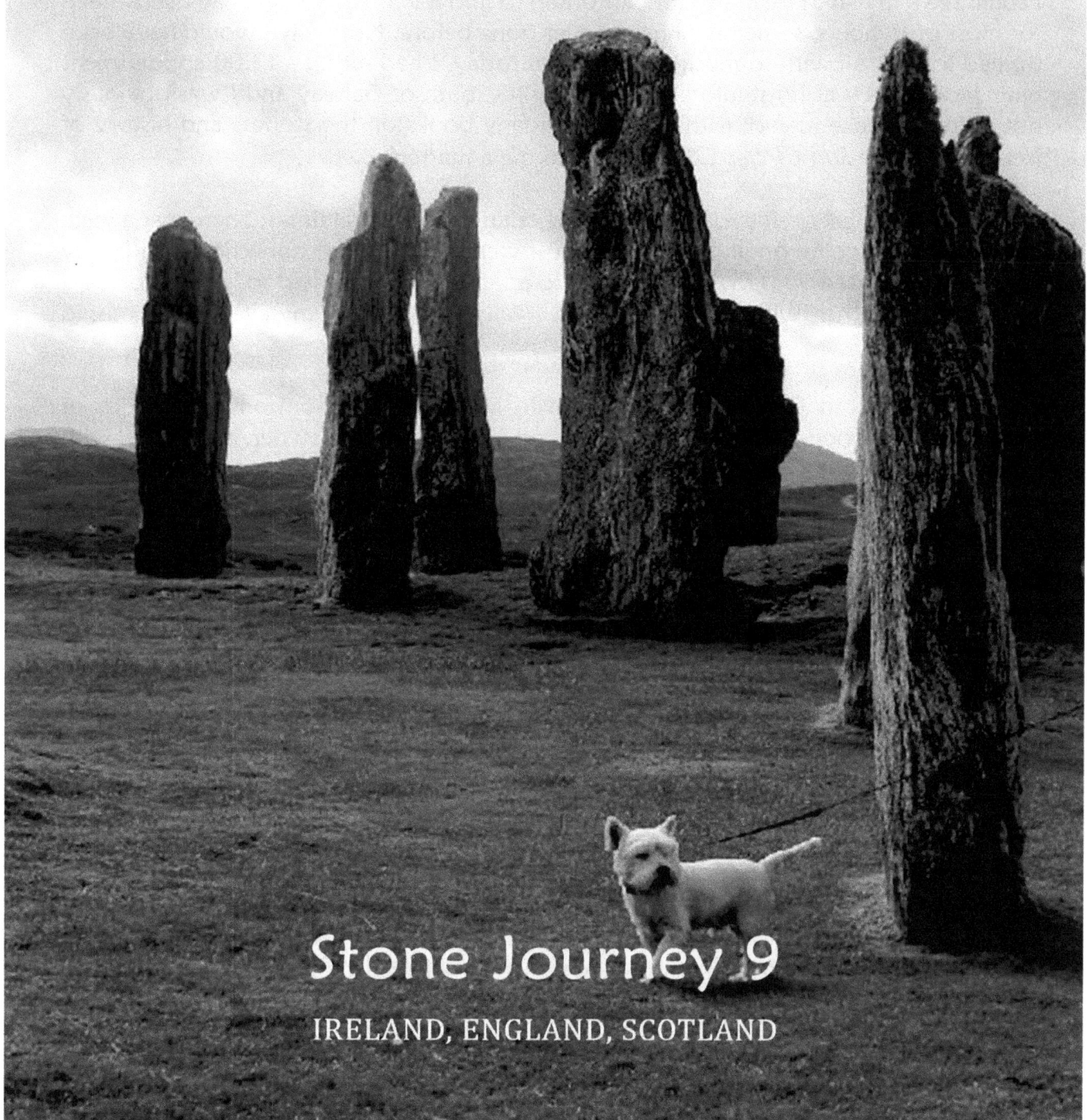

STONE JOURNEY 9 - July 18, 2017

After several long delays on both ends of our flight, a time consuming hassle from the car rental agency, and a two and a half drive from Dublin, Sharon and I finally arrived in Galway. We were both quite exhausted so we were in bed by 9:00 PM and I was soon out to the world.

7/19

When I woke up this morning I had no idea what time it was. I opened the curtain so I could see and was more than a little surprised to find it was 11:55 AM! I had been asleep for most of 15 hours, something I have never done before. Normally I would have been thrilled to start off with so much sleep but not today. I had set up a 12:00 appointment with Jack Roberts at his studio about 40 minutes south of Galway and I was obviously not going to make it. Jack is the author of many books on the stones and history of Ireland. His *The Sun Circles Of Ireland* is to me a masterful work.

We rushed to get on the road while I tried calling Jack several times. There was a huge electrical storm going on and the phones just were not making connections. Sadly, by the time we hooked up, Jack had left to go to another meeting. I had so looked forward to getting together with him and I was really upset with myself for this missed opportunity.

In route south to Tralee we stopped at Miss Marple's Tea Room on the outskirts of Limerick. It was good tea, good food, and good fun. We met the owner, and shared with her our joy of visiting tea rooms and collecting eclectic tea pots. When we went to pay our bill she surprised us by giving us a tea pot of a tearoom to add to our collection. I do love the Irish. We had missed Jack but Miss Marple's had put us back on track.

As it was quite a rainy day, when we arrived at the Ashe Hotel in Tralee we decided to call it quits. But even with the rain it was still great to be back in Ireland.

7/20

Unlike the night before, I got very little sleep due to the jet lag, so we were up and on our way early. The plan was to explore the Dingle Peninsula and first up was the Lugnagappul Ogham Stones and the Ardmore Stone Row which were said to be fairly close in proximity. After driving around for a while and having no luck finding any stones, we decided to visit Minard Castle, a lovely old ruin overlooking a charming small harbor on the southern coast. Just a short ways past the castle was the entrance to a path leading to Tobar Eoin, or St John's Well. It was a short pleasant walk along a wooded path and arriving at the site we were both very impressed by the horseshoe shaped, stone lined pool of clear water sitting at the base of an old tree. It was not only a beautiful location; it was also well maintained and felt of the earth.

Sharon commented that locations like this are very precious, because, as you stand there looking at the well, you get the feeling that Mother Earth intentionally picked this very spot from which to provide us with this blessing of water. We walked back to our car feeling thankful.

We next stopped in the town of Dingle at An Diseart to see the stained glass windows created by Harry Clark in the church there. We had been so impressed by his work at the church in Castletownsend on our last visit that we were up for more. And, the six pains in this chapel did not disappoint us. What a master he was.

Heading west on the R559 we were looking for a standing stone said to be right alongside the road just out of Dingle. For whatever the reason we did not find it. However, a few miles further along we saw a sign for Colaiste Ide where there was said to be a collection of Ogham stones that I had wanted to see. So we took the left and went in search.

Oghams are, by the way, the letters of an ancient alphabet used by the Irish/Celts a couple of thousand years ago. They were also used for divination purposes much as one would use the runes. After a couple of stops for directions we soon found the

stones right alongside the road approaching Burnham House. There are seven stones here which were gathered together from different locations by Lord Ventry of the manor. The tallest is about three and a half feet tall by a little over a foot wide. Many of the stones have very clear ogham markings, each letter designated by groups of lines carved into the stone.

When we had been looking for these stones one of the people we stopped to ask directions from was a delivery man. He told us that he had never heard of them and wished us luck. Later, while we were examining the stones he pulled up in his van, got out, and walked over to take a look for himself. He then showed us a tattoo he had on his arm which was of some oghams. When I asked him what it meant he said, "Freedom, which means very much to me." He explained he

Stone Journals

had grown up in Bulgaria where freedoms were much controlled by the State. In his search for a better life he became fascinated by the history of the Celtic culture, their pride and individual freedoms. The tattoo had represented his goal, and after several years he was able to immigrate to Ireland, where he told us he was now a very happy man. A free man! Great story.

Driving along on the Dingle Peninsula Loop we made several stops to see various ancient stone structures. The Beehive Huts located on the Slea Head Drive portion of the loop were part of what was once a community situated right on the bluffs overlooking the sea. Though abandoned long ago, the construction had been done to withstand time and the elements and much still remained as solid as when built. Walking among the ruins made one think about just how hard life must have been for these people.

Further along, just off the R559 about four miles northeast of Ballyferriter, was the Gallarus Oratory. This is an impressive little chapel made of stone with one small window opening and a doorway. It looks like the hull of a ship sat upside down on the earth. It is dark inside and there are no furnishings of any kind. Once again I found myself thinking about what it must have been like for the people living and worshipping here. Not easy, but also few distractions other than life itself.

Last stop on the R559 loop was at Kilmalkedar, which is the remains of an early Christian site and was once said to be the home of Saint Brendon, the Irish Saint believed to have sailed to America via the northern route long before Chris Columbus. Saint Brendon's home was closed off to the public but I was actually there to find a bullaun stone somewhere in the area. A bullaun stone is a rock into which large spherical depressions have been carved. No one knows for sure what their purpose was. In many areas they are referred to as wishing, stones. If you place a round rock into the depression and then spin it in a clockwise direction while making your wish, it will be granted. Spinning the rock in the other direction can bring about a curse. The depressions were also said to have been created as places into which milk could be poured as an offering to the fairies.

Though St. Brendon's home was closed off I was able to wander around the chapel grounds and graveyard. I found some wonderful old Celtic crosses in the graveyard along with a sundial stone and a really cool long, narrow, ogham stone with a hole drilled through the top. But no bullaun stone. I did come across a groundskeeper and asked if he had any idea where I might find the stone, but he was at a loss. He showed me around the grounds but still no success.

Then he asked me to follow him into the chapel, which is just a shell with no roof. As we got to the back he pointed to a slot in the wall that had been a narrow window opening. He asked me if I could climb through it? I said I thought so, but why? He told me to go ahead and do it. So while he walked outside and around to the back I climbed up to squeeze through the opening. As I came through to the outside he was standing there waiting for me and pronounced that I would now be blessed with a hundred years of good luck and live to be 110 years of age! I had found no bullaun stone but I had gained a lifetime of good luck! I could not have been happier as I rejoined Sharon and told her my story.

Continuing on I suggested we give the Ardmore Stone Row another try as I was now blessed with good luck. We returned to the area in which I thought the stones should be found, just off the N86, and as we drove along we saw a fellow standing beside the road and stopped to ask if he knew of these stones. He was quite a friendly guy and was, in fact, an American transplant. He informed us that he did know of the stones and that they were well worth the visit. However, we were going the wrong way. After he gave us very clear directions we said our goodbyes, turned around, and renewed our search.

As we came to the top of a hill, off to the right I saw what I was sure was the Graigue Standing Stone, which I had read about on the megalithicire land.com site. I had also seen photographs and it was easy to spot. The stone had been split in two centuries ago, with one half still standing upright while the other half had fallen and is only held up off the ground by another smaller stone upon which it rests. It appeared to be about 12 feet tall and quite wide. Finding this stone was a pleasant surprise, and though I wanted to go out to the stone I did not have permission, and I had read that the locals don't mind you visiting the stones but they want you to ask first. So we continued on.

We soon pulled into the farm where the Ardmore Stone Row was said to be located and saw a fellow working on a piece of equipment. He came right over and introduced himself. His name was Paul. He was a really good guy and we hit it off right away. I told him we were looking for the stone row and he said it was not far. As we talked he walked me back behind the farm buildings and pointed the way. He said he was happy for Sharon and I to visit the stones but to look out for the bull. At first I thought he was joking but he assured me that they did have a bull up in those fields that were not averse to charging a trespasser on his turf.

Sharon joined me and we took the walk. We soon found not only the three wonderful large row stones, but about 100 yards out was an outlier stone of similar size and shape. Though close, it was not actually in alignment with the three row stones. This surprised me.

The stones were all tall and thin. The tallest was at the northeast end of the alignment and stood about 10 feet tall, with the other two stones being under seven feet. The row is aligned northeast/southwest to the Winter Solstice sunset. Their color was a very intriguing purple that I have not seen before and they were all topped with a light green growth of some kind. They really were quite striking and I could feel their energy as we approached. And, happily, there was no bull!

For some reason I felt drawn to walk past the row to visit the outlier first. What a joy, as placing hand on stone my feet settled into the earth and I was flooded with strong earth energy, and I knew I was welcome. This stone is about 10 feet high, by six and a half feet wide, by one and a half feet thick, and as I looked closely at it I soon began to make out several cups and rings carved into its surface. Obviously this stone was important, but why?

Looking back at Sharon standing by the Ardmore Row Stones I wondered why this stone was out of alignment with them? Paul had said the stones were lined up with the winter solstice, but this stone must have been placed where it was for a different purpose.

I returned to the stone row, where Sharon commented on how calming this place was. Placing my hands on each stone they felt warm, with a mild pulse of energy emitting from the surface. Sharon was right. The stones were very comforting, and as we had been on the road for the better part of the day it was very appreciated. I thanked them as we prepared to leave.

Returning to the farm I asked Paul if he knew of the Lugnagappul Ogham stones, said to be somewhere in the vicinity. Though he had not seen them himself he pointed off in the distance and said he thought they were located alongside the road in that direction. Thanking him, we decided to try once again.

After a couple miles I was beginning to doubt our directions and stopped at a house to ask if we were on the right track. The nice gentleman told me we were going the wrong way. As it was getting later in the day I said, "Maybe we'll just let this spot go." To which he replied, "No you won't. I've never seen them but I know where they are." He gave me clear directions and sure enough, while driving back along the road to Minard Castle I saw the stones through a gated opening in the wall which ran alongside the road. My Irish luck was holding!

Sharon decided to wait in the car, which ended up being a good choice. Climbing the metal gate I crossed through the field to the remains of a rather insignificant looking cairn around the outside of which were a number of standing and fallen small stones. Two of these were Ogham stones, one looking like a large stone egg about one and a half feet tall and maybe three feet around. I had noticed there were a lot of cows in the field but had paid them no mind. However, as I approached the stones several of the cows seemed to get agitated and began advancing towards me rapidly. I must admit I was becoming quite nervous as even more cows began their advance. I had only had time to take one photograph when they broke into a charge and I decided it was time for me to get somewhere a little safer. I took off running for the field wall which was a tall rock wall about six feet high and covered with a variety of plants. I saw a place where it seemed I could get up on top and with the cows only about 10 feet behind me I scrambled up. The thing is, there was no way down from there to the road below, as it was all nettles and thistles. I was stuck.

Though the cows continued to stand there staring at me I knew I had to make a run for it. So, jumping down into the field I took off with a heard of cows in close pursuit. When I reached the gate I was up on top in no time. As Sharon turned to look I said, "We've got cows!" as they pressed up against the gate. I had found the ogham stones but did not get to spend any time with them. Maybe next trip. If there are no protector cows!

Looking back on the day, it had been quite a success. We had, in fact, circled the Dingle Peninsula with all its natural beauty, found many ancient stone structures, two locations with Ogham stones, standing stones and stone rows, and the stained glass work of Clarke. And, remembering the words of the groundskeeper at Kilmalkedar, I thought there just might be something to this Irish luck thing!

7/21

Though there were no stones today, we had a fun day driving around the area north of Tralee. I must mention Collin's Hot Seaweed Baths in Ballybunion. What a wonderful experience it was. We each had our own room with a porcelain tub in which fresh seaweed had been placed. You add as much water as you like, as warm as you want, and slip in. It is a very unique feeling, with the seaweed releasing the lightest imaginable oil which soon coats your body and begins doing its magic. I can honestly say I have never in my life felt more relaxed, and, in fact, when I did go to stand up my legs almost buckled under me. It was most amazing. And the really cool things is, the oil easily wipes off with a towel and leaves no oily residue at all. It cost 20 Euro for 45 minutes and was worth much more.

7/22

Destination Kenmare. A lovely drive and a happy return to the Rockcrest House, Room 4.

This evening we walked into town to the Kenmare Stone Circle and what a magical place it is. An ellipse 49 feet by 56 feet, it is made up of mostly boulder type stones. This was my third visit to these stones and I once again found myself overwhelmingly charmed by them. As I walked over the carpet of green grass I could feel the energy bubbling just below the surface and soon the stress of the drive was sucked down into earth as a warming energy flowed up and through me.

On a more subtle level this circle reminded me of Brisworthy Stone Circle, in that even though I was first drawn to the east stone, each stone here had a presence and each seemed to have a voice, barely audible, but there. Soon Sharon and I were both sitting on the north stone, quite happy and content. It was good to be back. Opening to the stones, I felt their welcome. It was enough.

Casting my gaze around the circle I once again wondered what it would have looked like before all the landscaping that has been done. I would love to have seen it. But I will also say that what they have done has created a very personal and protected feeling circle of stones, and they do seem quite content.

7/23
Our first stop today was the Bonane Heritage Park, and what a wonderful surprise it was. This park, just east of the N71, was developed and is maintained by a community organization and they are doing a marvelous job. The trail you walk is basically a large loop about one and a half miles long. It is somewhat steep in the beginning but it takes you through a lovely wooded environment. The first site along the way was an earth Ring Fort. You enter through an outer earth wall and an inner earth wall which are separated by a deep ditch. They form a protective barrier around the center in which the people would have lived, or gone to, for security. Really, it is still in pretty good shape.

From there we were back on the main trail which took us by a single insignificant looking standing stone that was small and leaning over. Not much happening but I did find a good northeast/southwest energy line running under it. A little further along we came to a bullaun stone that was an impressive large block-shaped rock in which several cups were carved. This was not really what I think of as a bullaun stone but that is how they had it labeled.

As the trail began looping back we came across a Fulacht Fiadh, or ancient cooking pit. It was interesting, but the real jewel in this walk was just ahead. Located to the left of the main trail sits the Bonane Stone Circle (also known as Dromagorteen) with its boulder burial stone in the center. Unlike at Kenmare, these stones sit as they did long ago, out in the open, surrounded by the natural landscape. Walking downslope towards this circle I could not help but get excited as I could feel its presence. The really wonderful thing is that it was a happy place, and I was smiling as Sharon and I interred this ring of stones.

Bonane is a near perfect circle about 33 feet across made up of 11 beautiful, irregular shaped stones, one of which has a number of large veins of quartz running through it. When I placed my hands on it I felt strong energies coming from this quartz infused rock. In the center of the ring sits the large boulder burial stone. A couple of other smaller stones also sit inside the circle. There is what appears to be a recumbent stone across from two portal stones (one being the previously mentioned stone lined with quartz) that do, according to the information board, line up with the summer solstice.

Though the circle is being maintained, it is also being allowed to remain a natural part of its environment. There is a tree growing just inside the circle off to the southwest. There are also patches of heather growing in the circle and, in fact, one stone was almost covered with the beautiful purple blooms of heather. It only added to the charm of the place.

It felt so right being there that I really thought I was going to get some kind of personal interaction with these stones. That did not happen, but the energies of the circle were very strong just below the surface and I was quite content with that.

As I dowsed the circle I found an energy line entering the circle slightly west of the south stone. It crossed under the center boulder stone and continued about half way to the north stone before it turned east. Then following the curve of the circle it went as far as the quartz lined stone where it turned, passed under the stone, and continued off in the direction of the Fulacht Fiadh, which also happens to be the direction of the summer solstice sunrise.

As we prepared to leave I placed my hand on the west stone and centered. "Come back," I heard. I thanked the stones and as we walked away I knew that I wanted to return to this place. It is a precious jewel and the caretakers are to be commended.

Next we stopped to see the gardens at Bantry House and to have afternoon tea. It was a lovely garden with grand views across Bantry Bay below. Good fun.

Feeling refreshed we went looking for the Mill Little Stone Circle complex with its boulder burial, stone pair, and other individual stones. I had seen photos of, and read about, this site and was anxious to find it. However, this was not to be the day. We had no success at all.

Eventually we decided to see if we could find the Kealkill Stones located just a little to the southeast of Kealkill Village. Happily, it was well signed and no trouble to find. This is another of those unique Irish stone complexes consisting of a five stone circle with recumbent stone and portals, a two stone alignment, and a radial stone circle. It

is one of the coolest sites I have seen and the views over Kealkill Village and Bantry Bay were amazing.

As we walked around the site I was drawn to the circle while Sharon was pulled to the two tall standing stones. The circle is roughly eight feet in diameter. The stones are not all that big, with the recumbent stone being only two and a half feet tall and the portals the tallest at about four feet. Dowsing the circle I found an energy line coming from the west which wound south around the circle about five feet out. At the recumbent it turned north, passed under it, crossed the circle and exited under the left portal. It turned east and went straight about 20 feet until it came to the the southern of the two tall standing stones. It then curled around its east side and started north just a few inches away from the stone. After only about a foot it turned and passed under the stone and then ran up the west side of the stone. When it was half way across the gap between these two megaliths the line turned back right and then north passing alongside the east side of the second stone. After it had passed the second stone I followed it quite aways into the next field but saw nothing more ahead and turned back.

As I returned I noticed that the pair was set in a northeast/ southwest alignment which was also the same as the alignment that crossed between the portals and the recumbent stone. Obviously intentional, but for what purpose?

Sharon had been spending time with the two alignment stones and had been very impressed by them. The tall, narrow stone stood 13 feet and its shorter and wider partner was eight feet tall. Sharon called the tall stone the Madonna Stone, as it not only had the look of a stone woman, it also had a very motherly, comforting, feel to it. I too, was impacted by the presence of this goddess rock.

The shorter stone was definitely the male of the pair. I could immediately pick up on its energy and felt my body "strengthen" as I stood with hand on stone. I was soon energized by this fellow and thanked him. Sharon told me that when she had been spending all her time with the Madonna stone she had suddenly felt the shorter stone demand her attention. She said it wasn't really a voice as much as a strong emotional pull from the stone. "Sounds like a guy rock" I said. "Hey, look at me!"

It was interesting that with this pair it was the tall thinner stone that was the feminine rock and the shorter and wider that was the male. I think this is the first time I have encountered this.

The radial circle, which was 26 feet in diameter, stood about seven feet to the southeast from the stone pair. There were 18 short uprights placed around the outer edge of the circle with the interior covered with smaller rocks. I still do not really understand these circles and have yet to make any connection with the ones I have found.

Returning to the five stone circle I went to the recumbent and placed my hands on the top of the stone. I immediately felt my feet sink into the earth. Placing my head on my hands, I felt the energy flow from the ground up through the stone, through my hands and forehead, back down through my body, and out my feet into the earth. What a purifying and exhilarating moment. I was soon ready for whatever this day had to offer. Thanking the stones we said our farewells and returned to the car. What a great place.

7/24

Today we were going to return to The Ring of Beara, a portion of which we had driven last year. First stop was to be the Uragh Stone Circle which was located several miles to the southeast off the R571. I was so impressed by this site last year that it made it to my all-time Top 5 list, and I could not wait to return. And, unlike last year, today was a beautiful sunny day.

Once we had parked the car we took the walk alongside a creek and then up the hill to the top where you have the most wonderful view of the stones below, overlooking Lough Inchiquin. This place is worth the visit just for the views, but we were here for the stones, and what fun it was to join their company once again.

As we walked up to the circle a large ram and a young male companion appeared from behind the large outlier stone. They just stood there looking at us, as if trying to decide if we were there with good intent. I did not move but did say, "Greetings, we are here to honor these stones. I am here to learn." It just seemed like the right thing to do. After another minute or so of this standoff the old fellow looked at the younger one and then they turned and walked away. I had the impression he was the protector of the stones and the young fella was his apprentice. I guess we were approved.

I decided to start with the tall outlier stone. It really is an impressive rock some 10 feet tall. I placed my hands on the stone and began rubbing them against it while asking for its blessing. I slowly worked my hands up the stone and as I did so I could feel the earth energy begin pushing up through the rock as well. At the same time I could also feel the energy rushing up through my feet. We were both being infused with this force and it was like we were sharing in the experience. There was something very sensual about it and I was loving it. After several minutes it was like I was full up and so was the stone, so I removed my hands and just stood there with a smile on my face. "Here we are the same, we are of the Mother" said the stone.

Walking around the interior of the small circle, which is only eight feet in diameter and said to be the smallest circle in Ireland, I stopped at the recumbent stone and placed my hands on the flat surface. Closing my eyes I soon felt the energy flowing around and around the circle reminding me of my experience at Bohonagh Stone Circle last year. No visualizations, but it was wonderful just to share with the stones. "We are one" I said.

Sharon had gone up to the top of the hill and was enjoying the spectacular view. I joined her and we both stood there looking down at this perfect circle, in this perfect location, and knew, once again, we were the luckiest of people.

Next stop was at the Derreen Gardens just north of Lauragh on the R573. We spent about an hour and a half walking the grounds of this wonderful natural garden. We also got a kick out of looking for Derreeny homes which are located in one portion of the garden. A Derreeny is like a garden fairy about two inches tall, and in this one part of the garden, if you look close, you will find a wide variety of little homes in which they are said to live. In fact, there has not been an actual Derreeny sighting since 1855 and though many of the homes are not all that impressive, it was still good fun looking for them.

From Derreen we continued back along the R571 to just east of Ardgroom to make a return visit to the Ardgroom Outer Stone Circle. It continued to be a beautiful sunny day and provided quite a contrast from our visit last year when it was cold and rainy. This time we could fully appreciate the grand view overlooking the entrance to the Kenmore River below.

These really are some gnarly old stones. Though they are in a variety of sizes and shapes, many tend to be long and narrow and do have the appearance of incisor teeth protruding from the earth. Last year, in the thick mist, they gave the overall site quite a foreboding, if not dangerous, appearance.

Sharon had gone her own way and after a while she came to me and asked if I had seen the lady in the outlier stone, which sits about 15 feet to the east of the circle and is over nine feet tall. I said I had noticed the lion face on the western side of the stone which I had also seen last year, but she said to look on the other side. Walking over to take a look I was quite surprised to see the face of a lady who was, as Sharon pointed out, gazing up at the sky. Looking to the stars maybe? I was most impressed and can only guess it was the inclement weather that kept me from noticing her last year.

Placing my hand upon the stargazer I said I was happy to meet her and felt my hand go warm. "Thank you" I said.

Returning to to the circle, which is only 23 feet in diameter, I stoped to spend a little time with each of the nine standing stones (there are two others fallen over). The north stone in particular grabbed my attention. Located pretty much in the center of its drab gray inner surface was a round, lime green lichen growth creating the appearance of an eye in the middle of the stone. As I stood there with my hand on the stone, gazing at this "inner eye," I sensed concern. After having stood there for all these years this stone was concerned that no one cared. I was quite impacted by this revelation. Suddenly this place felt very sad to me and there was nothing I could do to help.

Stone Journals

Moving to the other stones they all seemed withdrawn into themselves. I have never experienced this response before as it was quite emotional. Standing in the center I said a prayer for the stones, then, preparing to leave, I went back to the north stone and said I was very sorry. I felt a subtle surge of energy, thanked the stone, and walked back to the car feeling a bit low.

Continuing on to the west side of the peninsula we arrived at Casteltownbere. Our goal was to find Derreenataggart Stone Circle which was said to be located on a small road just northwest of town. The lady at the information center in the middle of town gave us directions which were quite misleading, but after getting on the right road and stopping to ask directions twice, we arrived at what is one of the most beautiful stone circles I have ever seen. Consisting of some kind of white/light grey rock, the stones, which were sitting in a field just up off the road, seemed to glow as we approached them and the sadness I had been carrying since we had left Ardgroom was dispelled. This was a very happy place!

I was so taken by the appearance of the stones that I spent my initial time taking photos and checking alignments. I noticed that there was a rather large recumbent stone sitting to the west. It is four feet high and seven feet wide. The tops of the two flanker stones were sloped down towards it. In fact, the stones of this circle were graded in such a way as to go from the recumbent which was the shortest, around to the portals, which at over seven feet, were the tallest (one portal is now but a stump). There are nine standing stones, three lying on the ground, and it appears that several are missing. The circle is about 28 feet in diameter.

Deciding it was time to get acquainted with the stones I started with the south stone and was immediately impressed with its strong male energy. It stood about seven feet high, was narrow and thin, with a pointed knife blade top. Once again, it was while I moved my hands up the stone that I began to receive the energy flowing up from the earth. This is a really cool effect and quite different than I had ever previously experienced, until earlier this day at Uragh.

Seeing that Sharon was enjoying relaxing against the standing portal stone I decided to move on to others in the ring. However, it was at this moment that a family (two adults and two teenagers) arrived, being quite loud and speaking a language I did not understand. I thought they would not stay long so I went and sat with Sharon awaiting their departure. Sadly, they laughed and carried on with no concern for us or the environment, and when I saw them settle on the fallen south stone and pull out candy bars, I knew they were not leaving anytime soon. It was time for us to go. I was sad to leave these wonderful stones as I felt a strong connection here. But it would have been even worse to sit in this amazing place and be bummed.

7/25

My main goal today was to find the Feaghna Bullaun Stone which was supposed to be sitting in a field between the road and St Fiachna's Cemetery, about two miles south of the Bonane Heritage Park. Sharon and I had no problem finding the cemetery but finding the stone proved to be another matter. The thing is, the cemetery is enclosed by a massive stone wall much of which is too tall to see over. And the road is also lined on both sides by high overgrown walls which completely block the view so we could not see the field from the road. I was just about to give up when I noticed a gap in the growth on the wall on the far side of the road. I climbed up on the wall to get high enough to see across the road and over the other wall. Happily, there was

the field, and there was the stone. Having no access from this point we went back into the cemetery and I found a place where some stones could be stacked to allow me to climb up and over the stone wall and into the field. I was not disappointed with my discovery. I can honestly say this rock was one of the most impressive stone monuments I have ever been to.

 The stone is a massive square shaped block which appears as if it is being absorbed back into the earth. One side sits at ground level but the earth drops off about three feet on the opposite side. There are seven depressions carved into the surface, three in a row on one side and four in a semicircle on the other. They each have a rounded oval shaped stone sitting in them which was used for making wishes or maybe curses. In the center of the bullaun stone is a round, flat, disk with a hole in the center in which a rounded, long, oval shaped stone is standing, sort of phallic in appearance. There are also three smaller, marble sized depressions on the outer edge of this disk stone. One contained a rock marble. I have no idea what this was all about, but this place felt of serious power.

Deciding to dowse the stone I found the most intriguing thing. Walking clockwise I came across an energy line which ran right across the middle of the stone and continued on. Then walking around the stone widdershins, about 10 feet out, I came to a line which began spiraling around the stone working its way towards the stone's center. The spirals were about three feet apart and after three turns around the stone the line crossed to the center phallic stone where it went to ground. Standing there in the center of the stone I could feel the rush of energy flowing around me as if I was standing in the middle of a whirlpool. I began seeing, or was it just imagining, people standing by the rock, twirling one of the bullaun stones clockwise as they made their wish for a healthy baby, a better life, a good crop, and so on. Some were poor and disheveled, some were obviously well off landholders, a few appeared to be priests. The images spun through my mind like a carousel. I began laughing as I felt the joy and hope this stone has provided to so many people over thousands of years. And I thanked the stone for giving me this moment of joy as well.

After the Feaghna Bullaun Stone we decided to stop at The Ewe Experience, which I recommend if you are in the area. It is a wonderful art garden.

We then went looking for the Ballycommane House B&B. Located on the grounds are three standing stones that I had seen photos of and always wanted to visit. As the B&B was not far to the south of the N71, along which we were driving, this was going to be the day.

Upon our arrival I had knocked on the door to ask permission to see the stones. We were met by a gracious fellow named Andy who said we were welcome to visit them. He then offered to prepare us tea and scones which, along with his pleasant company, we enjoyed while sitting at a table out in the garden. Once done he took us to see the stones. We walked up a slight ridge that was topped with a small grove of Monterey pines. The stones sat right on top, out in the open, with a magnificent view of the valley below and the hills beyond. Even without the stones it was a lovely place. The site consists of a large quartz boulder burial with a stone pair about six feet away, and the pair is not in alignment with the boulder. Andy said that when he and his partner bought the place the top of the hill was covered with brush and brambles and you could not see the stones. He had no idea they were even there until his neighbor told him about them and they had immediately began clearing off the hill top to reveal this hidden treasure.

Though there are only three stones at this site, they could not be more unique or more impressive. The boulder burial is a large, rough shaped boulder of white quartz sitting up off the ground on three smaller stones. As for the stone pair, they sit 10 feet apart with the northeast stone being just under three feet tall and the southwest stone being just over three feet tall. They are quite striking in appearance and look like sections of tree trunk sitting  on the ground. The surface of these rocks even looks like petrified wood and I can understand why this combination of tree and stone would have seemed special to the ancients.

Wondering if the stones were in alignment with an astronomical event I asked Andy. He said yes, but they were surprised to find that it was not the stone pair that were in an alignment. In fact, it was the boulder burial stone and the northern row stone that lined up with the sunrise on summer solstice.

I tried to dowse the site but soon gave up as I kept finding lines going every which way and could not make sense of it all. Definitely a place of energy but beyond my skills to decipher.

I then made an effort to get acquainted with the stones. Standing by the boulder burial I was surprised not to feel much. I mean, this was a huge block of quartz, the prime energy rock! I had expected to feel some serious energies here and was a little saddened by this lack of connection. Maybe if I came back another time?

I then walked over to the southeast stone in the pair. Right away I placed my hands on the stone and just as quickly my feet were rooted in the earth and my hands felt as if they were being pulled into the stone. It was like I was being stretched, with my hands and forearms being pulled deeper and deeper into the rock while my feet remained firmly planted in the ground. It was a very disturbing experience and soon I pulled myself back, feeling an immediate disconnect. That was very weird!

Moving to the other stone I didn't get much of a response but I was ok with that.

I walked over and sat on a bench with Sharon, explaining to her what had just happened. Taking her hand in mine I began to relax and we just sat there sharing in the peace of this most charming of settings. Thinking about what I had just experienced I remembered a similar event at Dowth, when I felt as if I was being drawn down into the earth. There, I had actually been sorry when I found myself back on the surface, but here, I don't know. Ballycommane was a wonderful and intriguing place and I was sorry we had not booked a room for the night.

7/28

In route back to Dublin we stopped to visit the Athgreany Stone Circle (Pipers Stones) on the east side of N81. When Sharon and I had visited this circle last year she had been in quite a negative mood due to her interaction with another couple who had been there. I had been very impressed by this circle and I wanted Sharon to have another chance for a better experience. I am glad we stopped as we were alone with the stones and Sharon thoroughly enjoyed herself.

The Pipers Stones is a ring of 16 granite stones, many with veins of quarts running through them. I find it to be a circle for serious contemplation, and if you want to go deep into yourself the stones will be quite supportive. But, it is also a very happy circle, and if you just walk in among the stones open to what they have to offer, you will feel their joy.

At one point I found myself leaning backwards up against the large northeast stone, with my hands held together behind my back and up against the rock. I soon felt the earth energy flowing out of the stone, in through my hands, down my body, and out my feet. This cycling of energy was very subtle and soothing and continued until I stepped away from the stone.

Moving on to the Cyclops stone (which is so named because it is shaped like a head with a long curved groove carved into it like a smile, and one cup carved above that like a single eye), I sat down on it and was soon smiling with as big of a smile as the stone itself. Like I said, this is a happy place!

Now a most interesting thing happened. Sharon had been standing up against a stone and after a time she came over to me and told me the stone had made her feel welcome. I said that was great. She then said, "But then it told me I needed to let go of not having had a child by natural birth." When I said I did not know it had been bothering her, she said that she didn't either. I found this to be quite heavy but it led to some serious and positive discussion by us both, and when we left there we were better for it. I continue to be surprised by what might happen when in the company of stones and Athgreany was just one more fine example.

Before leaving we walked over to check out the large outlier stone with the cross carved into its top, much like the top of a loaf of Irish soda bread. It sits about 60 yards northeast of the circle in alignment with the portal stones. Sharon wondered about the alignments of the lines carved in the top of the stone and I found one ran due north/south and the other just a little off east/west, for whatever its worth.

Looking back at this magical circle, with the fairy tree growing up among the stones and its smiling cyclops, we were so glad we had stopped for another visit. We thanked the stones, returned to our car, and drove back to Dublin.

This was the end of our stay in Ireland and we were more than satisfied with our time spent here. Once again Ireland and its people had filled us with joy. I had been granted a lifetime of good luck, and the stones, well the stones had touched us deeply and personally.

7/29

We flew into Bristol, England, got our rental car, and took off for Chagford where we were to spend the night, and where I hoped to find the Scorhill Stone Circle which had alluded me back in 2009. In route we took a little detour to make a stop in South Zeal at the Oxham Arms, a 12th century monastery that was long ago converted into an Inn and is only about five minutes off the A30. It is a very charming place but the real reason for stopping was to see the South Zeal Stone which is actually located in the snug room just in back of the bar. It seems that the structure was built around the standing stone. This is a good sized menhir that sits right in a wall running from floor to ceiling, and actually, the top few feet protrude through the floor into the room above. It was good fun to sit in the room by this ancient stone having tea. Why had the monks chosen to build around the stone at a time when far too often such stones were removed or destroyed as being some kind of devil worship? No-one knows but I am glad they made that choice. Cool place.

When we arrived in Chagford I went in search of Scorhill Circle. The roads were oh so narrow, lined with thick hedges and stone walls, and there was too much traffic. It was also raining. Several times I had to back up a hill to find a place to let an approaching car get by. Eventually I began to get burned out and in the end I gave it up. No Scorhill Circle once again. Bummer.

7/30

Taking off for Tavistock I told Sharon I wanted to return to Soussans Common Stone Circle which was located on Dartmoor, alongside a small lane about a mile off the B3212, just out of Postbridge. I had visited this circle on my first stone journey back in 2009 and had grown quite attached to those stones, thinking of them often over the last nine years.

When we arrived I could not help but smile as everything looked the same as before, except that this time the weather was much nicer. No rain.

As I approached the ring I was drawn into its embrace, and as one voice I could hear the welcome of the stones. Walking among them (there are 21 stones I think) was pure joy and looking closely at each stone I began seeing their individuality and to appreciate it. The south stone, however, really stood out. It is a rather pink, very chunky sort of crystalline like stone, with little purple gems spread throughout. It is quite different from the other stones in the circle. It is very irregular in shape and is about twice the height of the other stones, though it is still small, being only about two feet in height. Another fun thing about the south stone is that we found several faces in it with the one on the west side looking like the Hag. You could feel a powerful energy in this stone. Sharon had felt a strong sense of youth and innocence at Soussans and I wondered if the Hag was the protector of that energy.

Dowsing the site I found energy lines running both north/south and east/west. Walking along the outside of the circle, as I passed the south stone I felt a strong pull into the circle and heard the voice of an old woman saying, "Follow me." I looked down at the Hag and said, "Are you talking to me?" There was only a chuckle as I turned and followed the line to the center where it felt like I was being pulled down into the earth as the energy line descended deeper and deeper. This was a little like the experience I had at Dowth, and with the stone at Ballycommane in Ireland, but with no negativity attached. It was a very strong energy and I was not afraid to follow, but I just couldn't figure out how to do it. I have heard and read many stories about the underworld and for just a moment I thought maybe I was going to enter it. I was actually disappointed when I realized it wasn't going to happen. Still the experience was a powerful one.

Though we needed to move on Sharon and I had both been touched significantly by this lovely little circle of stones and I was once again grateful to have been able to return.

Continuing on west across Dartmoor along the B3357 we next stopped at the Merrivale Complex. At this site are the remains of ancient settlements, cairns, standing stones, cists, stone circles, and stone rows. The stones are, for the most part, quite small but impressive nonetheless.

When last here the weather was some of the very worst I have ever experienced and what I most remember about the visit is finally getting back into the car, turning on the heater, changing into dry cloths, and being thankful it was over. Not a very rewarding experience.

Today was a beautiful sun and clouds kind of day. The ground was dry and I could see the hills in the distance. It was a bit cold but nothing like on my previous visit.

It was only about a ten minute walk from the car park before we arrived at the stone avenues. There are actually two separate stone avenues and each is created by rows of mostly small stones, set maybe three feet apart, running in straight lines pretty much East/West. The avenues are separated from each other by a small leat, which is a manmade water channel. The one to the north, about 600 feet long, is the least impressive and, in fact, most of its stones are being absorbed back onto the earth.

The southern avenue, which is 865 feet long, has much more to offer. At its western end stand two pillar stones forming an entrance to the avenue and at the eastern end is a single triangular stone which stands in the end of the avenue to block it. Near the center of the avenue is a small 12 foot circle, consisting of seven or eight stones, which surround what appears to be a small barrow.

There is also an impressive cist 285 feet west of the triangular stone and about 45 feet to the south. It is seven feet long, by three feet wide, by three and a half feet deep. The covering slab is quite massive and the cist is worth a visit.

After having walked the southern row we turned to look south to where I could see, maybe a hundred and fifty yards away, the lone standing stone to which I had gravitated on my last visit. On that day in 2009, cold, wet, and miserable, I had looked out through the rain to see it standing like a beacon of hope, and it is the only positive memory I have of this place on that day. So off we went.

It was so fun to be comfortably walking across the firm ground of the moor, with the backdrop of Kings Tor proudly overlooking the area. Last time I could not even see the tor for the rain. Before we reached the lone stone we came across a stone circle, 67 by 58 feet across, consisting of 11 stones from one foot to one and a half feet tall. Nice circle but we spent little time there. Just another 50 yards south we came to the 10 foot tall megalith. As soon as I placed my hands on it I heard its welcome. My hands became warm and I was flooded with emotion as I remembered the comfort the stone had tried giving me on that cold and rainy day. The stone was still here, and

happy that I had returned. I just stood there sucking in its energy and warmth, and looking up at Sharon, I smiled. "I think it remembers me" I said. Could that even be possible I thought? "Thank you" I said.

There is actually much more to see at this location, including another small row or two, many cairns, remains of round houses and enclosures, and a route marking stone for those crossing the moor. We, however, were finished for today. I left Merrivale a much happier and content person this time around and once again was so thankful we had stopped.

We ended the day at the pleasant Queen's Head Hotel in Tavistock where we stayed two nights.

7/31

Because the weather had been so bad on my last stone journey to Cornwall/Devon I found myself returning to many of the same sights on this trip in hopes of a better experience.

Stone Journals

Yesterday had been just that. And today we were making a return visit to The Hurlers Stone Circles on Bodmin Moor, just outside of Minion. I say circles because there are, in fact, three large circles set close together in a line pretty much north/south. When we arrived the sky was overcast but it did not seem too threatening, so we took the walk over to the first of the three circles. Standing there looking out across the circles I felt a real sense of satisfaction. I was back. But then, while enjoying our walk among the stones I felt the first raindrop. Within five minutes it was pouring and we were getting soaked. This was a real bummer. We ran back to the car and went back into Minion for a tea and a change of clothes. After about 20 minutes the rain stopped and the sky began clearing so we decided to try again.

Upon our return I decided to begin with some dowsing and soon found an energy line running south through the middle of the northern circle which then exited and entered, and continued south through, the middle of the center circle. It then exited and entered the southern circle under the north stone and went about 10 feet straight on before turning left. It curled around the circle to the east about a quarter of the way before turning back on itself about a yards or so further in, and then went counterclockwise until it came to the south stone. There it exited and headed off to who knows where? All three circles were connected by this line and who knows what other sites in the area it connected up with? Once again I find myself wishing I had the time to just keep following one of these lines. I have found this same thing on Machrie Moor, at the Clava Cairns, in the Kilmartin Valley, and numerous other sites. I need to make such an effort to keep going a future priority.

We spent quite a while at the Hurlers. It became another beautiful sun and clouds kind of day, constantly changing. The rains had passed, we were dry and happy, and the stones were welcoming. This was one of those places where just being in the company of these stones was enough. There was a strong feeling of contentment. Standing in the middle of the northern circle I thanked them. "The earth is to be honored and life is to be cherished" echoed through my mind in response.

Concerning the circles, the northern one is 114 feet across and is made up of 16 stones. The middle circle is about 135 feet across and consists of 17 stones. The southern circle has been severely damaged in the past and now has only nine stones.

The stones are all pretty much of a similar height with the tallest five feet 10 inches. Many of the granite stones seem to have been shaped and are to my eyes some of the most pleasant I have seen.

Having read about two outlier stones called The Pipers, said to be located nearby, we went in search of them. They sit around 100 yards to the west and we found them with no problem. They are placed about seven feet apart in an east/west alignment, with the west stone being five and a half feet tall and the east stone being four feet nine inches tall. They radiated strength and we could both feel it. Sadly, they were surrounded by boggy soil and a pool of water so we could not get close enough to put hands on.

Before returning to the car we took one more walk back through the Hurlers Circles. Nothing dramatic happened here but what a wonderful place and what wonderful stones. I had the strong feeling I would need to return yet again.

High marks for my Hoka One hiking boots. They are really light, very comfortable, and keep my feet dry!

From the Hurlers I planned to take Sharon to see the Duloe Circle, one of my all-time favorites. However, the road was blocked by a major traffic accident and we decided to pass and go on to visit Cotehele House and gardens. Walking the gardens gave us a nice break from the narrow hedge lined country roads which were, I must admit, getting to me. The fear of those solid hedges, on those narrow roads, scratching the side of the rental car, kind of messes with you.

At this point I want to mention *The Three Hares Trail* which has nothing to do with stones but is great fun. Throughout Devon and Dartmoor there are a total of 17 churches in which you will find one or more motifs of three hares chasing each other in a circle and connected at the ears. This is an ancient symbol though no-one knows what it meant. They appear as bosses carved into the ceilings of the different churches and there are a total of 29 of them. You can get a nice Three Hares Trail map, created by Eleanor Ludgate, an artist in Chagford, which will show you were they are located. As two of these bosses were to be found at St. Michael the Archangel in Chagford and one in St.

Stone Journals

Eustachius in Tavistock, we made sure to search them out. They are not all that easy to find but well worth the effort. In fact, it was the organist at St. Eustachius (who was, thankfully, practicing for an evening performance and saw me staring up at the ceiling) that pointed out the one there. Also, in Chagford, the locals had created beautiful needlepoint cushions for the benches with this same three hare motif. It was a fun diversion and were we ever to return to that area I can see making an effort to find as many as possible.

8/1

Today we were on our way to the west coast. Our first stop was going to be Tintagel, claimed by some to have been King Arthurs Castle, which we had visited on a trip many years ago. However the town was packed with people and had doubled in size from when we were there before. We decided to keep going and drove on up the B3263 to visit Saint Nectan's Glen. This is a very special place. It is said to have been the location of Saint Nectan's hermitage and is considered by many to be a sacred site. After a beautiful walk to the glen, once there you will find many ribbons, prayers, and other objects tied to trees, and in the river bed itself there are stacks of stones, known as fairy stacks. There are also several logs into which coin offerings have been pounded over the years. I have not seen this before and it is pretty cool.

From where you park your car it is about a 20 minute walk, half of which wanders up a narrow valley of ancient woodlands and alongside the River Trevillet. Eventually you come to a shop and restaurant where you can purchase entrance into the waterfall area. There are actually three waterfalls along this walk. The largest has about a 60 foot drop at the base of which the stream has carved a large basin. Over the centuries the stream then carved a hole through the side of the basin out of which the water cascades and runs on down the valley. Saint Nectan's is one of those places you will never forget, and you will always be very thankful that you found your way there. There is magic in the air, you can feel it, and you can see it in the eyes, and on the faces, of others you meet along the way.

The only stones you encounter are the ones over and through which the stream flows, and the ones which were used to build stone walls. Nonetheless, you do find yourself noticing them, and noticing the ways in which they have been carved by nature as well as by human hands. Rock is a big part of the experience at Saint Nectan's.

The staff was very pleasant, and in fact, Sharon was convinced that this one girl in particular was in reality a fairy. She did have a most enchanting appearance and manner, and I, too, would not have been surprised if she had suddenly disappeared or sprouted wings.

Then it was on to Boscastle which is a wonderful little port village on the sea. I had wanted to stop there to visit The Museum of Witchcraft with its interesting collection of historical witchcraft artifacts. Fun stop.

At this point I think I should mention something. On this day I had written in my journal, "Note to self. Do not go to Cornwall July through mid-August." The schools are out at this time and an amazing number of the English choose Cornwall as their vacation spot, making the roads and some locations way overcrowded and uncomfortable. I really do recommend staying away at this time of year.

8/2
We began the day enjoying the charm of the small town of Wadebridge and then we drove on to Padstow. While this is a beautiful coastal town it had been overrun by tourists to the point of Disneyland type crowds. It really was not enjoyable at all and we quickly left. However we did visit Prixdeaux Place just outside of town and that was great fun. It is a wonderful old home and gardens and is well worth a visit.

8/3
After a stop to visit the Tremenheere Sculpture Garden above Penzance we went to check in at Mount Haven Hotel. It sits up on the hillside with a spectacular view overlooking the Cornish coastline, with Marazion below, Penzance in the distance, and the inspiring presence of Saint Michael's Mount standing just off the shore. When we arrived you could still see most of the causeway going from the shore out to the mount, but the tide  was coming in and it was not long before it disappeared under the rising sea, leaving just the boat shuttles running back and forth. What a special place.

On that first Stone Journey it was here at Mount Haven that I met Orange, one of the owners, who gave me *Spirits Of The Stones* by Alan Richardson to read while I was there. That book had a big impact on me. It is also where I had spent time with Joseph, who I had met earlier in the day on the path to Boscawen-Un Stone Circle. Both memorable experiences for me.

After having tea and scones on our balcony, with that amazing view overlooking St Michaels Mount, umbrellas in hand we went for a walk to a path I remembered that lead down to the seashore. The really cool thing about this place is that as you walk along the beach you can find the most wonderful "quartz lingams," as Orange had named them. They are chunks of milky white quartz, quite small to maybe eight inches in size, that have been rounded over the years by the actions of the sea rolling in and out on the beach. I had brought three home with me last time I was there. One, the size of a small egg still sets on the nightstand next to our bed. Another, sort of a five inch oval, moves from rock to rock in my large stone circle.

Sharon and I spent some time walking the beach, evaluating quartz lingam stones as we went, until we each found one that spoke to us. Stones in hand we headed back. Great fun and a wonderful way to end our day.

8/4

Unlike the off and on rainy weather we have been having for days now, today was a beautiful sunny day, so we decided to take the walk out to St Michael's Mount, a strong energy place full of history and legend. If you have not been, Saint Michael's is a castle surrounded by gardens sitting on top of a mass of rock out in the bay. It is connected to the mainland by a granite cobblestone causeway over which you can walk or drive when the tide is out. However, when the tide is in you only have access by boat. As the tide was out the causeway was open, so it was the perfect time to go. It really is a treat to be walking across to the mount on the causeway of cobblestones which only a few hours before was completely submerged.

We did the tour of the castle and then walked the gardens, which are amazing. It was a good day to be alive and we were taking full advantage of it. By the time we started the walk back the tide had turned and there was a long section of the causeway in the middle that was now covered over by several inches of water Though the boats were once again shuttling people we had on our hiking boots and splashed on across. This is a must visit if you are in the area.

In the afternoon we decided to take a drive out to visit Lanyon Quoit and Men An Tol, a couple of standing stone sites that Sharon and I had found on our very first trip to Cornwall. They are both easily accessed off the Madron-Morvah Road. Lanyon Quoit is just off the road to the north but there is a tall hedge which blocks your view and you can easily miss it when coming at it from the east, as we did. However, we kept looking and further down the road we saw it on the moor back behind us and turned around. There is a small turnout where you can park and then cross over into the field in which the quoit sits. It stands tall and proud out on the open moor and consists of three uprights upon which sit a nine feet by 17 feet by one and a half foot thick stone slab, said to weigh 13 and a half tons. The top sits seven feet off the ground and the quoit looks for all intent and purposes like a giant stone table, and is, in fact, called by many locals The Giants Table.

We did not spend a lot of time at Lanyon Quoit but I did appreciate the strength of its presence. No special recognition here, just good feeling earth energy.

We were then on to Men An Tol just a short drive on to the west. Upon parking the car it was about three quarters of a mile walk up a rocky road to where you could see the stones sitting off to the right, out on the moor. We arrived at the site about the same time as two other couples, one couple with their little boy. We decided to just sit back and allow the others to have their moment with the stones. It was not long before they were off again leaving us alone with this most eclectic of stone monuments.

This was my forth time to visit Men An Tol and once again I was excited to be there. I had on a previous trip dowsed the site and I found a number of buried stones which were, it seems, once a part of a stone circle. There remain only three standing stones, two normal uprights four feet tall, in-between which stands a round stone, four foot six inches in diameter, with a hole cut in its middle, looking much like a large rock donut. I have never seen another like it. According to tradition, passing a child through the center of the stone would heal the child of whatever troubles them. It was joyful to watch as the couple with the little boy had passed him through the stone. While he seemed just fine, they also seemed quite serious.

Dowsing the circle I found an energy line running east/west across the circle under two mostly buried stones, one directly to the east and the other directly to the west. I also found a line running mostly north/south which was slightly off center and passed right alongside of the donut stone.

Stone Journals

While we enjoyed our visit we had no special experiences. Each time I have been to this site I have done so thinking that surely these stones would have some kind of story to tell me, or some words of wisdom to impart, even if only on an emotional level. And each time I walk away a bit empty, as I just do not seem to be able to make a connect with Men An Tol.

That evening Sharon and I were driving out to Minnack to attend the theater when I suddenly said to Sharon, "We're near The Blind Fiddler, I can feel him!" It had been almost 10 years since I had met that most joyful of stones, and I had not realized that our drive would take us past him. I looked up at the tall hedge lining the road and sure enough I could just see the top foot or so of the Fiddler. I pulled the car into the same turnout I had used all those years ago and ran across the road to look out over the field in which the Fiddler sat. There he was! I was so very happy, and I hollered to him "I will be back tomorrow!"

8/5

What a great day this was! This was a "stones day" of the highest caliber. We began with a search for the Drift Standing Stones said to sit just off the A30 west of the village of Drift. We had no trouble finding them. The pair of stones were sitting out in a freshly tilled field where the farmer had obviously taken care to plow around them and to cause no harm. Sharon waited in the car for me to check them out and as I approached them I was immediately drawn to the southeast stone which was about nine feet tall and phallic in its appearance. It also had a rather dramatic crack running diagonally all the way around the stone. Standing with my back up against it my feet settled into the earth and I could feel a very strong masculine energy flowing up through my body. The energy was not overpowering but solid and steady and I thanked the stone.

I was soon welcomed by the stone and I could almost "feel" his smile, as he was very pleased by my visit. "How do I look?" he asked. Really? Was that humor from a stone? I had to laugh.

Not to be ignored, the northwest stone, standing about eight feet tall, gave me a strong tug and I moved over to place my hands on it. This time the energy was very calming, quite feminine, and just as welcoming. The two stones stand 18 feet apart and as I stood in-between them it felt as if I was standing between the Yin and the Yang, the two sides of the coin. The two stones were working together to create a perfect balance. Sharon soon joined me and she too, commented on the feeling of balance with these two stones.

We spent quite a while walking back and forth between these two megaliths, laughing and talking about how happy we were to be there. Looking at the female stone we both saw a Kwan Yin character in the stone, and when looking at the male stone we saw what appeared to be a man's head wearing some kind of hat, or cap, and looking kind of like an Egyptian priest.

Dowsing the site was good fun. I found a line running northwest/southeast passing directly under both stones. I also found another line coming from the southeast just a few feet to the west of, and running parallel with, the line that crossed under the two stones. This line curled around the southeast stone and then entered the space between the two stones heading towards the northwest. However, after having only gone a few feet it turned to the west and off it went across the field. I wonder where it was going? The Fiddler is in that direction.

Next up, just a little ways down the road was, in fact, The Blind Fiddler, and once again I could see it peeping over the hedge as we approached it. As I climbed over the gate and entered the field I was filled with happiness! I had long hoped I would get a chance to return to this wonderful old stone and here I was. This time it was a beautiful sunny day and the Fiddler stood ever so proudly just about 100 yards away, surrounded by a field of golden wheat. He looked very impressive and I could feel his welcome like a warm chuckle vibrating through the earth.

Stone Journals

Being very careful not to harm the wheat I made my way to the stone. As with the Drift Stones, the farmer here has respected this solitary megalith and had left an open space around it. I think there is still a little of the old customs in play here. It was believed that messing with these stones could bring a curse on you and I think some farmers today still feel you are better off just leaving them be.

Walking up to the Fiddler the earth pulsed with energy as I felt him welcome me back. What joy! After walking around the stone I crouched down with my back against it and settled in. I soon felt the embrace of the stone as If it were wrapping around me. I had this same "Old Man Willow" experience last time I was here. Then he spoke. "Look at the crop growing strong and healthy once again. But for how much longer? It is up to you." "Why me?" I asked. "Humans." said the Fiddler. "The scale is tipping faster than you seem to think. Embrace the earth while there is still time." That was it. "Getting a bit heavy on me Fiddler," I replied.

Standing, I stood looking at the stone and noticed three snails about a third of the way up the stone. I remembered seeing a lone snail about half way up on my last visit. Were these three on a pilgrimage to the top? Were they supporting each other or was it a race to see who got there first? In any case, I would not be around to see the finish.

Stepping back up to this lone menhir I embraced it and felt the comforting warmth of the stone, but there was also a sense of sadness. Was it for me or for mankind? Suddenly, I felt that mild rumble under my feet as once again the Fiddler chuckled and thanked me for visiting him again. "Sorry to be so heavy" he said.

"Thank you for caring Fiddler," I said. Returning to the car I found Sharon standing by the gate. She said she was really sorry not to have met The Blind Fiddler. She had been unable to get over the gate but said she could feel the strength and character of the stone from where she stood.

Last stop of the day was the Boscawen-Un Stone Circle. Again I was enjoying the fact that it was a nice sunny day. It had been so cold and rainy on my last two visits, and though I did not miss the cold and the rain I did find myself missing the moody atmosphere just a little. Still, I was happy to introduce Sharon to this most charming circle. There are nineteen stones, three to five feet tall in this 73 ft by 82 ft circle. With the exception of a gap on the west side the stones are all quite evenly spaced. All the stones are gray granite except one block to the west which is quartz. Why the one? There is also a lone finger of stone, about eight feet tall, standing off center near the middle of the circle and leaning at quite an angle. The whole thing is surrounded by a hedge of gorse and it really is a most magical place.

When we first arrived at Boscawen-Un Sharon had been having strong stomach pains, so she went to the quartz stone standing on the west side of the circle and stood with her tummy up against it. After about five minutes the pain went away and all was well. I was not surprised that it was the quartz stone she had been drawn to, as quartz is such a good healing stone, but I was surprised by just how quickly the stone had helped her with her pain.

We both enjoyed our time spent with these stones as they really do feel welcoming. Whether you are walking among the stones or just standing outside the ring gazing at them, you cannot help but get the sense that this is a place of celebration. Traditionally this circle has been used for rituals by both groups and individuals, and that practice continues even today. A group had gathered there just a little over a month ago to celebrate the Summer Solstice.

8/7

Today was to be our last in England and we were off to the Stanton Drew Stone Circles to meet up with Martin Ringer, the author of *Pictures Of The Past*. We arrived at the same time as he and after introductions we walked on to the Great Circle. There are three circles at Stanton Drew; the NE ring being 97 feet in diameter, The Great Circle being 368 feet sitting in the middle, and the SW ring being 145 feet across. I found Martin to be quite an enjoyable fellow and we were soon talking stones. I think Sharon wanted to give us a chance to get acquainted and so she decided to head off to the NE circle on her own.

Martin has made it his passion to look for the faces and figures revealed in the stones erected by ancient ancestors. It was quite rewarding to read his book on the subject and even more fun to be there with him having him show me figures in the stones. There are not that many stones still standing in the Great Circle so it was not long before we were off to

Stone Journals

the NE circle to join up with Sharon. Martin was soon revealing many of the images he had discovered in these rocks, some human and some animal. It was great fun and I was impressed by his knowledge and dedication.

Dowsing this ring I soon found an energy line to the north-northwest which passed under a stone there, crossed the center of the ring, and exited under a stone in the south-southeast. Outside the circle the line bent south and Sharon, Martin, and I followed it as it crossed alongside the Great Circle and continued on across the field. We were soon following it up a low hill at the top of which sat the SW circle. The line entered the ring from the northwest, crossed through the center of the circle, and exited to the southeast, similar to the NE circle. It then turned northeast towards where the Cove would be located (The Cove is a group of three stones I shall speak more of in a moment). I was, however, stopped by a stone wall. I am sure it would have gone on to connect with those stones. My thought was to try to pick up the line on the other side later. It was quite wonderful to find this one line connecting all three circles and probably the Cove as well.

In walking around the outside of the circle I did also find another line crossing the circle northeast/southwest but I did not try to follow it.

Sharon, Martin, and I spent quite a while at the SW Circle which is, in fact, one of my favorite stone rings. Nothing but comfort from these stones. The grasses were well mowed this time and all the stones were visible, or at least the portion that still remains above ground. This circle can appear quite insignificant at a glance. But, if you take some time to get acquainted with the stones, they continue to have a healthy energy which they are happy to share. We did not spend near the time I would have liked but I will return.

At this point we decided to go visit the Cove. This is a wonderful megalithic site composed of just three stones set in sort of a U shape, with the back stone having fallen over. Of the two

uprights, one is diamond shaped and the other has the appearance of an animals head. I have written about it in Stone Journey 7. It really is a cool place and provided for some good discussion about what its original purpose might have been.

Last stop was the Druids Arms for tea and a pint. Hanging with Martin was a distraction from the stones but well worth the tradeoff. I really enjoyed his company and his knowledge and was sorry we did not have more time. He was kind enough to bring me an autographed copy of *Pictures Of The Past* for which I am grateful. I hope our paths cross again.

8/9

After a short stop in Edinburgh, Scotland, and our first time at the Edinburgh Tattoo (which was great fun), we were headed to Pitlochry. In route we took the A827 off the A9 towards Loch Tay. The Tay Valley is another one of those places rich in megalithic sites that I have long wanted to get to. This was the day.

It was a beautiful sunny day and the drive alone was worth the trip. But, I was looking for standing stones and first up was the Lundin Farm Stone Circle which was easily found. Just a short drive up a farm road, as we came around a turn, there were the stones, and Sharon and I both exclaimed, "Oh my!" at the same time. Located up on a mound just to the left of the road you could feel the stones' presence from 50 yards away. Some were standing, some fallen, and I think some were missing. The ring was a little overgrown with grasses and brush, gorse maybe and there was a large oak tree growing up on its edge. Still, this haggard looking circle of stones coursed with energy, and though I could sense their desire to interact with us I could also sense their pride. I could not wait to meet them.

Arriving at the ring, which is actually more of a rectangle 11 ft. by 13 ft., we found four standing stones, with several lying on the ground. The stone to the northeast was much larger than the others being seven feet three inches tall and I immediately felt drawn to it. Leaning up against the stone I was flooded with a sense of happiness and heard, "Welcome, welcome." I could "feel" the stone's smile as he spoke to me, "We do look kind of rough don't we?" I had been thinking just that as we had walked up to the circle, and had to laugh.

I noticed that there was a narrow ledge carved on the inner side of the stone which made a perfect seat. So sitting there, leaning against the rock, I began to experience the sensation of my body merging into it, and at the same time, my feet seemed to sink into the earth. I do not know how long I sat there but as I stepped away I was fully charged and I said to Sharon, "This is a most wonderful stone!"

Walking among the other stones I felt a calm, flow of support but realized it was not just from the stones. The tree growing on the edge of the circle caught my full attention and once I centered on it I was made aware that this oak was there for a purpose, to provide company, and to a degree, protection, to these neglected stones. While I understood the company part I was not sure how it could provide protection? Then, I thought maybe the root system grows out under the rocks stabilizing them and keeping them from sinking into the earth? Whatever the case, there is no doubting the interaction of stone and tree here at Lundin Farm. In fact, I could feel the interaction of all the elements, especially on a day like this, with the sun shining down on tree and stones, all deeply rooted in the earth. All being supportive of, and protective of, each other. I had a wonderful sense of fullness, and gave the tree a hug.

Deciding to dowse the site I did find an energy line approaching the stones from the north that then wrapped around the outside of the ring to the east side, where it entered and crossed the circle to exit under the west stone. It then curled around the outside of the ring to the south side where it took off across a field towards a pile of stones I could see in the distance. Another site maybe? I am sorry I did not follow the line to see if it did, in fact, lead to those stones, and if so, what they might have been.

I also found the physical location of this ring to be interesting. It sits up on a natural platform which sits in a basin from which you can only see out to the west. I wondered if there was a solar or lunar alignment here?

This was a great way to start our time in Scotland. We had encountered a wonderful ring of stones here at Lundin Farm and they had made us welcome.

Continuing on along the A827, just about four miles past Aberfeldy, we came to the Croft Moraig Stone Circle. I must say this really is a complex site. In the center of it all there is a stone horseshoe about 24 feet across which is surrounded by a stone circle some 40 feet in diameter, both being made up of good sized boulder type stones from two to six and a half feet in height. These are then surrounded by a ring of stone rubble with the ring being some 60 feet across, and all of this is built up on a raised platform. There are two larger pillar/portal stones standing 18 feet outside the rubble ring, to the southeast. Also of interest there is to the south, lying flat on the ground in the rubble ring, a six foot six inch long stone which has a number of cup marks carved in it. Some of the Croft Moraig stones have fallen over and some seem to have been moved at some point in time, but overall this site is very well preserved.

Though the setting is quite impacted by the surrounding farm buildings one cannot help but be somewhat envious. It would be be amazing to be able to look out your windows and have this circle as your view.

When I dowsed the location I found an energy line running right between the two portal stones, straight across the circle, and out to the northwest.

We really enjoyed our time at Croft Moraig but as we had much to find before calling it a day, and as I was not getting any kind of interactions with these stones, we decided to continue on. Great place though!

After a stop at Castle Menzies for tea we went looking for the Dull Stone Circle, but with no success. Though I think we were looking in the right field I also think the crop had grown too tall and was covering up the stones.

Not all that much further along the B846 we had no trouble locating the Fortingall Stones. Out in a field to our left we could see what appeared to be the remains of three stone circles, the stones being two to four feet tall. So, parking the car, over the fence we went. Feeling the pull of the stones, I once again had a big smile on my face as we approached the first circle (southwest). Consisting of three irregular shaped boulders, a portion of the circle was overgrown with some plant that had actually grown taller than the stones. It made getting around a bit difficult but I did not care.

Walking around the outside, going from stone to stone, I felt a subtle surge of energy flowing up through my feet. As poorly as these stones had been treated over the years they remained strong and full of earth energy. I also noticed that these stones, between two and three feet tall, seemed to have been smoothed, probably by natural causes, but I could not help but wonder if humans had maybe had a hand in it?

Crossing to the northeast circle, only about 90 feet away, I found it was even more overgrown than the last,

Stone Journals

making it quite difficult to get around. There were four stones here and they were a little smaller than those in the southwest grouping, being only about two feet tall. I wondered if this was a four poster circle, but it was so overgrown it was hard to get a read of what was going on here. I was not making any connections with this ring but I was getting a strong pull from the stones to the south, so, I headed that way.

These stones were less than 200 feet from the others and although this group also consisted of three stones, here they seemed to be placed in a straight alignment running southeast/northwest. Interestingly, the three stones had sort of a recumbent stone and flankers look to them. Maybe they were once a part of a recumbent circle? The middle stone was long and flat topped. The would-be flankers were taller, thin, and shaped like an upside down U. They sat three or four feet to each side of the recumbent and were placed at ninety degree angles from it, to good effect. I was reminded of the stone circles in Ireland with their portal stones placed at angles.

Another thought was that maybe the three stones were not part of a circle but rather part of a row. There may originally have been even more stones in this row, maybe even an avenue? Did these stones align with the northeast circle and someplace further down towards the river? Lots of possibilities. There had obviously been some kind of megalithic complex here long ago, but who knows how extensive it was? Sadly, I had forgot my dowsing rods so I was not getting any help figuring out this place. Whatever the story, I loved these stones.

At one point Sharon and I settled in against the northern U stone of the alignment and we were both flooded with a sense of happiness and a sense of welcome. What a marvelous place. Looking down towards the River Lyon, just to the east, I understood why this place had been chosen for this complex. The earth was alive with energy here and you could feel the magic! And, I knew I would return here one day to properly dowse and explore this area.

As we returned to our car, I climbed up on the stone wall and looked back across the field at the three groupings of stones, partially buried in the grass and weeds.

These were not massive or dramatically shaped stones and some folks might even ignore them, but they would really be missing out. Standing there I closed my mind to all but the stones and thanked them, saying I would return one day, a promise I do not make lightly. I began to feel the energy rumbling under my feet, right up through the stone wall, and I was a happy lad.

Driving on to Fortingall we went to the abbey to see the Fortingall Yew, which is said to be 3000 to 5000 years old. It is the oldest tree in Britain and one of the oldest living organisms of any kind in all of Europe, and that is impressive in and of itself. Cool tree and worth the stop.

Another interesting tidbit about Fortingall is that it is said to be the birthplace and home of Pontius Pilate before his move to the Holy Land, for whatever that is worth.

It was time to get on to Pitlochry and the Annslea B&B where we were to stay for a few days. Driving back through the Tay Valley we felt blessed. It had been a beautiful sunny day and the stones had welcomed us. It doesn't get much better.

8/10
We had a fun visit to Blair Castle and gardens in the morning. Most impressive I think was Dana's Grove, an amazing collection of trees, including redwoods, that were taller than any I have seen in Scotland before.

In the afternoon we made a visit to Edradour Distillery just outside of Pitlochry which was charming and good fun. Then on our return to town we did a little searching and near the Moulin Inn we found the Danes Stone sitting all alone in a freshly mowed field. It is quite an oddly shaped chunk of rock and is about seven feet in height. Standing there looking at it I was suddenly surprised to see a man's face staring back at me. Though the face may be a natural occurrence it was still quite striking and I told him I thought he was pretty cool. We did not stay long but it was long enough for this solitary stone to impress me, and I left knowing he deserved a return visit.

Having spent the night in Ullapool we caught the morning ferry to Stornoway on the Isle of Lewis. It was a sunny day with cumulus clouds advancing rapidly across the sky. So very different than our last visit with the constant rain and strong winds. That said, upon arrival, knowing how quickly the weather can change we decided to go straight away to Callanish I, or just Callanish, which is how most people refer to it.

It is a 25 minute drive from Stornoway to the stones and as we approached the site we saw both Callanish II and III sitting out in the open to the left of the A858. There are actually four different stone circles in this area and they are numbered Callanish I thru IV, with Callanish I being the largest and most impressive. I really wanted to get to the main site while the weather held so we continued on.

After parking we walked past the information center on up to the top of the hill where we could look down upon the megaliths that are Callanish. What can one say about these stones? This really is as impressive a site as you will find anywhere and I was so thankful that I had been able to get back. Gazing down across this complex of stone circle and stone rows you know that each stone was placed where it is for a purpose. A purpose that they, the stones, can remember but that we have long forgotten.

When you stand up on the rocky outcrop of Cnoc an Tursa, looking below you and to the north, there stand the stones and they fill you with awe and a sense of sacredness. You are looking down along the southern row of stones which lead to the circle, from which short rows go out to the east and west and two long rows form and avenue going off to the north. The word impressive does not nearly do this site justice.

The stones are maybe the most spectacular you will find anywhere, in size, shape, and composition. They are tall, narrow, and thin, with the tallest being the circle center stone at 16 feet, and all have their own unique shape. They are composed of Lewissian gneiss which was formed in dramatic swirls of color with little chunks of crystals throughout. These really are about as cool as a rock can get. The overall layout is similar to that of a Celtic cross which covers an area 400 feet from end to end.

I think this is possibly the most "human" of all the stone sites. By that I mean that as I walk among the stones I can really sense them as individual beings and actually, many even have a humanlike appearance. It is as if they are all in communion with one another and if you listen closely you can, almost, hear their conversation.

As we moved among the stones I felt energy flows running along each of the rows down into the center. I had once again forgot to bring my dowsing rod but the flow was there and I could feel it. Some of the stones seemed happy with our presence with the occasional surge of warmth emitted by a rock here and there, but for the most part I felt almost an indifference. I got the impression that if I wanted to interact with the megaliths at Callanish It would require much more time and energy spent with the stones to prove my sincerity. That wasn't going to happen on this trip but maybe another time?

Sharon and I spent a couple of hours walking from stone to stone, feeling so very lucky that we were able to experience them without getting wet or being blown about. In fact, the sky continued to change moods the whole time we were there, but it did not rain. One moment the sky would be a brilliant blue with some white cumulous clouds and then a little later it would go all gray. After a short time it was back to blue again. So much nicer than last time. There were not many people there and those that were seemed quite respectful of the stones and of others and we weren't really impacted by them at all. The magic of Callanish Is just too strong. Earth, Water, and Sky were all around us and at the heart of it all were the wonderful stones.

Deciding we should move on to the other nearby circles before the changing weather turned bad, we got directions and a map from the information center and drove to the southeast on the B8011 to visit Cnoc Ceann A' Gharraidh, or Callanish II. From the parking area it was just a short walk across bogland to the circle and I must say I was quite intrigued. It sits out in the open just 100 yards up from Loch Roag. There are five standing stones of Lewissian gneiss (with several lying on the ground) that are the remains of a ring 71 feet by 62 feet. Once again this is a collection of large, uniquely shaped stones ranging from six foot six inches to 10 foot nine inches in height. Standing in the circle and looking to the northwest, there up on the ridge, standing against the skyline, were the stones of Callanish I and it was a most wondrous sight. I stood in awe looking up at the stones and imagined people long, long ago doing the same. Was there a lost ritual path that once led up to those stones? Intriguing thought.

From inside the circle of Callanish II, if you look around you cannot help but notice just how exposed these stones are. All three circles sit out in the open with no trees, bushes, or even tall grasses around them. Just peat bogs and water for as far as you can see (with the occasional structure of course). Then you realize that you, too, are exposed, with no place to hide. It is just you, the stones, and the elements. There is something about the atmosphere that is almost intimidating. Not in a frightening way, but more like a challenge. Why are you here? Do you really want to be here?

Leaning against a stone to the east I felt the embrace of the stone. It is a most comforting experience and one I am always grateful for. Sinking into the stone I knew why I was there, and that yes, I really, really wanted to be there!

We began feeling the first sprinkles from a darkening sky and so decided we better move on to Cnoc Fillibhir Bheag, or Callanish III, just a couple hundred yards walk to the east. This is a really interesting site and one I that still do not understand. The ring consists of eight standing stones but there are also four more standing stones within the circle along with several fallen ones. It is believed by some that the interior stones were part of an inner circle. Most of the stones are about five feet in height but there was one stone more like seven feet. Two of the inner standing stones were in a northeast/southwest alignment but whether by chance or purpose I do not know.

As we were getting cold, and a little wet, we decided to walk back. I thought to dowse the site first and found a line crossing through the middle of the circle from north to south. Upon exiting the circle the line turned to the west and I followed it down to Callanish II where it entered from the east, crossed the circle and exited to the west. It then turned northwest and headed in the direction of Callanish I. Wow! Were all three circles connected by one energy line? I do believe so. Might this be the ritual path? Another reason to return.

Our visit to Callanish II and III was not nearly long enough, but it was now full out raining and time to go. We returned to our car and headed back to Stornoway. Our first day on Lewis could not have been better.

8/13

This morning we decided to explore the northeast side of Lewis and driving along the A858 we soon found The Truiseil Stone. Lone and exposed, overlooking the north sea, this massive monolith is the tallest stone in Scotland, being about 20 feet tall. As is often the case with the stones on Lewis, it is also wide and thin. The top, which is covered with a light green lichen, is quite irregular in shape and appears as if it was broken off. It really is a magnificent rock.

As I approached the stone, which sits in an alley between two stone walls, I could feel its presence. This was a powerful, self-assured fellow, and loud and clear his message almost assaulted me as I walked up to him. "The earth is strength. Root deep and stand tall." My eyes filled with water as I placed my forehead to the stone and felt a surge of energy.

Sharon and I stood with this stone for quite a while, each accepting its strength and blessing. It was cold and windy but we just did not want to hurry away. Deciding to dowse it I soon found an energy line running northwest/southeast through the middle of the wide side of the stone and another running northeast/southwest through the thin side.

The closeness of some farm buildings was kind of disappointing but as I stood with back to stone, gazing out at the sea beyond, I was again struck by the precious melding of earth, sea, sky, and stone here in Scotland. When we said farewell to The Truiseil Stone, we left quite content.

Continuing further east along the A857 we saw a sign pointing to Steinacleit Cairn and Stone Circle. The site sits up on a hill overlooking a loch below and the sea beyond, and is quite interesting. Though the sign describes it as a circle and cairn, there is no confirmation of that. Some think it was just a farm house and enclosure. To my eye there does seem to be the remains of a stone circle here, with four or five stones still standing, and a lot of smaller stones lying around. There is definitely a low stone wall surrounding the entire site.

I did find an energy line running east/west across the middle of the circle and the place really did have a very different kind of feel to it. Many of the stones were a cool looking gneiss with pink swirls and deposits of quartz. And the view, was really spectacular. Whether it was a sacred site or someone's home they really thought about location, location, location. Whatever the case, it is a fun place to visit.

Continuing on we drove out the B8014 to the northern tip of the island, to the Butt Of Lewis. This was a very awesome location. We stood near the old lighthouse looking out across the 80 foot cliffs at lands end and to the sea beyond. It was cold, windy, and threatening rain, as the mighty waves of the North Atlantic crashed against the rocks. In one cliff we saw clearly the outline of the face of the Hag, watching protectively over the Isle. Gazing further out we knew there was nothing out there but the Arctic Icecap. We were at the end of the world. This was another of those places where it was great to just stand there and feel the elements.

Heading back along the B8014 we were looking for The Clach Stein Stones. This is a pair of stones located on a grassy hillside overlooking Port Nis. It is far from a pristine location with homes below on two sides, power lines, and some kind of tall cement tower not far away. Nonetheless, I let out an enthusiastic, "Yes!" when I first saw them. They only stood about three feet tall but had a real presence, and though I could feel the strong bond between them they were obviously as different as hard and soft. I could also feel their joy at my approach.

The first of the pair was smaller, a bit gnarly and irregular shaped, and lighter in color. This was the result of large amounts of milk white quartz in the stone. The second stone, located maybe 10 feet further on, was rounded and smooth with a flat top. It was black in color with thin bands of quartz running through it making lovely white patterns on the surface. As I said, these stones could not have been more different and yet you could feel they were bound together like the Yen and the Yang.

The lighter stone had a subtle, warm, feminine energy about it which was very pleasant, but I could not ignore the call from its darker partner. Its energy was a strong, jubilant, masculine energy and I laughed as I walked up and place a hand on its top. "Ok, I'm here" I said. My feet sunk into the earth and I soaked up what it had to offer. My hand became very warm and I was soon full up and ready to go. I began to hear a subtle laugh actually coming from the stone and a voice calling out, "Life should be lived to the fullest every day. Are you listening?" So simple, so direct, and yet it felt so personal.

I knew I wanted Sharon to meet these stones so I took the walk back to the car (where she had been waiting) and was able to calm down a bit along the way. As I approached her she rolled down the window and said, "I know that look. You found the stones didn't you?" I took her hand and we walked back up the hill.

The weather had once again improved so we took our time moving back and forth between this unique pair of stones. Sharon, too, picked up on the positive energy of both and enjoyed their company. She especially liked the calming energy which emanated from the lighter stone. "This stone feels so comforting" Sharon said.

Later, walking back to the car, I was full up with "enthusiasm," for whatever was next.

On our drive back to Stornoway we stopped to check out Dun Carloway, a most impressive broch tower, or fortress, made of stacked stones. It was in very good condition for how old it is and we had fun climbing around and through it.

Last stop of the day was to be Ceann Hulavig, or Callanish IV. I hated to just drive past the other Callanish sites but it was getting late and I was worried about rain, so we carried on. Located a couple of miles south of the other Callanish sites this circle sits up on a ridge about 400 yards off the B8011 and the tops of several of the stones can be seen from the road. We had experienced some rain off and on throughout the day but at the moment it was just overcast, so once we had parked we made the hike up to the stones. This ring sits quite alone on a vast, grass covered landscape overlooking Loch Hulavig.

The stones are quite similar to Callanish II and III in both size and shape. Here, however, an excavation of the site had been done which encompassed the entire circle. They had dug out the soil to a depth of several feet, from the center of the circle to a couple of feet out beyond the stones. This has created a marshy basin in which the stones sit and in which we could not walk. This was a real bummer. If I ever get back I will know to bring Wellies. We could also see the remains of a cairn in the center of the ring.

Dowsing the site I found lines running both northeast/southwest and northwest/southeast. I could not help but wonder if one of those lines heading north might not connect up with all the other Callanish circles?

As we explored the site Sharon and I were both attracted to two stones. They were positioned next to each other and separated by about eight feet. The one further to the north looked like the head of a lady and gave off an uppity, female kind of energy, while the other to its right had the appearance of a man and gave off a stubborn, male energy. The thing is, the lady was facing away from the man while he looked right at her. She had obviously turned her back on him for whatever the reason. Sharon said she could really feel the lady's energy and felt an emotional connection with her. As this does not happen often with Sharon this was a fun moment. We named them, "She Said, He Said."

Looking to the north you could not see the other circles but I could feel a strong pull in that direction. It seemed that if I was to follow the right one of those energy lines off to the north I would indeed find the old track that was once used to walk between the sites. That there had, in fact, once been just such a path. The desire to search out this path was strong but the reality was that it would not happen on this trip. As I turned to leave I knew I would have to return.

Callanish IV, as a whole, had a really good vibe to it and we enjoyed being in the company of these stones. It was just sad that we could not get up and personal with them.

8/16

After spending a night in Tarbert on Harris, and after another travel day to south of Fort William, today we were approaching the Kilmartin Valley from the north on the A816. I was in search of the Kintraw Stone and Cairn which I had unsuccessfully looked for on our previous trip to this area. It was raining, and the road is quite winding and narrow in the area where I thought we should find the stones. We passed the Kintraw House and after a mile or so I knew we must have missed them and turned around. Sure enough, headed back north, we soon saw the tall megalith standing just up off the road, to our right.

As it was raining pretty good Sharon decided to wait in the car, and out I went. The Kintraw

Stone stands 13 feet tall and seems quite resolute overlooking the stone pile that is the cairn, and Loch Craignish beyond. Even in this steady rain I could not have been more impressed with this lone sentinel. Walking up to the stone, I placed my hand on its surface and even though the day was quite cold, my hand instantly felt warm against the rock. I felt my feet sink into the earth and the energy flowed! And then, "Thank you for stopping." This stone was awake an aware.

I took a moment to explore the cairn before returning to the stone. I would have loved to spend more time but it was really raining, I had not worn rain gear, and Sharon was waiting in the car which was parked in a bit of a precarious location. Placing my hand back on the stone I said, "I am sorry but I have to go." For just the briefest moment I felt sadness, but just as quickly it turned to a warm, comforting energy. As I walked back to the car I was feeling both. This visit had not been near long enough. I can only hope that I will get a chance another day.

Arriving in Kilmartin we decided to stop at the information center for lunch. They have a lovely cafe. Revived by tea, soup, and scones, though it was windy and raining we took the walk to Glebe Cairn which sits down below the Center. We had not visited this cairn on our last trip. I must say I was quite disappointed. I said to Sharon, "It's just a pile of rocks." Sad really.

Returning to our car we took a drive out the B840, a lovely country road just north of Kilmartin, headed towards Ford. I had read that there were a couple of standing stones and cairns near the road and sure enough after just a mile or two we found the remains of The Creagantairbh Stone standing right alongside the road, next to the fence. This stone now stands about six feet tall but it once was 16 feet in height. You can see the top 10 feet of the stone lying on the ground behind it, where it has lain since a big storm broke it off back in 1879. As our car was blocking a one lane road, and as it was still raining, we did not stay long. Still, I am glad we found this pleasant rock.

It was time to check into the Duncraigaig B&B south of Kilmartin. We had stayed there last time and were happy to return. Once again, from our room we had that lovely view of the Ballymeanoch Stones in the field across the road. Anytime you look out the window there they are, where they have been standing for thousands of years, welcoming and inviting you to visit. Oddly, Sharon kept saying that the stones seemed to move location a little each time she looked. I left that between her and the stones.

After a nice dinner at the Kilmartin Hotel we decided to stop for a quick visit to "The Great X," or The Netherlargie Stones as they are properly called. It was getting late and was overcast but the mood in the Valley was grand. I told Sharon I would not be long and she waited in the car. As I approached this intriguing gathering of stones I met an "old timer" (a fellow about my age) who was traveling by himself and had stopped to check this site out. I sensed a kindred spirit and we were soon in conversation. At one point he asked, "What do you suppose they were up to with these stones?" He was impressed by not only each tall and individual standing stone, and the small stone circle in the middle of it all, but by the unique X shaped layout of the site. It really is quite different and one must wonder about its purpose.

We discussed possible astronomical alignments, ritual routes, and connections with other sites nearby. He said he really was not a "rock hugger" but it did seem to him that something special was going on with these stones and that it just felt good to be there with them. I could not have agreed more.

It was getting darker and colder so I said my goodbyes. I enjoyed his company.

8/17

We began the day with a return visit to Duncraigaig Cairn and the Ballymeanoch Stones. I really enjoyed the vibe around Duncraigaig. It sits in a beautiful location right off the A816 and though there are several far more impressive cairns in this valley, it has its own pride of place, and you can feel it.

From Duncraigaig we resumed our walk to the Ballymeanoch Stones. This is one of the most inviting locations I have visited and as we entered the field in which the

Stone Journals

stones sit I could feel their welcome. There are two parallel stone rows, one of two stones and the other of four stones, sitting in northwest/southeast alignments. They are good sized stones with the tallest at about 12 feet. Though the sky was dark and threatening rain, I was so happy to be back that I gave it no thought. The stones, too, were happy and I was overwhelmed with a feeling of contentment.

Going first to the stone pair to the west I was welcomed with a warm, comforting energy from the stone to the north. I remembered it having a similar female energy on my list visit. Moving to "the Martian" (as I named him last time) I received a strong jolt of male energy when I placed hand to stone. It was good to be back.

When I walked over to the four stone row I was once again wondering if there had not originally been more stones in this row? It just felt as if there should be. They have serious size and shape to them and a solid presence. The cup marks carved into the two stones in the middle grabbed our attention this time. It would be great to know what the intent had been with those. It was also interesting that the stone which had made both of us feel very queasy last time was much more subdued on this visit. There was still a little of that energy going on but nothing like before. Why the change?

Last of all, we went to check out the cairn remains and noticed that the large, holed stone was still lying nearby, being slowly absorbed into the earth. Sad really. I ask once again, "Why not stand it up?" Even if it is not placed in its original location does it not deserve to be standing, as was its original intent, rather than allowing it to sink into the earth? This seems a no brainer to me.

Fearing rain we said goodbye to these precious stones. I may never visit them again and I am so thankful to have had the opportunity. "So long Martian!"

Returning to Duncraigaig Cairn I remembered there was said to be a stone covered in rock art just up the road a ways. So we followed a path running north alongside the A816 and were soon led down to The Balnachraig Stone. The stone is a large flat slab which lies on the ground and is covered with lots of carvings. Some were simple cup marks while others were cups with one or two rings around them. They are placed in different groupings all over the rock surface. Pretty cool but once again, more questions.

Before it started to rain in earnest, and I knew it was coming, I wanted to take Sharon to Dunadd Hill Fort located at the south end of the valley. This ancient rock formation, which juts up from the valley floor and forms a natural fortification, was once the home to Scottish Kings and had impressed me when I was there a few years ago. Now, Sharon is very uncomfortable with heights and uneven surfaces, but I knew that if I could get her up on top she would be happy she had made the effort. It was indeed a bit of a struggle but in the end we stood side by side at the top of Dunadd, right alongside a large stone slab containing the footprint in which the ancient Scottish kings would place their foot when being crowned. The natural fortress, the footprint, the history, the views, it really is one of the best places ever!

Later in the day we went to find Ri Cruin Cairn which sits nestled into a grove of trees just south of the Netherlargie Stones. While the cairn is a nice one, I was more impressed with the atmosphere of the place, and with the trees. Near the entrance there is an old tree that looks like it has a severe case of arthritis, really gnarly. I felt a warm welcome from this tree as we entered the grove and before leaving we spent a little time with this old-timer of the wood. We had no conversations but we knew he was happy we had visited.

Of note, on one of the slabs in the kist located in the side of the cairn, there are several ax heads carved into the stone. They were kind of hard to see so it was fun to find them.

We finished out the day with a visit to Temple Wood Stone Circle. There was a group of ladies sitting in the middle of the main circle and they were enjoying each other's company. They were not leaving anytime soon so we did not stay long. I enjoyed our time there nonetheless.

There are actually two circles at this location. The main circle is 20 standing stones in a ring about 40 feet across and there is a cist in the center that is four and a half feet by two and a half feet. River rock covers the ground inside and out beyond the stone circle creating and even larger ring. To the north is a smaller ring 33 feet across created by just covering the ground with river rock. There is one small standing stone in the center and one on the outer rim but originally there was probably a complete circle of small standing stones. There is a real charm to these two circles sitting together in this wooded location, looking out upon the Netherlargie complex. Great spot.

Walking back to the car we stopped for a time at The Great X Stones giving special attention to the center standing stone. It has a unique shape and is larger at the top than at the bottom. It also has a large number of cup marks carved into it. This is a really fun stone.

Checking the energies at the site I once again found a strong line running through the middle of the complex, going from end to end, entering between one pair of standing stones at the north end and exiting between the second pair of standing stones at the south end. The line continued on and I wondered if maybe Ri Cruin Cairn might not be its next destination?

The last stop of the day was at Carmasserie was a nice walk up to this wonderful old ruin, sitting in a most beautiful location, with lovely views. As it was raining we did not stay long, but standing there in the castle, gazing across the rich green Scottish landscape was a great way to finish our time in Scotland.

So ended this journey, and so too ends this book. It has been challenging and rewarding in ways I never imagined when I started with that first trip to England, nine

Stone Journals

years ago. While I am already planning my next "Journey," it is not to be a part of this project and only time will tell what happens next. If after reading this book you, too, feel that fire of inspiration burning within, the desire to go and meet the stones, I encourage you to follow your heart. There is so much to experience, so much to learn, in the company of stones.

AFTERTHOUGHTS

In closing, let me take a moment to further clarify my understanding of the earth energies which I refer to throughout this book. I see the Earth as a living organism with energies flowing throughout. Those energies are the life force of the planet and they flow through rock, tree, and stream, as well as through humans. It is clear that, for whatever the reason, some stones become conduits by which those energies can concentrate and surface, and people who are susceptible to, and come in contact with those energies, then need to find a way to relate to them. The fact that some stones seem to take on personalities is, I think, a natural response for humans in trying to understand those energies and to better interact with them. My interaction with The Bowl Rock on my first "Stone Journey" is an example of this. When we think of a stone as more than just a rock, when we think of it as part of the creation, imbued with the same life force as we ourselves, then maybe we can treat it more respectfully. Maybe, just maybe, we will even begin to talk to it.

D.H. Lawrence wrote, "I am a part of the sun as my eye is a part of me. That I am part of the earth, my feet know perfectly, and my blood is a part of the sea." When we realize that everything is connected, then we also realize that what we do with our lives impacts far more than just ourselves, and, in fact, that we truly are the stewards of the Earth, all of it, even the rocks.

In *The Sun And The Serpent* by Hamish Miller and Paul Broadhurst, they write that "To begin to communicate with the Earth, an almost childlike reverence is necessary. Preconceptions must be held in check and the mind emptied of trivial everyday clutter. Then one enters a different world. Old stones appear as friends, relishing the contact of a willing mind and triggering revealing insights into their past." My own experiences with the stones completely support this view.

I am reminded of something I read many years ago in a biography of JRR Tolkien. Sadly, I no longer recall the author or the name of the book, but I do remember the episode about which he wrote. Tolkien was walking through one of his favorite gardens with a close friend. At some point the friend noticed that Tolkien was no longer with him. He turned to look back and saw Tolkien standing with head and hands pressed against a tree. Though he thought it a bit odd, he looked away and acted as though he had not noticed. When Tolkien rejoined him, he looked at his friend and with a subtle smile said, "They do talk you know." The friend, who was a well-educated and respected man, said he did not doubt for a moment that Tolkien had been talking with the tree.

To be clear, over the years I have tried to interact with many stones, rocks, trees, etc. with which I have been unsuccessful. I do not yet understand why on some occasions I connect and on others I do not. I do believe that, as with everything else from football to math, we are all born with different natural abilities. For some people certain things just come easy while others have to work at whatever it is, and some never seem to get it. My ability to open to, and interact with the stones (and trees), is a developing skill set, and one for which I am very thankful.

I think that one of the problems we have when trying to understand topics like this is simply in how we approach them. Instead of asking what a stone is (scientifically), maybe we should ask what it is to be a stone? In asking what it is to be a stone, "being" implies action, and action implies energy, or life of some kind. This simple change in perspective opens many new possibilities.

Greg Cajete, a Native American scholar, has written that "in indigenous ways of knowing, we understand a thing only when we understand it with all four aspects of our being: mind, body, emotion, and spirit." (Quoted from *Braiding Sweetgrass* by Robin Wall Kimmerer) This makes complete since to me.

For example, if you were to examine a honey bee, noticing its rich brown color, the speed at which its small wings work to propel it through the air, and the buzzing sound it created as it flew back and forth while gathering pollen on its legs to take back to the hive, and, even if you were to watch as the queen bee mated and lay her eggs, and as the workers created and filled the honey comb with its golden nectar, would you then really understand the bee if you were never to taste the honey? You would be missing something so very special about the bee.

When watching the water flowing down a creek is that all there is to it? Do you see the little whirlpools that are created along the way pulling floating items into their embrace? Do you notice the foaming waters at the base of the small waterfalls freeing oxygen into the air for all to breathe? Do the rocks worn smooth by countless years of water flowing over them not draw your attention with their beauty, and, if they have a thin layer of some kind of moss growing on them do they not warn you to take care when walking over them? What of the countless number of beings who live within, and around the waters, like the trout and carp, or the salmon who are returning from years at sea, to lay their eggs and continue the cycle. And what about the water skippers walking on the surface of the calm waters as if it was solid glass, or the orange bellied, brown skinned newts who move ever so slowly about their lives, seemingly unconcerned with all around them? Do you notice the kingfisher setting on the overhanging branch, watching the waters in hope of catching its next meal? When you take a drink from the creek is the water cold? How does it taste? Does it taste like rocks? Is it maybe one of the most refreshing things you have ever had the pleasure of drinking? How does it smell, how does it feel? What kind of memories does the creek bring up? Only through this process of observation and awareness can you really understand the water in the creek.

Likewise, if you were to walk up to a rock, chip off a piece, and have that analyzed, would you then "know" the rock? Is there not much more to find out? When you look at it what do you see? Is it may be made up of small, shining, colored crystals held together by some kind of matrix, or maybe it has a smooth flat surface of swirls of different colors? If it is a clear crystal and you stare into it, do you see rainbows of color as the light reflects off inner fractures, or do you maybe see what appears to be another whole world of mountains, valleys, and trees created by impurities within the crystal? If you gaze at an orb of labradorite do you find you are being drawn deeper and deeper into its depths, into a dark world of ever shifting colors? If you reach out and feel the texture of a stone is it rough, jagged, cracked or uneven, or is it may be smooth and slick like glass? If you lie down on a large stone on a cold windy day do you feel the stone radiating heat to warm you? If you get close and smell a rock what do you smell? You might at first think it is musty or earthy, but after a bit of comparing different rocks you begin to notice subtle differences. And, how can you really "know" a rock if you do not take the time to hold it if it is small, or sit with your back against it if it is large, and to open to the calm and comfort it has to offer, or, if you're lucky, to whatever else you might experience?

GLOSSARY

- Alignment - An arrangement of standing stones, stone circles, cairns, etc. which are placed in a straight line.

- Avenue - Passageways from one place to another which are lined on both sides with stones, trees, earth banks and/or ditches.

- Barrow / Tumulous - Burial site covered over with an earth mound.

- Cairn - burial tomb which is covered over a mound of river rocks.

- Cist - A box-shaped burial chamber made of stone slabs and covered with a stone lid.

- Cupmark - A small rounded hollow made in the surface of a stone.

- Dolmen / Cromlech - Freestanding megalithic chamber usually consisting of three or four uprights supporting a large capstone. May have originally been covered with earth.

- Fogous - Particular to Cornwall, these are underground passages built floor to ceiling of stacked stones, off of which there are chambers. These were not burial sites.

- Four-poster - A stone circle made up of just four stones.

- Henge - An enclosure consisting of an earth ring, usually with an inner or outer ditch.

- Kerb-cairn - A cairn consisting of smaller stones held in place by large stones which line the base, called kerbstones.

- Ley - An alignment of ancient sites with ancient trackways.

- Longbarrow - A barrow which is more rectangular in shape.

- Megalith / Menhir / Monolith - Tall standing stone.

- Outlier - A stone standing outside, and away from, a stone circle or henge.

- Passage Tomb - a circular tomb covered with earth, with a long passage lined with stone slabs leading to a central chamber.

- Recumbent stone - A stone lying down on the ground rather than standing.

- Recumbent Stone Circle - A stone circle which contains a recumbent stone with upright flanker stones on each side.

- Trilithon - Two tall upright stones with a third stone placed across the tops of, and connecting, both.

Stone Journals

SUGGESTED READING and RESOURCES

1. Beckensall, Stan - *Circles In Stone* - Tempus Publishing - 2006
2. Bennett, Paul - *The Old Stones Of Elmet* - Capall Bann, Milverton - 2001
3. Bord, Janet & Colin - *Mysterious Britain* - Paladin Publishing - 1977
4. Burl, Aubrey - *Megalithic Brittany* - Thames & Hudson, New York - 1985
5. Burl, Aubrey - *A Guide To The Stone Circles of Britain, Ireland, and Brittany* - Yale University Press, New Haven & London - 1995
6. Burl, Aubrey - *The Stone Circles of the British Isles* - Yale University Press - 1976
7. Burl, Aubrey & Piper, Peter - *Rings Of Stone* - Ticknor & Fields - 1980
8. Cajete, Gregory - *Look To The Mountain* - Kivaki Press
9. Callaway, Paul - *Stone Circles Of Southern England* - 2014
10. Chippindale, Christopher - *Stonehenge Complete* - Thames & Hudson - 2004
11. Cooke, Ian - *Mermaid To Merrymaid* - Men An Tol Studio - 1987
12. Cope Julian - *The Modern Antiquarian* - Thornsons / HarperCollins Publishers, London - 1998
13. Cope, Julian - *The Megalithic European* - Element / HarperCollins Publishers, London - 2004
14. Corio, David & Lai Ngan - *Megaliths* - Jonathan Cape - 2003
15. Devereux, Paul - *Places Of Power* - Blandford - 1990
16. Devereux, Paul - *Symbolic Landscapes* - Gothic Umage Publications - 1992
17. Farrah, Robert W.E. - A Guide To The Stone Circles Of Cumbria - Hayloft - 2008
18. Graves, Tom - *Needles Of Stone* - Gothic Image Publications - 1986
19. Gray, William - *The Rollright Ritual* - Skylight Press, Cheltenham - 2011
20. Hadingham, Evan - *Circles And Standing Stones* - Walker Publishing Co - 1975
21. Legg, Rodney - *Stanton Drew* - Wincanton Press, Somerset - 1998
22. Matthews, John & Stead, Michael J. - *Landscapes Of Legend* - Cassell/Blandford Publishing - 1997
23. Meaden, Terence - *The Secrets Of The Avebury Stones* - Souvenir Press - 1999
24. Milligan, Max / Burl, Aubrey - *Circles Of Stone* - The Harvill Press - 1999
25. Michell, John - *Simulacra* - Thames & Hudson
26. Michell, John - *The Old Stones Of Land's End* - The Garnstone Press Ltd - 1974
27. Miller, Hamish & Broadhurst, Paul - *The Sun And The Serpent* - Pendragon Press - 1994
28. Murphy, Cornelius J. - *The Prehistoric Archeology Of The Beara Peninsula* - Beara Historical Society - 2014
29. O Nuallain, Sean - *Stone Circles In Ireland* - Country House - 1995
30. Pohribny, Jan & Richards, Julian - *Magic Stones* - Merrell Publishers - 2007
31. Ponting, Gerald - *Callanish* - Wooden Books - 2002
32. Ponting, Gerald & Curtis, Margaret - *New Light On The Stones Of Callanish* - 1984
33. Richardson, Alan - *Spirits Of The Stones* - Megalithic Books/Skylight Press (also titled *The Inner Guide To The Megaliths*) - 2011
34. Roberts, Jack - *The Sun Circles Of Ireland* - Bandia Publishing, Galway - 2013
35. Roberts, Jack - *The Sacred Mythological Centres Of Ireland* - Bandia Publishing - 2016
36. Rafferty, Andrew & Crossley-Holland, Kevin - *The Stones Remain* - Rider/Century Hutchinson Ltd - 1989
37. Service, Alastair & Bradbery, Jean - *Megaliths And Their Mysteries* - J.M.Dent - 1993
38. Sink, David - *The Ancient Stones Speak* - E. P. Dutton - 1979
39. Soskin, Rupert - *Standing With Stones* - Thames & Hudson - 2009

40. Strong, Gordon - *The Sacred Stone Circles Of Stanton Drew* - Skylight Press - 2012
41. Tuck, Cathrine & Bull, Alun - *Landscapes And Desire* - Sutton Publishing - 2003
42. Waterhouse, John - The Stone Circles Of Cumbria - Phillimore & Co. - 1985
43. Watson, David - *Guide to the Stone Circles Of The Lake District - 2009*
44. Watson, David - *A Guide To The Stone Circles And Standing Stones Of Perthshire* - 2007
45. Weatherhill, Craig - *Cornovia* - Cornwall Books - 2000
46. Wheatley, Maria & Taylor, Busty - *Avebury / Sun, Moon, and Earth* - Wessex Books
47. Wildwood, Rob - *Magical Places Of Britain* - Wyldwood Publishing - York 2014

The *Standing With Stones* DVD by Rupert Soskin and Michael Bott is spectacular. I can think of no better way to introduce someone to this topic.

The following web sites provide great information about the stones:

www.megalithicportal.com
www.stonepages.com
www.ancient-wisdom.co.uk
www.megalithics.com
www.visitcumbria.com
www.themodernantiquarian.com
www.megalthomania.com
www.megalithicireland.com
www.ancient-scotland.co.uk
www.roaringwaterjournal.com
cornishancientsites.com

The following web sites provide valuable map information when trying to find stone locations:

www.getamap.ordnancesurvey.co.uk
www.multimap.com
www.panoramio.com
www.streetmap.co.uk
www.maps.google.com
www.bing.com/maps

Index

A
Adam and Eve, 98
Ales Stenar, 120-122, 124
An Diseart, 233
Ardgroom, 206-207, 244, 246
Ardgroom Stone Circle, 206
Ardmore row stones, 237
Ardmore Stone Row, 232, 235-236
Athgreany, 186, 211, 250-251
Athgreany Stone Circle, 186, 211, 250
Avebury, 7-8, 14, 16-18, 21, 38, 50, 59, 68, 72, 88, 92-96, 98-101, 110, 169-170, 193, 292-293
Avebury Circle, 99-100

B
Ballycommane, 248, 250, 253
Ballymeanoch, 146-147, 149, 152, 155-156, 280-281
Ballymeanoch standing stones, 146
Ballymeanoch Stones, 147, 152, 155-156, 280-281
Balnachraig Stone, 283
Balnuaran of Clava, 136
Beaghmore, 221, 223
Beaghmore Stone Circles, 221
Belas Knap, 173-174, 220
Belas Knap Long Barrow, 173
Beltane, 94, 99-100, 110
Birkrigg Stone Circle, 161
Blarney Castle, 196-197
Bohonagh, 190-191, 194-196, 244
Bohonagh Stone Circle, 190, 244
Bonane, 239, 247
Bonane Heritage Park, 239, 247
Bonane Stone Circle, 239
Boscawen-Un, 25, 27, 29-32, 36, 259, 264-265
Boscawen-Un Stone Circle, 259, 264
Brimham, 166
Brimham Rocks, 166
Brisworthy, 41, 43, 45, 239
Brisworthy Circle, 43
Brisworthy Stone Circle, 41, 239
Broadleas, 184-187
Broadleas Stone Circle, 184
Brown's Hill Dolmen, 189
Burgatia Stone, 192

C
Cairnholy, 57, 85-86, 179
Callanish, 64-68, 76, 271-275, 278-279, 292
Callanish I, 271-272, 274-275
Callanish II, 272-275, 278
Callanish III, 274
Callanish IV, 278-279
Callanish Stone Circle, 64
Callanish stones, 64-65
Carn Euny, 27
Carrowmore, 216-217, 219
Carrowmore Megalithic Cemetery, 216
Castlerigg, 58, 66, 158, 170
Castlerigg Stone Circle, 58, 158
Castleruddery Stone Circle, 188
Cherhill White Horse, 97
Church of St. Barrahane, 192
Clach Stein Stones, 277
Clava Cairns, 136, 256
Corrimony, 140-143, 147, 208
Croft Moraig, 268-269
Croft Moraig Stone Circle, 268
Cullerlie, 128-129
Cullerlie Stone Circle, 128

D
Danes Stone, 271
Derreen Gardens, 244
Derreenataggart Stone Circle, 246
Devil's Arrows, 167
Disa's Ting, 120-121
Dowth, 223-225, 250, 253
Drift Standing Stones, 262
Dromagorteen, 239
Drombeg, 193-196
Drombeg Stone Circle, 193
Druids Circle, 161, 163
Duloe, 35-37, 257
Duloe Circle, 37, 257
Duloe Stone Circle, 36
Dunadd, 155, 217, 283
Dunadd Fort, 155
Dunadd Hill Fort, 283
Dunchraigaig Cairn, 147, 150, 156

E
Eire, 144

F
Fairy Glen, 144-145
Feaghna Bullaun Stone, 247-248
Fortingall Stones, 269
Fortingall Yew, 271

G
Gallarus Oratory, 234
Giants Grave, 212
Girdle Stanes, 112, 114-117
Girdle Stanes Stone Circle, 112

Glantane, 200, 204
Glastonbury, 101-104, 136
Glastonbury Tor, 103
Glebe, 212-213, 215, 280
Glebe Cairn, 280
Glebe Stones, 215
Glenquicken Stone Circle, 57, 87, 179
Graigue Standing Stone, 235
Grange, 75, 203, 209, 211, 213, 223, 225, 230
Gurranes, 193

H
Havangsdosen, 123-124
Hill Of Tara, 227, 229

J
Janus Stones, 220

K
Kealkill Stones, 241
Kenmare Circle, 208
Kenmare Stone Circle, 202, 207, 238
Kilmalkedar, 234, 238
King Stone, 16, 176
Kintraw Stone, 279
Kintraw Stone and Cairn, 279
Kirkmadrine Stones, 109
Kivik Kungagraven, 123, 137
Knockdrum Stone Fort, 192
Knocknakilla, 200-202, 204
Knocknarea, 216-219
Knockraheen, 198-200, 210
Knockraheen Stone Circle, 198
Knowth, 223, 225

L
Listoghil, 217
Little Meg, 62-63, 83
Loanhead, 132-133, 138
Loanhead Of Daviot Stone Circle, 138
Long Meg, 59, 61-62, 94, 113, 116, 143
Loughcrew, 226-227
Loughcrew Cairns, 226
Loupin Stanes, 110-111, 114, 117, 187
Loupin Stanes Circle, 111, 114
Loupin Stanes Stone Circle, 110
Lugnagappul Ogham Stones, 232, 237
Lundin Farm, 267-268
Lundin Farm Stone Circle, 267

M
Machrie Moor, 105, 108, 111, 113-114, 146, 168, 256
Machrie Moor Stone Circles, 105
Machrie Moor stones, 108

Maeshowe, 67, 73-75
Maeves Tomb, 216-218
Maiden Stone, 135
Mayburgh, 115-117
Mayburgh Henge, 115
Meg, 59-63, 83, 94, 113, 116, 143
Meg's daughters, 60
Men An Tol, 7, 33-34, 260-262, 292
Merrivale, 43-45, 254-255
Merrivale Complex, 254
Merry Maidens, 30-32, 34, 50
Mid Cairn, 153
Midmar, 129, 131
Midmar Kirk Stone Circle, 129
Minchinhampton Long Stone, 172
Minchinhampton Stone, 172-173

N
Nether Largie North, 153
Nether Largie South, 153
Nether Largie Stones, 151-152, 154

P
Pipers Stones, 34, 186, 250
Punchestown Longstone, 182
Punchestown Stone, 183-184, 201

R
Rollright, 13-14, 16, 18, 21, 38, 45, 168, 172, 174-175, 292
Rollright Circle, 14, 16, 21, 38, 175
Rollright Stone Circle, 14, 16, 168, 174
Rollright Stones, 21, 172, 175

S
Scara Brae, 75-76
Seven Sisters Stone Circle, 197
Shronebirrane, 204-205
Shronebirrane Stone Circle, 204
Silbury Hill, 19, 50, 92, 97
Soussans, 45, 252-253
Soussans Common, 45, 252
Soussans Common Stone Circle, 45, 252
South Zeal Stone, 252
Stanton Drew, 19-22, 24, 50, 95, 176-179, 265, 292-293
Stanton Drew Circles, 21
Stanton Drew Stone Circles, 20, 265
Stanton Drew Stone Circles, 20, 265
Stenness, 67-68, 70, 72-74, 76, 88, 107, 134, 185
Stenness stones, 70, 73

Stone Circle, 7, 10, 14, 16-17, 25-26, 30-31, 33, 35-36, 39-41, 44-46, 50, 52, 55-60, 64, 67, 72, 80, 83, 87-89, 93, 106-107, 110-112, 114, 116, 128-131, 133, 135, 137-138, 143, 151, 153, 158-159, 161, 168-169, 174, 178-179, 184-186, 188, 190, 193, 195, 197-198, 200-211, 215, 221-223, 230, 238-239, 241-244, 246, 250, 252, 255, 259-261, 264, 267-269, 272, 276, 281, 285, 290-291
Stonehenge, 6-7, 14, 17, 47, 50, 64, 68, 76-78, 105, 120-121, 170-171, 292
Stones of Stenness, 68, 70, 72, 107, 185
Stoney Littleton, 101
Sunhoney Stone Circle, 131
Sunkenkirk, 159-161, 163
Sunkenkirk Circle, 161

T
Temple Wood, 151-152, 154, 285
Temple Wood Stone Circle, 151, 285
Templebryan, 195
Templebryan Stone Circle, 195
The Apostles, 54
The Blind Fiddler, 25, 27-28, 34, 43, 63, 74, 162-163, 262-264
The Bowl Rock, 22-24, 43, 66, 287
The Carles, 58
The Cove, 170, 176-177, 179, 266
The Fiddler, 28-29, 262-264
The Great X, 151, 154, 281, 285
The Hurlers, 37, 50, 256-257
The Hurlers Stone Circles, 37, 50, 256
The Lios, 209, 211
The Longstones, 98, 184
The Merry Maidens Stone Circle, 30-31
The Pipers, 34, 186, 250, 257
The Truiseil Stone, 275-276
The Twelve Apostles, 52, 55, 57, 83-84, 158, 178
The Twelve Apostles Stone Circle, 52, 83, 158, 178
Tobar Eoin, 232
Tomb of The Eagles, 67-68
Torhouse, 55-58, 81, 85
Torhouskie, 55
Trencrom Hill, 23

U
Uragh, 203-205, 207, 243, 247
Uragh Stone Circle, 203, 243

W
Wayland's Smithy Long Barrow, 168
West Kennet Avenue, 19, 94
West Kennet Long Barrow, 19, 50, 97
Whispering Knights, 16, 175-176

Patrick has spent the better part of his life involved in the music business, as a musician, songwriter, producer, band leader, and owner of his own record label, Blue Rock'lt Records. Over the years he toured and recorded with many blues greats, including Brownie McGhee, Lowell Fulson, Charlie Musselwhite, and Jimmy Witherspoon. He also performed and recorded with his brothers Mark and Robben Ford and since 1988 Patrick has fronted his own band, The Ford Blues Band.

He has been intrigued by the European megalithic standing stones since he saw his first photographs of Stonehenge as a young boy. However, he did not get to actually visit any standing stone sites until 1986, when he was in his mid 30's, and Stonehenge was the first one he visited. Over the years since, he has continued to make return trips to northern Europe to find and explore more than 150 stone sites in as many as six different countries. Many of those locations were returned to on numerous occasions.

Beginning in 2009, Patrick began what he called his "Stone Journeys," with the explicit purpose of finding out what he could both about the stones, and from the stones. On his travels he kept journals which provided the base material for his book, Stone Journals.

On many of these journeys Patrick was accompanied by Sharon, his wife of 49 years. Their home is on five acres in the small rural community of Redwood Valley, Ca. near where they both grew up.

www.ingramcontent.com/pod-product-compliance
Lightning Source LLC
Chambersburg PA
CBHW080532170426
43195CB00016B/2542